BIBLIOGRAPHY OF H[illegible]

(PART I[illegible]

COMPILED IN HONOR OF

DR. NELSON GLUECK

BY

ELEANOR K. VOGEL
(CINCINNATI)

Reprint from Hebrew Union College Annual, Volume XLII (1971)

third printing, 1982

WITH FOREWORD BY

G. ERNEST WRIGHT (HARVARD DIVINITY SCHOOL, CAMBRIDGE, MASS.)

ISBN 0–87820–626–4

FOREWORD

Eleanor K. Vogel's "Bibliography of Holy Land Sites," originally printed in the *HUCA,* Vol. XLII (1971), is in such demand that it is now made available as a separate monograph. This was predicted when Professor M. Tsevat first discovered that Mrs. Vogel had such a reference aid and asked whether she might prepare it for publication.

Mrs. Vogel had been archaeological research assistant to Nelson Glueck for over three decades. Her husband had been a classmate of mine at McCormick Theological Seminary. After graduation he and his wife settled in the Cincinnati area where Eleanor began graduate work which she hoped would lead to a doctoral degree in ancient history and archaeology. Coming under the spell of Nelson Glueck, she laid aside her own plans for his. The monograph here published is one of several collections of information made for her own and Dr. Glueck's use over the years. It demonstrates the meticulousness of the ideal compiler of reference information.

It is a pleasure to see some of Eleanor K. Vogel's work finally in print, even though it was never intended for publication. We archaeologists are greatly in her debt, both for this invaluable bibliographical material, and for her years of hard work, without which Nelson Glueck, in his years as a burdened administrator, would never have been able to publish as much of his archaeological work as he did.

G. Ernest Wright
Harvard University

BIBLIOGRAPHY OF HOLY LAND SITES

compiled in honor of
DR. NELSON GLUECK

ELEANOR K. VOGEL

Hebrew Union College-Jewish Institute of Religion, Cincinnati

ABBREVIATIONS

AASOR	*Annual of the American Schools of Oriental Research*, Cambridge, Mass.
ADAJ	*Annual of the Department of Antiquities of Jordan*, Amman, Jordan.
ADHL	*Archaeological Discoveries in the Holy Land*, New York: Thomas Y. Crowell Co., 1967.
AJA	*American Journal of Archaeology*, Archaeological Institute of America, New York.
ANEP	Pritchard, J. B., ed., *The Ancient Near East in Pictures*, Princeton, 1969.
ANET	Pritchard, J. B., ed., *Ancient Near Eastern Texts*, Princeton, 1969.
AOTS	Thomas, D. W., ed., *Archaeology and Old Testament Study*, Oxford: The Clarendon Press, 1967.
Archaeology	Archaeological Institute of America, New York.
A and S	*Antiquity and Survival*, The Hague and Jerusalem.
Ariel	State of Israel, Jerusalem.
ᶜAtiqot	Department of Antiquities and Museums, Israel.
BA	*The Biblical Archaeologist*, American Schools of Oriental Research, Cambridge, Mass.
BASOR	*Bulletin of the American Schools of Oriental Research*, Cambridge, Mass.
Berytus	*Berytus Archaeological Studies*, American University, Beirut.
Biblica	Pontifical Biblical Institute, Rome.
BJPES	*Bulletin of the Jewish Palestine Exploration Society*, Jerusalem.
BMH	*Bulletin of the Museum Haaretz*, Tel Aviv.
BTS	*Bible et Terre Sainte*, Paris.
CNI	*Christian News from Israel*, Government of Israel, Jerusalem.

EAEHL	*Encyclopaedia of Archaeological Excavations in the Holy Land*, Israel Exploration Society and Massada Ltd., Jerusalem.
EI	*Eretz-Israel*, Israel Exploration Society, Jerusalem.
Expedition	The University Museum, University of Pennsylvania, Philadelphia.
HUCA	*Hebrew Union College Annual*, Cincinnati.
IDB	*The Interpreter's Dictionary of the Bible*, Abingdon Press, New York, 1962.
IEJ	*Israel Exploration Journal*, Israel Exploration Society, Jerusalem.
ILN	*Illustrated London News*, London.
Iraq	British School of Archaeology in Iraq, London.
JAOS	*Journal of the American Oriental Society*, New Haven.
JBL	*Journal of Biblical Literature*, Philadelphia.
JNES	*Journal of Near Eastern Studies*, University of Chicago.
JPOS	*The Journal of the Palestine Oriental Society*, Jerusalem.
LA	*Liber Annuus*, Studii Biblici Franciscani, Jerusalem.
Levant	*Journal of the British School of Archaeology in Jerusalem*, London.
Muse	*Annual of the Museum of Art and Archaeology*, University of Missouri-Columbia.
NEATC	Sanders, J. A., ed., *Essays in Honor of Nelson Glueck: Near Eastern Archaeology in the the Twentieth Century*, Garden City, N. Y.: Doubleday and Co., Inc., 1970.
Orientalia	Pontifical Biblical Institute, Rome.
PEFA	*Palestine Exploration Fund Annual*, London.
PEFQS, PEQ	*Palestine Exploration Quarterly* (*Quarterly Statement*), London.
Perspective	Gowan, D. E., ed., *Perspective: Essays in Memory of Paul W. Lapp*, Pittsburgh: Pittsburgh Theological Seminary, 1971.
Qadmoniot	Israel Exploration Society, Jerusalem.
QDAP	*Quarterly of the Department of Antiquities of Palestine*, London.
Raggi	*Zeitschrift zur Kunstgeschichte und Archäologie*, Zürich.
RB	*Revue Biblique*, Paris.
Symbols	Goodenough, E. R., *Jewish Symbols in the Greco-Roman Period*, New York: Pantheon Books, Inc., 1953.
Syria	*Revue d'art oriental et d'archéologie*, Paris.
VT	*Vetus Testamentum*, Leiden.
ZAW	*Zeitschrift für die alttestamentliche Wissenschaft*, Berlin.
ZDPV	*Zeitschrift des deutschen Palästina-Vereins*, Wiesbaden.

'Abdah, Eboda, Avdat

R. Jaussen, M. Savignac, H. Vincent, *RB* 13, 1904, pp. 403–424; *RB* 14, 1905, pp. 78–89, 235–244; C. L. Woolley, T. E. Lawrence, "The Wilderness of Zin," *PEFA* 3, 1914–1915, pp. 28, 93–107, 143–145, figs. 24–41, pls. 23–25; A. Alt, "Aus der ᶜAraba II," *ZDPV* 58, 1935, pp. 38–40; C. L. Woolley, T. E. Lawrence, *The Wilderness of Zin*, 1936; G. E. Kirk, "Archaeological Exploration in the Southern Desert," *PEQ* 1938, pp. 211–235, esp. p. 231; *id.*, "The Negev or Southern Desert of Palestine," *PEQ* 1941, pp. 57–71, esp. p. 61; N. Glueck, *BASOR* 131, 1953, pp. 10–11; *id.*, *BASOR* 137, 1955, pp. 10–11.

Clearing and Excavation by the Department for the Preservation of Landscape and Conservation of Antiquities of Israel, under the direction of M. Avi-Yonah, A. Negev, Y. Cohen, 1958–1960.

A. Negev, "Abdah," *IEJ* 9, 1959, pp. 274–275; A. Biran, "Abdah," *CNI* 11:2, 1960, pp. 18–19, pl. 3; M. Avi-Yonah, "Abdah," *RB* 67, 1960, pp. 378–381, pls. 21, 22a; M. Avi-Yonah, A. Negev, "A City of the Negeb: Excavations in Nabataean, Roman and Byzantine Eboda," *ILN* Nov. 26, 1960, pp. 944–947, figs. 1–21; A. Negev, "Nabataean Inscriptions from ᶜAvdat (Oboda)," *IEJ* 11, 1961, pp. 127–138, pls. 28b, 29–31; *id.*, "Avdat, a Caravan Halt in the Negev," *Archaeology* 14, 1961, pp. 122–130; *id.*, "Nabataean Inscriptions from ᶜAvdat (Oboda)," *IEJ* 13, 1963, pp. 113–124, pls. 17–18; *id.*, "Stonedressers' Marks from a Nabataean Sanctuary at ᶜAvdat," *EI* 7, 1964, pp. 29–32, pls. 3–5 (Hebrew); N. Glueck, *Deities and Dolphins*, 1965, pp. 6–7, pl. 8a on p. 20, pp. 332–333, 520, pl. 219b on p. 525 and pl. 220b on p. 526; A. Negev, "Avdat in the Negev," *Ariel* 16, 1966, pp. 12–22, pls. 13–19; *id.*, "Oboda, Mampsis, and Provincia Arabia," *IEJ* 17, 1967, pp. 46–55; J. Naveh, "Some Notes on Nabataean Inscriptions from ᶜAvdat," *IEJ* 17, 1967, pp. 187–189; N. Glueck, *Rivers in the Desert*, 1968, pp. 271–276, fig. 44; A. Negev, "Avdat," *EAEHL*, 1970, pp. 424–431, figs. (Hebrew).

Abu Ghosh, Qaryet el 'Enab

Excavation by Abbé Moreau, 1901.

Bibliography, *QDAP* 1, 1932, p. 86; R. deVaux, A. M. Stève, *Fouilles à Qaryet el-ᶜEnab, Abû Ghosh, Palestine*, 1950, figs. 1–37, pls. 1–20; J. Perrot, "Le Néolithique d'Abou Ghosh," *Syria* 29, 1952, pp. 119–145, figs. 1–6, pls. 7–14.

Excavation by Centre de recherches préhistoriques français de Jérusalem, Jean Perrot, Director, 1967–1968, 1970.

J. Perrot, "Abu Ghosh," *IEJ* 17, 1967, pp. 266–267; *id.*, "Abu Ghosh," *RB* 75, 1968, pp. 264–266, pl. 33; A. Biran, "Abu Ghosh," *CNI* 19:3–4, 1968, p. 43; J. Perrot, "Abu Ghosh," *IEJ* 19, 1969, pp. 115–116; *id.*, *RB* 76, 1969, pp. 421–423, pl. 22; A. Biran, "Abu Ghosh," *CNI* 20:3–4, 1969, p. 46; M. Lechevallier, G. Dollfus, "Les deux premières campagnes de fouilles à Abou Ghosh (1967–1968)," *Syria* 46, 1969, pp. 277–287, figs. 1–5, pls. 22–24; J. Perrot, "Abu Ghosh," *EAEHL*, 1970, p. 1, fig. (Hebrew); M. Avi-Yonah, "Abu Ghosh," *EAEHL*, 1970, pp. 2–4, figs. (Hebrew); M. Lechevallier, "Abu Gosh," *IEJ* 20, 1970, pp. 222–223; *id.*, "Abou-Gosh," *BTS* 132, 1971, pp. 6–8, figs.

Achzib, ez-Zib, Akzibi.

Seventy rock-cut tombs excavated in 1941–42 by I. Ben-Dor, N. Makhouly, for the Department of Antiquities, Government of Palestine. I. Ben-Dor, *IDB*, 1962, "Achziv," pp. 27–28.

Excavations by M. W. Prausnitz, Department of Antiquities of Israel, and S. Moscati, University of Rome, 1958, 1960, 1963, 1964, 1970.

A. Biran, "Achzib," *CNI* 10:1–2, 1959, pp. 27–28, pl. 2; M. W. Prausnitz, "Achzib," *IEJ* 9, 1959, p. 271; *id.*, "Achzib," *RB* 67, 1960, p. 398, pl. 25; *id.*, "Achzib," *IEJ* 10, 1960, pp. 260–261; *id.*, "Achzib," *RB* 69, 1962, pp. 404–405, pl. 44b; *id.*, "Achzib," *IEJ* 13, 1963, pp. 337–338; A. Biran, "Achzib," *CNI* 15:2–3, 1964, pp. 29–30, pls. 6:2, 7:2, M. W. Prausnitz, "Achzib," *IEJ* 15, 1965, pp. 256–258; *id.*, "Achzib," *RB* 72, 1965, pp. 544–547, pls. 27b, 28b; A. Biran, "Achziv," *CNI* 16:4, 1965, p. 15, pl. 1:2,3; M. W. Prausnitz, "A Phoenician Krater from Akhziv," *OA* 5, 1966, pp. 177–188, figs. 1–5; *id.*, "A Phoenician Krater from Akhziv," *EI* 8, 1967, pp. 95–98 (Hebrew); M. Prausnitz, "Akhziv," *EAEHL*, 1970, pp. 9–10, figs. (Hebrew); *id.*, "Achzib," *IEJ* 20, 1970, p. 232.

Acre, Tell el-Fukhar, Akko, Ptolemais, St. Jean d'Acre, el-Makr.

C. N. Johns, *Palestine of the Crusades*, 1937, booklet with plan; M. Avi-Yonah, "Syrian Gods at Ptolemais-Accho," *IEJ* 9, 1959, pp. 1–12, fig. 1.

Excavation by S. Applebaum for Department of Antiquities, Israel, 1959.

S. Applebaum, "Accho," *IEJ* 9, 1959, p. 274; Y. H. Landau, "A Greek Inscription from Acre," *IEJ* 11, 1961, pp. 118–126, fig. 1, pl. 28a; Z. Goldmann, "The Refectory of the Order of St. John in Acre," *CNI* 12:4, 1962, pp. 15–19, fig. 1, pls. 1–4; *id.*, "Newly Discovered Crusaders' Inscription in Acre," *CNI* 13:1, 1962, pp. 33–34, pl. 4; Department for Landscaping and the Preservation of Historical Sites, *Acre, The Old City, Survey and Planning*, 1962; H. Seyrig, "Divinités de Ptolémais," *Syria* 39, 1962, pp. 193–207, pls. 13–14; A. Biran, "Acre" *CNI* 16:4, 1965, p. 20, pl. 3:3.

Excavation in 1966 by Dr. Elisha Lindner, Israel Underwater Exploration Society, Dr. Gershon Edelstein, Department of Antiquities, Israel, Dr. Edward Hall, Oxford University Research Laboratory for Archaeology and History of Art, Dr. Alexander Flinder, British Sub-Aqua Club.

A. Biran, "Acre," *CNI* 18:1–2, 1967, p. 28, pl. 3:1; Z. Goldmann, "The Hospice of the Knights of St. John in Akko," *Archaeological Discoveries in the Holy Land*, 1967, pp. 199–206.

Cemetery excavated in 1967 by V. Tsaferis and Y. Margovsky, Department of Antiquities, Israel.

E. T. Hall, A. Flinder, E. Lindner, "Acre," *RB* 75, 1968, pp. 421–422; A. Biran, "Acre," *CNI* 19:3–4, 1968, pp. 40–41; Z. Goldmann, "Akko," *EAEHL*, 1970, pp. 455–459, figs. (Hebrew); M. Benvenisti, *The Crusaders in the Holy Land*, 1970, pp. 78–113, figs.

'Ader

W. F. Albright, "The Archaeological Results of an Expedition to Moab and the Dead Sea," *BASOR* 14, 1924, pp. 1–12, see pp. 1, 10; N. Glueck, "Further Explorations in Eastern Palestine," *BASOR* 51, 1933, pp. 9–19, see pp. 17–18.

Soundings by W. F. Albright, ASOR, R. G. Head, Department of Antiquities, Transjordan, November, 1933.

W. F. Albright, "Soundings at Ader, a Bronze Age City of Moab," *BASOR* 53, 1934, pp. 13–18; N. Glueck, *AASOR* 14, 1934, pp. 3, 45–47, 63; W. F. Albright, J. L. Kelso, T. J. Palin, "Early Bronze Pottery from Bâb ed-Drâ in Moab," *BASOR* 95, 1944, pp. 3–13, see p. 6; R. L. Cleveland, "Soundings at Khirbet Ader," *AASOR*

34–35, 1960, pp. 79–97, figs. 8–15, pls. 19–24; N. Glueck, *The Other Side of the Jordan*, 1970, p. 149; P. W. Lapp, *NEATC*, 1970, pp. 115, 129; W. G. Dever, *NEATC*, 1970, pp. 134, 153, 162; M. Kochavi, "Ader," *EAEHL*, 1970, p. 5 (Hebrew).

'Affûlah

E. L. Sukenik, "Late Chalcolithic Pottery from ᶜAffuleh," *PEFQS* 1936, pp. 150–154, pls. 1–2.

Excavations by E. L. Sukenik, March, 1937 for Department of Antiquities, Palestine.

E. L. Sukenik, "Affûleh," *QDAP* 8, 1939, p. 157; *id.*, "Archaeological Investigations at ᶜAffûla," *JPOS* 21, 1948, pp. 1–78, figs. 1–12, pls. 1–26.

Excavations in 1951, 1952 by I. Ben-Dor, M. Dothan, Department of Antiquities, Israel.

I. Ben-Dor, "Affule," *IEJ* 1, 1951, p. 249; M. Dothan, "Affule," *IEJ* 2, 1952, p. 142; *id.*, "The Excavations at ᶜAfula," *Atiqot* 1, 1955, pp. 19–70, figs. 1–20, pls. 2–6; M. Dothan, "Afule," *EAEHL*, 1970, pp. 464–466, figs. (Hebrew).

'Ai, et-Tell

W. F. Albright, "Ai and Beth-aven," *AASOR* 4, 1924, pp. 141–149; *J. Garstang, Director of the Department of Antiquities, Palestine, made a sounding in 1928.*

J. Garstang, "The Destruction of Ai," *Joshua, Judges*, 1931, pp. 149–161, 355–356, pls. 28–32.

J. Marquet-Krause excavated in 1933–1935 for the Baron Edmond de Rothschild Expedition.

J. Marquet-Krause, "et-Tell," *QDAP* 4, 1935, pp. 204–205; *id.*, "La deuxième campagne de fouilles à Ay (1934) rapport sommaire," *Syria* 16, 1935, pp. 325–345, figs. 1–7, pls. 50–59; L. H. Vincent, "Les fouilles d' et-Tell-ᶜAi," *RB* 46, 1937, pp. 231–266, figs. 1–4, pls. 1–6; J. Marquet-Krause, *Les fouilles de ᶜAy (et-Tell) 1933–35*, 1949.

J. A. Callaway directed excavations in 1964, 1966, 1968, 1969 for the Southern Baptist Theological Seminary, Perkins School of Theology, Drew Theological Seminary, Harvard Semitic Museum, American Schools of Oriental Research, Department of Antiquities, Jordan, Asbury Theological Seminary, Waterloo Lutheran University, Evangel College, Palestine Exploration Fund.

J. A. Callaway, *Pottery of the Tombs at ᶜAi (et-Tell)*, 1964; *id.*, "The 1964 ᶜAi (et-Tell) Excavations," *BASOR* 178, 1965, pp. 13–40, figs. 1–17; J. A. Callaway, M. B. Nicol, "A Sounding at Khirbet Ḥaiyân," *BASOR* 183, 1966, pp. 12–19, figs. 1–5; J. B. Hennessy, "The Sanctuary at ᶜAi," *The Foreign Relations of Palestine during the Early Bronze Age*, 1967, pp. 24–25, pls. 14–16; R. Amiran, "Khirbet Kerak Ware at Ai," *IEJ* 17, 1967, pp. 185–186, fig. 1; K. Schoonover, "et-Tell (Ai)," *RB* 75, 1968, pp. 243–247, pl. 25; J. A. Callaway, "New Evidence on the Conquest of ᶜAi," *JBL* 87, 1968, pp. 312–320; K. Schoonover, News, *RB* 76, 1969, pp. 423–426, pl. 23; J. A. Callaway, "The 1966 ᶜAi (et-Tell) Excavations," *BASOR* 196, 1969, pp. 2–16, figs. 1–11; *id.*, "Ai," *IEJ* 19, 1969, pp. 236–239; P. W. Lapp, *Biblical Archaeology and History*, 1969, pp. 74, 109, 118, pl. 19; J. A. Callaway, News, *PEQ* 1969, p. 56; A. Biran, "ᶜAi," *CNI* 20:3–4, 1969, pp. 45–46; J. A. Callaway, "The 1968 ᶜAi (et-Tell) Excavations," *PEQ* 1970, pp. 42–44, fig. 1, pl. 12; J. A. Callaway, *et al.*, "The 1968–1969 ᶜAi (et-Tell) Excavations," *BASOR* 198, 1970, pp. 7–31, figs. 1–16; K. M. Kenyon, *Archaeology in the Holy Land*, 1970, pp. 115, 322, 336–337, 343; G. E. Wright, "The Significance of Ai in the Third Millennium B. C.," A. Kuschke, E. Kutsch, eds., *Archäologie und Altes Testament*, 1970, pp. 299–319, figs. 1–5; J. A. Callaway, "Ai,"

RB 77, 1970, pp. 390–394; S. Kaplan, "Haᶜai," *EAEHL*, 1970, pp. 433–437, figs. (Hebrew); R. Amiran, "The Egyptian Alabaster Vessels from Ai," *IEJ* 20, 1970, pp. 170–179, figs. 1–6, pls. 39–43.

ʻAin Duq, Naʻaran

Excavations by École Biblique et Archéologique in 1919, 1920.

L. H. Vincent, "Le sanctuaire juif d' ᶜAïn Douq," *RB* 28, 1919, pp. 532–563, figs. 1–2; *id.*, "Le sanctuaire juif d' ᶜAïn Douq," *RB* 30, 1921, pp. 442–443, fig. 2, pl. 8; L. H. Vincent, B. Carrière, "La synagogue de Noarah," *RB* 30, 1921, pp. 579–601, pls. 15–16; E. L. Sukenik, *Ancient Synagogues in Palestine and Greece*, 1934, pp. 6, 28–31, 65, 72–77, figs. 4–6, pl. 18; *id.*, "Naᶜaran," *Bulletin Rabinowitz* 1, 1949, pp. 9–11, 14, figs. 1, 7, pls. 1–3; E. R. Goodenough, *Symbols* 1, 1953, pp. 253–257; P. Benoit, "Un Sanctuaire dans la Région de Jéricho la Synagogue de Naᶜarah," *RB* 65, 1961, pp. 161–177, pls. 3–23; M. Avi-Yonah, "Naᶜaran," *EAEHL*, 1970, pp. 414–416, figs. (Hebrew).

ʻAin el-Fawara, see Kabri

ʻAin el-Jarba

Excavations in 1966 by J. Kaplan for the Museum of Antiquities, Tel-Aviv-Jaffa.

J. Kaplan, "ᶜEin el-Jarba, Chalcolithic Remains in the Plain of Esdraelon," *BASOR* 194, 1969, pp. 2–38, pls. 1–6; B. Arensburg, "The Human Remains from ᶜEin el-Jarba," *BASOR* 197, 1970, pp. 49–52, figs. 1–4.

ʻAin el-Qudeirat, Kadesh-barnea

C. L. Woolley, T. E. Lawrence, "The Wilderness of Zin," *PEFA* 3, 1914–1915, pp. 59–71, pls. 13–15.

Soundings in 1956 by M. Dothan for the Department of Antiquities, Israel.

B. Rothenberg, "Cadès Barné," *BTS* 32, 1960, pp. 4–13, figs.; Y. Aharoni, "Kadesh-barnea and Mount Sinai," *God's Wilderness*, 1962, pp. 117–182, pls. 10, 11, 17, 90; M. Dothan, "The Fortress at Kadesh-barnea," *IEJ* 15, 1965, pp. 134–151, figs. 1–7, pls. 25–31; N. Glueck, *Rivers in the Desert*, 1968, pp. 96–98; M. Dothan, "Qadesh-barnea," *EAEHL*, 1970, pp. 498–500, figs. (Hebrew).

ʻAin es-Sâmiyeh, see Dhahr Mirzbaneh

ʻAin et-Tabgha, Heptapegon, ʻEin Ha-Shivʻah

Excavated by A. E. Mader and A. M. Schneider for the Görresgesellschaft, 1932, 1936.

A. E. Mader, "ᶜEin et Tabigha," *QDAP* 2, 1933, pp. 184–185; B. Bagatti, "ᶜAin et Tābigha," *QDAP* 5, 1936, p. 194; C. F. Close, "The Tabgha Mosaics," *PEFQS* 1937, pp. 59–61, pl. 6; A. M. Schneider, *The Church of the Multiplying of the Loaves and Fishes at Tabgha on the Sea of Gennessaret and its Mosaics*, 1937; B. Gauer, "Werkbericht über die Instandsetzung der Boden-Mosaiken von Heptapegon am See Tiberias," *JPOS* 18, 1938, pp. 233–253, pls. 45–49; J. W. Crowfoot, *Early Churches in Palestine*, 1941, pp. 73–77, 122–124, pls. 12, 13; Unesco, *Israel Ancient Mosaics*, 1960, pp. 16–17, 20, 22, pls. 1–3; J. Meysing, "Tabgha," *BTS* 77, 1965, pp. 6–16, figs.

Excavated by B. Bagatti and S. Loffreda for the Custody of the Holy Land, 1968.

S. Loffreda, "The First Season of Excavations at Tabgha (near Capharnaum)," *LA* 18, 1968, pp. 238–243, figs. 1–2; A. Biran, "et-Tabgha," *CNI* 20:3–4, 1969, p. 40;

J. Finegan, *The Archeology of the New Testament*, 1969, pp. 48–50, figs.; M. Avi-Yonah, "En-Shevaᶜ," *EAEHL*, 1970, pp. 448–451, figs. (Hebrew).

ʻAin Feshkha

G. M. Crowfoot, "Linen Textiles from the Cave of ᶜAin Feshkha in the Jordan Valley," *PEQ*, 1951, pp. 5–31, figs. 1–5, pls. 1–8.

Excavation by R. deVaux for the Department of Antiquities, Jordan, École Biblique et Archéologique Française and the Palestine Archaeological Museum, 1958.

R. deVaux, "Fouilles de Feshkha," *RB* 66, 1959, pp. 225–255, figs. 1–3, pls. 2–12; *id.*, "Excavations at ᶜAin Feshkha," *ADAJ* 4–5, 1960, pp. 7–11, pls. 1–2; J. B. Poole, R. Reed, "The Tannery of ᶜAin Feshkha," *PEQ*, 1961, pp. 114–123, pl. 16; R. deVaux, "Feshkha," *EAEHL*, 1970, pp. 188–189, figs. (Hebrew). See Qumran.

ʻAin Kârim

G. E. Wright, "The Chronology of Palestinian Pottery in Middle Bronze I," *BASOR* 71, 1938, pp. 27–34, esp. pp. 28–31.

Excavated for the Franciscan Order by B. Bagatti, 1938, by S. Saller, 1941–42.

B. Bagatti, "ᶜAin Karim," *QDAP* 8, 1939, pp. 170–172; S. Saller, *Discoveries at St. John's, Ein Kârim, 1941–42*, 1946; B. Bagatti, *Il Santuario della Visitazione ad ᶜAin Karim*, 1948; J. Finegan, *The Archaeology of the New Testament*, 1969, pp. 3–5.

ʻAin Shems, see Beth-shemesh

Akko, see Acre

Ala-Safat, see Damiya

Amatha, see Ḥammat-Gader

ʻAmmân, Rabbath Ammon, Philadelphia

D. Mackenzie, "The Megalithic Monuments of Rabbath Ammon at Amman," *PEFA* 1, 1911, pp. 1–40, pls. 1–6; C. C. Torrey, "A Few Ancient Seals," *AASOR* 2–3, 1923, pp. 103–108, esp. pp. 103–105.

Excavation by Museo Nazionale Romano, directed by G. Guidi, 1927.

News, *PEQ*, 1928, pp. 3, 61; W. F. Albright, "An Anthropoid Clay Coffin from Sahab in Transjordan," *AJA* 36, 1932, pp. 295–306, pl. 12; N. Glueck, "Explorations in the Land of Ammon," *BASOR* 68, 1937, pp. 13–21; *id.*, *AASOR* 18–19, 1939, pp. 155–157, 159–160, 165–174, 201–204; E. Henschel-Simon, "Note on the Pottery of the ᶜAmman Tombs," *QDAP* 11, 1945, pp. 75–80; G. L. Harding, "Two Iron Age Tombs from ᶜAmman," *QDAP* 11, 1945, pp. 67–74, figs. 1–66, pls. 17–18; G. R. Driver, "Seals from ʻAmman and Petra," *QDAP* 11, 1945, pp. 81–82.

Excavations by the Jordan Department of Antiquities, 1947–

G. L. Harding, "An Iron Age Tomb at Sahab," *QDAP* 13, 1948, pp. 92–102, figs. 1–2, pls. 34–35; *id.*, "An Iron-Age Tomb at Meqabelein," *QDAP* 14, 1950, pp. 44–48, pls. 13–17; *id.*, "A Roman Family Vault on Jebel Jofeh, ᶜAmmân," *QDAP* 14, 1950, pp. 81–94, fig. 1, pls. 24–31; *id.*, "Unique Statues of the Iron Age Discovered at Amman," *ILN*, Feb. 18, 1950, pp. 266–267, figs. 1–8; Y. Aharoni, "A New Ammonite

Inscription," *IEJ* 1, 1950–51, pp. 219–222, figs. 1–3; G. L. Harding, "Excavations on the Citadel, Amman," *ADAJ* 1, 1951, pp. 7–16, figs. 1–5, pls. 1–5; *id.*, "A Roman Tomb in Amman," *ADAJ* 1, 1951, pp. 30–33, fig. 1, pl. 9; R. D. Barnett, "Four Sculptures from Amman," *ADAJ* 1, 1951, pp. 34–36, pls. 10–13; G. L. Harding, "Two Iron-Age Tombs in Amman," *ADAJ* 1, 1951, pp. 37–40, fig. 1, pl. 14; N. Avigad, "An Ammonite Seal," *IEJ* 2, 1952, pp. 163–164, fig. 1; R. T. O'Callaghan, "A Statue Recently Found in ᶜAmmân," *Orientalia* 21, 1952, pp. 184–193, pl. 26; G. L. Harding, "A Middle Bronze Age Tomb at Amman," *PEFA* 6, 1953, pp. 14–18, figs. 6–9, pl. 2; B. S. J. Isserlin, "Notes and Comparisons,"*PEFA* 6, 1953, pp. 19–22; G. L. Harding, "The Tomb of Adoni Nur in Amman," *PEFA* 6, 1953, pp. 48–65, figs. 18–20, pls. 6–7; O. Tufnell, "Notes and Comparisons," *PEFA* 6, 1953, pp. 66–72, figs. 21–23; G. R. Driver, "Seals and Tombstones," *ADAJ* 2, 1953, pp. 62–65; W. F. Albright, "Notes on Ammonite History," *Miscellanea Biblica B. Ubach*, 1953, pp. 131–136; G. L. Harding, "Excavations in Jordan 1953–1954," *ADAJ* 3, 1956, pp. 74–82, esp. p. 80; *id.*, "Recent Discoveries in Jordan," *PEQ*, 1958, pp. 7–18, esp. pp. 10–12; F. S. Maᵓayeh, "Recent Archaeological Discoveries in Jordan," *ADAJ* 4–5, 1960, pp. 114–115, pl. 3:1; *id.*, "Amman," *RB* 67, 1960, p. 226; G. M. Landes "The Material Civilization of the Ammonites," *BA* 24, 1961, pp. 66–86, esp. pp. 76–82, figs. 1–10; *id.*, "Ammon, Ammonites," *IDB*, 1962, pp. 108–114; R. W. Dajani, "A Neo-Babylonian Seal from Amman," *ADAJ* 6–7, 1962, pp. 124–125, pl. 4:8; W. A. Ward, "Cylinders and Scarabs from a Late Bronze Temple at Amman," *ADAJ* 8–9, 1964, pp. 47–55, pls. 21–22; *id.*, "Scarabs, Seals and Cylinders from Two Tombs at Amman," *ADAJ* 11, 1966, pp. 5–18, pls. 19–21; R. W. Dajani, "An Iron Age Tomb from Amman," *ADAJ* 11, 1966, pp. 41–47, pls. 2–9; *id.*, "Jabal Nuzha Tomb at Amman," *ADAJ* 11, 1966, pp. 48–52, pls. 10–18; *id.*, "Archaeological News," *ADAJ* 11, 1966, pp. 102–106; J. B. Hennessy, "Excavation of Late Bronze Age Temple," *PEQ* 1966, pp. 155–162, fig. 1, pls. 32–36; G. R. H. Wright, "The Bronze Age Temple at Amman," *ZAW* 78, 1966, pp. 350–357; J. B. Hennessy, "Supplementary Note," *ZAW* 78, 1966, pp. 357–359; R. Tournay, "Un Cylindre Babylonien découvert en Transjordanie," *RB* 74, 1967, pp. 248–254, fig. 1, pl. 17; G. L. Harding, *The Antiquities of Jordan*, 1967, pp. 32–33, 44–46, 49, 61–70, pls. 6–7; S. K. Tell, "New Ammonite Discoveries," *ADAJ* 12–13, 1967–68, pp. 9–12, pls. 1–4 (Arabic); R. W. Dajani, "The Amman Theater Fragment," *ADAJ* 12–13, 1967–1968, pp. 65–67, pl. 39; *id.*, "An EB-MB Burial from Amman," *ADAJ* 12–13, 1967–1968, pp. 68–69, pl. 40; S. H. Horn, "The Amman Citadel Inscription," *ADAJ* 12–13, 1967–1968, pp. 81–83, pl. 54; S. Ben-Arieh, "The Late Bronze Age Temple at Amman," *Qadmoniot* 1, 1968, pp. 98–99 (Hebrew); F. Zayadine, "A Greek Inscription from the Forum of Amman-Philadelphia, A. D. 189," *ADAJ* 14, 1969, pp. 34–35, pls. 22–23; S. K. Tell, "Notes on the Archaeology of Amman," *ADAJ* 14, 1969, pp. 28–33, pl. 21; S. H. Horn, "The ᶜAmmân Citadel Inscription," *BASOR* 193, 1969, pp. 2–13, figs. 1–3; F. M. Cross, Jr., "Epigraphic Notes on the ᶜAmmân Citadel," *BASOR* 193, 1969, pp. 13–19, fig. 1; J. B. Pritchard, ed., *ANEP*, 1969, nos. 64, 853a–b; N. Glueck, *The Other Side of the Jordan*, 1970, pp. 28, 141, 173, 180; W. F. Albright, "Some Comments on the ᶜAmmân Citadel Inscription," *BASOR* 198, 1970, pp. 38–40; R. Amiran, *Ancient Pottery of the Holy Land*, 1970, pp. 294–297, figs. 301–312; M. Avi-Yonah, "Rabbat ᶜAmmon," *EAEHL*, 1970, pp. 510–513, figs. (Hebrew).

ʿAmwās, see ʿEmmaus

Antipatris, see Apheq

Apheq, Rosh ha-ʿAyin, Antipatris, Tell Râs el-ʿAin

W. F. Albright, "The Site of Aphek in Sharon (=Antipatris or Râs el-Ein)," *JPOS* 3, 1923, pp. 50–53; *id.*, "Some Archaeological and Topographical Results of a Trip through Palestine," *BASOR* 11, 1923, pp. 3–7, fig. on p. 1.

Excavated by J. Ory for the Department of Antiquities, Palestine, 1934–1936.

J. H. Iliffe, "Pottery from Râs el-ᶜAin," *QDAP* 5, 1936, pp. 113–126, figs., pls. 64–67; J. Ory, "Excavations at Râs el-ᶜAin," *QDAP* 5, 1936, pp. 111–112, figs. 1–2, pls. 61–63; *id.*, "Excavations at Râs el-ᶜAin, II," *QDAP* 6, 1937, pp. 99–120, figs. 1–6, pls. 25–34; W. F. Albright, "New Egyptian Data on Palestine in the Patriarchal Age," *BASOR* 81, 1941, pp. 16–21.

Excavations carried out by J. Kaplan for the Department of Antiquities, Israel, 1958.

J. Kaplan, "Excavations at Wadi Rabah," *IEJ* 8, 1958, pp. 149–160, figs. 1–6, pl. 29b.

Excavations carried out by A. Eitan for the Department of Antiquities, Israel, 1961.

A. Eitan, "Aphek," *IEJ* 12, 1962, pp. 151–152; *id.*, "A Sarcophagus and an Ornamental Arch from the Mausoleum at Rosh haᶜAyin," *EI* 8, 1967, pp. 114–118, figs. 1–2, pls. 18–19 (Hebrew); *id.*, "Afeq Basharon," *EAEHL*, 1970, pp. 12–14, figs. (Hebrew); R. Gofna, "Nahal Šoreq," *EAEHL*, 1970, pp. 412–413, figs. (Hebrew).

Arad

Excavations by Hebrew University, Israel Exploration Society, Department of Antiquities, Israel, directed by Mrs. R. Amiran, Dr. Y. Aharoni, 1962–

Y. Aharoni and R. Amiran, "Tel Arad," *IEJ* 12, 1962, pp. 144–145; Y. Aharoni, "Tel Arad," *IEJ* 13, 1963, pp. 334–337; R. Amiran, Y. Aharoni, "Arad: A Biblical City in Southern Palestine," *Archaeology* 17, 1964, pp. 43–53, figs.; A. Biran, "Tell Arad," *CNI* 15: 2–3, 1964, pp. 20–21, pl. 2; Y. Aharoni, R. Amiran, "Tel Arad," *IEJ* 14, 1964, pp. 280–283; *id.*, "Excavations at Tel Arad," *IEJ* 14, 1964, pp. 131–147, figs. 1–5, pls. 31–38; Y. Aharoni, "The Second Season of Excavations at Tel Arad (1963)," *Yediot* 28, 1964, pp. 153–175, figs. 1–4, pls. 7–11 (Hebrew); B. Mazar, "The Sanctuary of Arad and the Family of Hobab the Kenite," *EI* 7, 1964, pp. 1–5 (Hebrew); Y. Aharoni, "Arad," *RB* 71, 1964, pp. 393–396, pls. 18b, 19; Y. Yadin, "A Note on the Stratigraphy of Arad," *IEJ* 15, 1965, p. 180; Y. Aharoni, R. Amiran, "Tel Arad," *IEJ* 15, 1965, pp. 249–252; R. Amiran, "A Preliminary Note on the Synchronisms between the Early Bronze Strata of Arad and the First Dynasty," *BASOR* 179, 1965, pp. 30–33, figs. 1–3; A. Biran, "Tell Arad," *CNI* 16:3, 1965, pp. 15–16, pls. 2–3; B. Mazar, "The Sanctuary of Arad and the Family of Hobab the Kenite," *JNES* 24, 1965, pp. 297–303, pls. 51; Y. Aharoni, R. Amiran, "Tel Arad," *RB* 72, 1965; pp. 556–560, pls. 29a, 30a; Y. Aharoni, "Hebrew Ostraca from Tel Arad," *IEJ* 16, 1966, pp. 1–7, figs. 1–2, pl. 1; S. Yeivin, "A Hieratic Ostracon from Tel Arad," *IEJ* 16, 1966, pp. 153–159, pl. 17a; A. Biran, "Arad," *CNI* 17:1, 1966, p. 19; Y. Aharoni, "Errata," *IEJ* 16, 1966, p. 152; R. Amiran, "Arad," *IEJ* 16, 1966, pp. 273–274; Y. Aharoni, R. Amiran, "Tel Arad," *RB* 74, 1967, pp. 68–72, pls. 7–8; A. Biran, "Arad," *CNI* 18:1–2, 1967, p. 34, pl. 4:3; Y. Aharoni, "Tel Arad," *BTS* 92, 1967, pp. 8–16, pls.; R. Amiran, Y. Aharoni, "Ancient Arad," *Israel Museum Guide*, 1967, pp. 1–36, figs. 1–25; Y. Aharoni, "Seals of Royal Functionaries from Arad," *EI* 8, 1967, pp. 101–103, pl. 13 (Hebrew); *id.*, "Excavations at Tel Arad, Preliminary Report on the Second Season, 1963," *IEJ* 17, 1967, pp. 233–249; *id.*, "Arad," *IEJ* 17 1967, pp. 270–272; R. Amiran, Y. Aharoni, "Arad: An Early Bronze Age City and a Biblical Citadel," *Archaeological Discoveries in the Holy Land*, 1967, pp. 89–99, figs.; Y. Aharoni, "The Negeb," *AOTS*, 1967, pp. 384–403, fig. 1, pl. 17; *id.*, "Arad: Its Inscriptions and Temple," *BA* 31, 1968, pp. 2–32, figs. 1–18; A. Biran, "Arad," *CNI* 19:3–4, 1968, p. 45; Y. Aharoni, "The Arad Ostraca," *Qadmoniot* 1, 1968, pp. 101–104, figs. (Hebrew); R. Amiran, Y. Aharoni, "Tell Arad," *RB* 75, 1968, pp. 388–392, pls. 40–41; B. A. Levine, "Notes on a Hebrew Ostracon from Arad," *IEJ* 19, 1969, pp. 49–51; D. N. Freedman, "The Orthography of the Arad Ostraca," *IEJ* 19, 1969, pp. 52–56; K. J. Cathcart, "*TRKB QMḤ* in the Arad Ostracon and Biblical Hebrew *REKEB*, 'Upper Millstone'," *VT* 19, 1969, pp. 121–123; Y. Aharoni, "Roots in the Past," *Ariel* 24, 1969, pp. 21–36; R. Amiran, "A Second Note on the Synchronism between Early Bronze Arad and the First Dynasty," *BASOR* 195, 1969, pp. 50–53, fig. 1; Y. Aharoni, "Three Hebrew Ostraca from Arad," *EI* 9, 1969, pl. 3 (Hebrew); *id.*, "The Israelite Sanctuary at Arad," *New Directions in Biblical Archaeology*, 1969, pp. 25–39, pls. 40–55; J. B. Pritchard, ed., *ANEP*, 1969, nos. 806, 807, 864, 872, 873; Y. Aharoni, "Three Hebrew Ostraca from Arad," *BASOR* 197, 1970, pp. 16–42, figs. 1–9; R. Amiran, "The Beginnings of Urbanization in Canaan," *NEATC*, 1970, pp. 83–96, fig. 6, pls. 9–12; B. Otzen, "Noch einmal das Wort *TRKB* auf einem Arad-ostracon," *VT* 20, 1970, pp. 239–242; K. M. Kenyon, *Archaeology in the Holy Land*, 1970, pp. 322, 337, 348–349; Y. Aharoni, "Notes and News," *PEQ* 1970, p. 80; Y. Aharoni, "ʿArad," *EAEHL*, 1970, pp. 469–477, figs. (Hebrew); A. F. Rainey, "A Hebrew 'Receipt' from Arad," *BASOR* 202, 1971, pp. 23–29, figs. 1–3.

ʿArâ ʿir, ʿArôʿer

N. Glueck, *AASOR* 14, 1934, p. 49, fig. 21a, p. 50, pl. 11a; *id.*, *AASOR* 18–19, 1939, pp. 246–250.

Excavated by Casa de Santiago for Biblical and Oriental Studies, directed by E. Olávarri, 1964–1966.

E. Olávarri, "Sondages à ʿArôʿer sur l'Arnon," *RB* 72, 1965, pp. 77–94, figs. 1–3, pls. 1–4; *id.*, "Aroër sur l'Arnon," *BTS* 72, 1965, pp. 2–3, figs.; R. W. Dajani, "Excavation at ʿArâʿir, 1964," *ADAJ* 11, 1966, p. 105; P. W. Lapp, *The Dhahr Mirzbâneh Tombs*, 1966, p. 95; S. Mittman, "Aroer, Minnith und Abel Keramim," *ZDPV* 85, 1969, pp. 63–75; E. Olávarri, "Fouilles à ʿArôʿer sur l'Arnon. Les niveaux du Bronze Intermédiaire," *RB* 76, 1969, pp. 230–259, figs. 1–5, pls. 1–5; P. W. Lapp, *NEATC*, 1970, pp. 111, 129; W. G. Dever, *NEATC*, 1970, pp. 150, 162–163; N. Glueck, *The Other Side of the Jordan*, 1970, pp. 32, 34, 142, 147, 153.

ʿArâq el-Emîr

H. C. Butler, *Publications of the Princeton University Archaeological Expeditions to Syria*, IIA, 1919, pp. 1–22, pl. 3; N. Glueck, *AASOR* 18–19, 1939, pp. 154–156; C. C. McCown, "The Araq el-Emir and the Tobiads," *BA* 20, 1957, pp. 63–76, figs. 1–10; B. Mazar, "The Tobiads," *IEJ* 7, 1957, pp. 137–145; *id.*, *IEJ* 7, 1957, pp. 229–238; W. F. Albright, *The Archaeology of Palestine*, 1960, pp. 149–150; M. Avi-Yonah, *Oriental Art in Roman Palestine*, 1961, p. 14.

Excavations by P. W. Lapp in 1961–1962 for the American Schools of Oriental Research, Concordia Seminary, Department of Antiquities, Jordan.

P. W. Lapp, "Soundings at ʿArâq el-Emîr (Jordan)," *BASOR* 165, 1962, pp. 16–34, figs. 1–11; *id.*, "The 1961 Excavation at ʿAraq el-Emir," *ADAJ* 6–7, 1962, pp. 80–89; G. E. Wright, *Biblical Archaeology*, 1962, fig. 149 on p. 207; P. W. Lapp, "The Second and Third Campaigns at ʿArâq el-Emîr," *BASOR* 171, 1963, pp. 8–39, figs. 1–15;

M. J. B. Brett, "The Qasr el-ᶜAbd: A Proposed Reconstruction," *BASOR* 171, 1963, pp. 39–45, figs. 1–2; D. K. Hill, "The Animal Fountain of ᶜArâq el-Emîr," *BASOR* 171, 1963, pp. 45–55, figs. 1–5; P. W. Lapp, "The 1962 Excavation at ᶜArâq el-Emîr," *ADAJ* 10, 1965, pp. 37–42, pls. 16–20; N. Glueck, *Deities and Dolphins*, 1965, p. 226, pl. 168 on p. 370; B. Porten, *Archives from Elephantine*, 1968, pp. 116–118, 300; P. W. Lapp, "ᶜAraq el-Emir," *EAEHL*, 1970, pp. 467–469, figs. (Hebrew).

'Arô'er, see 'Arâ'ir

'Arqûb el-Dhahr

N. Glueck, "ᶜArqûb ez-Zahar," *AASOR* 25–28, 1951, pp. 146–147, 425–426, pl. 2:2; P. J. Parr, "A Cave at ᶜArqub el-Dhahr," *ADAJ* 3, 1956, pp. 61–73.

Ascalon, Ashkelon

C. Schick, "Statues at Askalon," *PEFQS* 1888, pp. 22–23, fig. 1.

Excavations by the British School of Archaeology Jerusalem, for the Palestine Exploration Fund, 1920–22, directed by John Garstang and W. J. Phythian-Adams.

J. Garstang, "The Fund's Excavation of Ashkalon," *PEFQS* 1921, pp. 12–16, pls. 1–3; *id.*, "The Excavation of Ashkalon, 1920–1," *PEFQS* 1921, pp. 73–75, pls. 1–2; W. J. Phythian-Adams, "History of Askalon," *PEFQS* 1921, pp. 76–90; J. Garstang, "Askalon Reports. The Philistine Problem," *PEFQS* 1921, pp. 162–163; W. J. Phythian-Adams, "Askalon Reports. Stratigraphical Sections," *PEFQS* 1921, pp. 163–169, pl. 1; J. Garstang, "The Excavations at Askalon," *PEFQS* 1922, pp. 112–119, pls. 1–3; W. J. Phythian-Adams, "Report on the Stratification of Askalon," *PEFQS* 1923, pp. 60–84, figs. 1–4, pls. 1–4; J. Garstang, "Askalon," *PEFQS* 1924, pp. 24–35, figs. 1–5, pls. 1–3; J. H. Iliffe, "Third-Century Portrait Busts," *QDAP* 2, 1933, pp. 11–14, pls. 3–4; *id.*, "A Copy of the Crouching Aphrodite," *QDAP* 2, 1933, pp. 110–112, pl. 42; *id.*, "Vaulted Tomb Near Askalon," *QDAP* 2, 1933, pp. 182–183, fig. 1, pl. 48; *id.*, "A Hoard of Bronzes from Askalon," *QDAP* 5, 1936, pp. 61–68, pls. 29–34; J. Ory, "A Painted Tomb Near Ascalon," *QDAP* 8, 1939, pp. 38–44, figs. 1–2, pls. 25–29; M. Avi-Yonah, "Greek Inscriptions from Ascalon, Jerusalem, Beisan, and Hebron," *QDAP* 10, 1944, pp. 160–169, pl. 35; H. L. Ginsberg, "An Aramaic Contemporary of the Lachish Letters," *BASOR* 111, 1948, pp. 24–27; J. Bright, "A New Letter in Aramaic," *BA* 12, 1949, pp. 46–52; J. Perrot, "Ashkelon," *IEJ* 5, 1955, pp. 270–271; A. Malamat, "A New Record of Nebuchadrezzar's Palestinian Campaign," *IEJ* 6, 1956, pp. 251–252; G. Radan, "Helmet Found Near Ascalon," *IEJ* 8, 1958, pp. 185–188, pl. 32c; J. Prawer, "The City and Duchy of Ascalon in the Crusader Period," *EI* 5, 1958, pp. 224–237, pl. 26 (Hebrew); J. Leibowitz, "Ashkelon," *CNI* 9:1–2, 1958, p. 23, pl. 2a; W. F. Stinespring, "Ashkelon," *IDB*, 1962, pp. 252–254; A. Biran, "Ascalon," *CNI* 17:2–3, 1966, p. 26, pl. 4:1,2; *id.*, *CNI* 18:1–2, 1967, p. 42; V. Tsaferis, "Ashkelon-Barnea," *RB* 75, 1968, pp. 414–415, pl. 49; Y. Tsafrir, "A Painted Tomb at Or ha-Ner," *IEJ* 18, 1968, pp. 170–180, figs. 1–6, pls. 13–19; J. B. Pritchard, ed., *ANEP*, 1969, no. 334; *id.*, *ANET*, 1969, p. 256; K. M. Kenyon, *Archaeology in the Holy Land*, 1970, pp. 224, 230, 305; U. Rappaport, "Gaza and Ascalon in the Persian and Hellenistic Periods in Relation to their Coins," *IEJ* 20, 1970, pp. 75–80; J. Apel, "Ashqlon," *EAEHL*, 1970, pp. 20–21, fig. (Hebrew); M. Avi-Yonah, "Ashqlon," *EAEHL*, 1970, pp. 22–25, figs. (Hebrew); M. Benvenisti," *The Crusaders in the Holy Land*, 1970, pp. 114–130, figs.; P. R. Diplock, "The Date of Askalon's Sculptured Panels and an Identification of the Caesarea Statues," *PEQ* 1971, pp. 11–16, pls. 5–10.

Ashdod, Tell Mor

M. Dothan, "Tell Mor (Tell Kheidar)," *IEJ* 9, 1959, pp. 271–272; *id.*, "Tell Mor," *IEJ* 10, 1960, pp. 123–125; *id.*, "The Ancient Harbor of Ashdod," *CNI* 11:1, 1960, pp. 16–19, pls. 1–4; M. Avi-Yonah, "A New Fragment of the Ashdod Chancel Screen," *Bulletin Rabinowitz* III, 1960, p. 69, pl. 14:4.

Excavations by D. N. Freedman, M. Dothan, J. L. Swauger, for the Carnegie Museum, Pittsburgh Theological Seminary, Department of Antiquities and Museums, Israel, 1962–63, 1965, 1968, 1969, 1970.

M. Dothan, "Ashdod," *IEJ* 12, 1962, pp. 147–148; W. F. Stinespring, "Ashdod," *IDB*, 1962, pp. 248–249; E. F. Campbell, "In search of the Philistines," *BA* 26, 1963, pp. 30–32, figs. 13–14; M. Dothan, "Tell Ashdod," *IEJ* 13, 1963, pp. 340–342; A. Biran, "Ashdod," *CNI* 14:2, 1963, pp. 13–14, pl. 2; M. Dothan, "Ancient Ashdod," *ILN*, November 30, 1963, pp. 904–906, figs. 1–20; *id.*, "Ashdod," *ILN*, December 7, 1963, pp. 944–946, figs. 1–20; D. N. Freedman, "The Second Season at Ancient Ashdod," *BA* 26, 1963, pp. 134–139; M. Dothan, "Ashdod, Preliminary Report on the Excavations in Seasons 1962–1963," *IEJ* 14, 1964, pp. 79–95, figs. 1–4, pls. 17–23; A. Biran, "Ashdod," *CNI* 15:2–3, 1964, pp. 24–26, pl. 3; F. M. Cross, D. N. Freedman, "The Name of Ashdod," *BASOR* 175, 1964, pp. 48–50; M. Dothan, D. N. Freedman, "Ashdod," *RB* 71, 1964, pp. 401–405, pl. 20c–d; M. Dothan, "Remains of Muslim Buildings at Ashdod," *EI* 7, 1964, pp. 98–101, pl. 21 (Hebrew); *id.*, "Ashdod," *BTS* 71, 1965, pp. 8–16, figs.; *id.*, "Ashdod," *IEJ* 15, 1965, pp. 259–260; A. Biran, "Ashdod," *CNI* 17:1, 1966, p. 20, pl. 4:3; G. E. Wright, "Fresh Evidence for the Philistine Story," *BA* 29, 1966, pp. 70–86, figs. 1–8; M. Dothan, "Ashdod," *RB* 74, 1967, pp. 78–80, pl. 11b–c; *id.*, "Ashdod: A City of the Philistine Pentapolis," *Archaeology* 20, 1967, pp. 178–186, figs.; *id.*, "Ashdod: A City of the Philistine Pentapolis," *ADHL*, 1967, pp. 129–137, figs.; M. Dothan, D. N. Freedman, "Ashdod I," *ᶜAtiqot* 7, 1967, pp. 1–171, figs. 1–47, pls. 1–28; H. Tadmor, "Fragment of a Stele of Sargon II from the Excavations of Ashdod," *EI* 8, 1967, pp. 241–245, pl. 41 (Hebrew); M. Dothan, "Tel Ashdod," *IEJ* 18, 1968, pp. 253–254.

Excavations at Ashdod-Yam by J. Kaplan, November 1965—March 1968, for Museum Haaretz, Tel Aviv.

J. Kaplan, "The Stronghold of Yamani at Ashdod-Yam," *IEJ* 19, 1969, pp. 137–149, figs. 1–8, pl. 13; J. B. Pritchard, ed., *ANET*, 1969, pp. 284, 286–288, 291, 294, 308; *id.*, *ANEP*, 1969, no. 773; A. Biran, "Ashdod," *CNI* 20:3–4, 1969, pp. 50–51, pls. 5b, 6b, 7; M. Dothan, "Tel Ashdod," *IEJ* 19, 1969, pp. 243–245; J. Kaplan, "The Stronghold of Yamani at Ashdod-Yam," *EI* 9, 1969, pp. 130–147, pl. 38 (Hebrew); M. Dothan, "Ashdod," *RB* 76, 1969, pp. 569–572, pl. 29; *id.*, "Ashdod of the Philistines," *New Directions in Biblical Archaeology*, 1969, pp. 15–24, pls. 1–33; O. Bar-Yosef, "Prehistoric Sites near Ashdod, Israel," *PEQ* 1970, pp. 52–64, figs. 1–3; M. Dothan, "Tel Ashdod," *RB* 77, 1970, pp. 402–405, pls. 25, 26a; R. Gophna, D. Meron, "An Iron Age I Tomb Between Ashdod and Ashkelon," *ᶜAtiqot* 6, 1970, pp. 1–5, pl. 1 (Hebrew); M. Dothan, "A Stand with 'Musicians' Motif from Ashdod," *Qadmoniot* 3, 1970, p. 94, pl. 1(Hebrew); M. Dothan, "Ashdod," *IEJ* 20, 1970, pp. 119–120; *id.*, "Ashdod," *EAEHL*, 1970, pp. 16–20, figs. (Hebrew); *id.*, "The Musicians of Ashdod," *Archaeology* 23, 1970, pp. 310–311, figs.; M. Dothan, "Tel Mor," *EAEHL*, 1970, pp. 587–588, figs. (Hebrew).

Ashkelon, see Ascalon

aṣ-Ṣinnabra, see Beth-Yeraḥ

ʻAtar Haroʻa

Excavated by R. Cohen in 1965, 1967 for the Department of Antiquities, Israel.

R. Cohen, "Atar Haroᶜa," *ᶜAtiqot* 6, 1970, pp. 6–24, pls. 2–5 (Hebrew);

ʻAthlit

Excavated by C. N. Johns for the Department of Antiquities, Palestine, 1930–33.

C. N. Johns, "Excavations at Pilgrims' Castle (ᶜAtlit)," *QDAP* 1, 1932, pp. 111–129, figs. 1–29, pls. 40–53; *id.*, "Excavations at ᶜAtlit (1930–31): The Southeast Cemetery," *QDAP* 2, 1933, pp. 41–104, figs. 1–94, pls. 13–37; *id.*, "Medieval Slip-ware from Pilgrims' Castle, ᶜAtlīt (1930–1)," *QDAP* 3, 1934, pp. 137–144, pls. 49–57; *id.*, "Excavations at Pilgrims' Castle, ᶜAtlit, (1932); the Ancient Tell and the Outer Defences of the Castle," *QDAP* 3, 1934, pp. 145–164, 173, pls. 48–65; *id.*, "Excavations at Pilgrims' Castle, ᶜAtlīt (1931–2): An Unfinished Church in the Suburb," *QDAP* 4, 1935, pp. 122–137, pls. 71–75; *id.*, "Excavations at Pilgrims' Castle, ᶜAtlīt (1932–3): Stables at the South-west of the Suburb," *QDAP* 5, 1936, pp. 31–60, pls. 22–28; *id.*, "Excavations at Pilgrims' Castle, ᶜAtlīt (1933): Cremated Burials of Phoenician Origin," *QDAP* 6, 1937, pp. 121–152, pls. 35–42; D. Harden, *The Phoenicians*, 1963, pp. 60, 105–106, 114, 149, 152, fig. 44; A. Biran, "Athlit," *CNI* 17:1, 1966, p. 18, pl. 2; J. B. Pritchard, ed., *ANEP*, 1969, no. 71; C. N. Johns, "ᶜAtlit," *EAEHL*, 1970, pp. 478–483, figs. (Hebrew).

ʻAuja el-Hafir, Nitsanah, Nessana

C. L. Woolley, T. E. Lawrence, "The Wilderness of Zin," *PEFA* 3, 1914–15, pp. 117–121, figs. 52–54, pl. 29; J. H. Iliffe, "Nabataean Pottery from the Negeb," *QDAP* 3, 1934, pp. 132–135, pls. 45, 47, 48.

Excavations by the Colt Archaeological Expedition, for the British School of Archaeology in Jerusalem, 1934–1938, directed by H. D. Colt.

H. D. Colt, "Discoveries at Auja Hafir," *PEFQS* 1936, pp. 216–220; J. L. Myres, "Chairman's Address," *PEQ* 1938, pp. 150–151; G. E. Kirk, "Archaeological Exploration in the Southern Desert," *PEQ* 1938, pp. 211–235, figs. 1–4, pls. 16–17; *id.*, "The Negev or Southern Desert of Palestine," *PEQ* 1941, pp. 57–71, pl. 5; M. E. Kirk, "Short History of Palestinian Excavation," *PEQ* 1944, pp. 131–144, esp. p. 143; *id.*, "An Outline of the Ancient Cultural History of Transjordan," *PEQ* 1944, pp. 180–198, esp. p. 197; N. Lewis, "New Light on the Negev in Ancient Times," *PEQ* 1948, pp. 102–117, esp. pp. 102–103; L. Casson, E. L. Hettich, *Excavations at Nessana* 2, 1950; C. J. Kraemer, *Excavations at Nessana* 3, 1958; H. D. Colt, *Excavations at Nessana* 1, 1962; *id.*, "Castles in Zin," *ADHL*, 1967, pp. 187–192, pls.; N. Glueck, *Rivers in the Desert*, 1968, pp. 26, 29, 262–263; M. Avi-Yonah, "Nitsana," *EAEHL*, 1970, pp. 416–419, figs. (Hebrew).

Avdat, see Abdah

Azekah, see Tell ez-Zakariyeh

Azor

J. Perrot and M. Dothan conducted excavations since 1955 for the Department of Antiquities, Israel.

J. Leibovitch, "Azor," *CNI* 6:3–4, 1955, p. 33, pl. 4:3–4; J. Perrot, "Azor," *IEJ* 8, 1958, p. 133; M. Dothan, "Asor," *IEJ* 8, 1958, pp. 272–274; J. Perrot, "Azor,"

IEJ 9, 1959, pp. 266–267; A. Biran, "Azor," *CNI* 10:1–2, 1959, pp. 28–29, pl. 3; J. Perrot, "Azor," *RB* 67, 1960, pp. 255–257, pl. 17b; M. Dothan, "Azor," *RB* 67, 1960, pp. 395–396, pl. 24:b; *id.*, "Azor," *IEJ* 10, 1960, pp. 259–60; R. Amiran, "The Pottery of the Middle Bronze Age I in Palestine," *IEJ* 10, 1960, pp. 204–225, figs. 1–10, esp. p. 208, fig. 2:3; J. Perrot, "A Group of Curious Ceramic Ossuaries from Azor," *ILN*, December 3, 1960, pp. 998–1000, figs. 1–16; *id.*, "Azor," *BTS* 37, 1961, pp. 14–17; A. Biran, "Azor," *CNI* 12:2, 1961, pp. 16–17, pl. 3; J. Perrot, "Une tombe à ossuaries du IVe millénaire à Azor, près de Tel-Aviv," *ᶜAtiqot* 3, 1961, pp. 1–83, figs. 1–43, pls. 1–10; M. Dothan, "An Inscribed Jar from Azor," *ᶜAtiqot* 3, 1961, pp. 181–184, fig. 1, pl. 28:2–3; *id.*, "Excavations at Azor," *IEJ* 11, 1961, pp. 171–175, fig. 1, pls. 33–35; A. Biran, "Azor," *CNI* 18:1–2, 1967, p. 41; N. Glueck, *The River Jordan*, 1968, p. 157, fig.; V. Tsaferis, A. Druks, "Tell Azor," *RB* 77, 1970, p. 578, pl. 40b; J. Perrot, "Azor," *EAEHL*, 1970, pp. 6–7, figs. (Hebrew); M. Dothan, "Azor," *EAEHL*, 1970, pp. 7–8, figs. (Hebrew).

Bâb edh-Dhrâʻ

W. F. Albright, "The Archaeological Results of an Expedition to Moab and the Dead Sea," *BASOR* 14, 1924, pp. 2–12, esp. pp. 5–7; *id.*, *AASOR* 6, 1926, pp. 53–66; G. E. Wright, "The Chronology of Palestine in the Early Bronze Age," *BASOR* 63, 1936, pp. 12–21, esp. pp. 15, 20, figs. 1–5; *id.*, "The Chronology of Palestinian Pottery in Middle Bronze I," *BASOR* 71, 1938, pp. 27–34, figs. 1–2; J. P. Harland, "Sodom and Gomorrah," *BA* 5, 1942, pp. 17–32, esp. pp. 27–28, figs. 1–8; W. F. Albright, J. L. Kelso, J. P. Thorley, "Early Bronze Pottery from Bâb ed-Drâᶜ in Moab," *BASOR* 95, 1944, pp. 3–13, pls. 1–3.

Excavated by P. W. Lapp for the American Schools of Oriental Research, 1965–67.

S. Saller, "Bâb edh-Dhrâᶜ," *LA* 15, 1965, pp. 137–219, figs. 1–34; P. W. Lapp, "The Cemetery at Bab edh-Dhraᶜ," *Archaeology* 19, 1966, pp. 104–111, figs.; G. L. Harding, *The Antiquities of Jordan*, 1967, pp. 31–32; P. W. Lapp, "The Cemetery at Bâb edh-Dhrâᶜ Jordan," *ADHL*, 1967, pp. 35–40, figs.; *id.*, "Bâb edh-Dhrâᶜ," *RB* 75, 1968, pp. 86–93, fig. 1, pls. 3–6a; *id.*, "Bâb edh-Dhrâᶜ Tomb A 76 and Early Bronze I in Palestine," *BASOR* 189, 1968, pp. 12–41, figs. 1–16; *id.*, "Bâb edh-Dhrâᶜ, Perizzites and Emim," *Jerusalem Through the Ages*, 1968, pp. 1–25, fig. 1, pls. 1–3; W. F. Albright, *Yahweh and the Gods of Canaan*, 1968, p. 63, n. 27; M. Tadmor, "Excavations at Bab edh-Dhraᶜ," *Qadmoniot* 2, 1969, pp. 56–59, figs. (Hebrew); K. M. Kenyon, *Archaeology in the Holy Land*, 1970, p. 323; N. Glueck, *The Other Side of the Jordan*, 1970, p. 149; P. W. Lapp, "Palestine in the Early Bronze Age," *NEATC*, 1970, pp. 103–112, 114–116, 118, 121; M. Kochavi, "Bab edh-Dhraᶜ," *EAEHL*, 1970, p. 27 (Hebrew).

Balûʻah

G. Horsfield, L. H. Vincent, "Un Stele Égypto-Moabite au Balouᶜa," *RB* 41, 1932, pp. 417–444, figs. 1–7, pls. 1–15; É. Drioton, "À propos de la Stèle du Balouᶜa," *RB* 42, 1933, pp. 353–365, figs. 1–10; J. W. Crowfoot, "An Expedition to Baluah," *PEFQS* 1934, pp. 76–84, pls. 1–3; A. H. van Zyl, *The Moabites*, 1960, pp. 31–33, 108–111; W. F. Albright, *The Archaeology of Palestine*, 1960, pp. 79, 186–187, pl. 12; W. A. Ward, M. F. Martin, "The Baluᶜa Stele: A New Transcription with Palaeographical and Historical Notes," *ADAJ* 8–9, 1964, pp. 5–29, pls. 2–6; G. L. Harding, *The Antiquities of Jordan*, 1967, pp. 27, 38, 109, pl. 3b; J. B. Pritchard, ed., *ANEP*, 1969, no. 488; N. Glueck, *The Other Side of the Jordan*, 1970, pp. 142, 153, 158, fig. 76 on p. 159, p. 163, fig. 94 on p. 187, p. 188, fig. 96 on p. 189.

Beersheba, Bir Abu Matar (Tell Abu Matar), Bir eṣ-Ṣafadi, Khirbet el-Bitar (Ḥorvat Beter)

C. L. Woolley, T. E. Lawrence, "The Wilderness of Zin," *PEFA* 3, 1914–1915, pp. 46, 107–108, figs. 42, 43, pp. 134–135.

Excavated by J. Perrot for the Centre National de la Recherche Scientifique and the Department of Antiquities, Israel, 1952–1960.

J. Leibovitch, "Khirbet el-Bitar," *CNI* 5:1–2, 1954, pp. 26–27, pl. 3a; *id.*, "Beersheba," *CNI* 5:1–2, 1954, pp. 27–28, pl. 4; J. Perrot, "The Excavations at Tell Abu Matar, near Beersheba," *IEJ* 5, 1955, pp. 17–40, figs. 1–14, pls. 2–8; *id.*, "The Excavations at Tell Abu Matar, near Beersheba," *IEJ* 5, 1955, pp. 73–84, figs. 15, 16, pls. 9–18; *id.*, "Beersheba: Bir eṣ-Ṣafadi," *IEJ* 5, 1955, pp. 125–126; *id.*, "The Excavations at Tell Abu Matar, near Beersheba," *IEJ* 5, 1955, pp. 167–189, figs. 17–22, pls. 21–24a; R. Amiran, "The 'Cream Ware' of Gezer and the Beersheba Late Chalcolithic," *IEJ* 5, 1955, pp. 240–245, fig. 1, pl. 34C:2–4; T. Josien, "La Faune chalcolithique des gisements Palestiniens de Bir es-Safadi et Bir Abou Matar," *IEJ* 5, 1955, pp. 246–256; M. Negbi, "The Botanical Finds at Tell Abu Matar, near Beersheba," *IEJ* 5, 1955, pp. 257–258, pl. 35; E. Anati, "Subterranean Dwellings in the Central Negev," *IEJ* 5, 1955, pp. 259–261, figs. 1–2.

Excavations at Ḥorvat Beter conducted by M. Dothan for the Department of Antiquities, Israel, 1953–1955.

M. Dothan, "Radioactive Examination of Archaeological Material from Israel," *IEJ* 6, 1956, pp. 112–114; J. Perrot, "Beersheba: Bir eṣ-Ṣafadi," *IEJ* 6, 1956, pp. 126–127; H. deContenson, "La céramique chalcolithique de Beersheba, étude typologique," *IEJ* 6, 1956, pp. 163–179, figs. 1–9, pp. 226–238, figs. 10–13; J. Perrot, "Les fouilles d'Abou Matar près de Beersheba," *Syria* 34, 1957, pp. 1–38, figs. 1–25, pls. 1–4; *id.*, "Bir es-Safadi," *IEJ* 9, 1959, pp. 141–142; M. Dothan, "Excavations at Horvat Beter (Beersheba)," *ᶜAtiqot* 2, 1959, pp. 1–42, figs. 1–19, pls. 1–6; E. Yeivin, "The Flint Implements from Horvat Beter (Beersheba)," *ᶜAtiqot* 2, 1959, pp. 43–47, figs. 1–2, pl. 7; D. V. Zaitchek, "Remains of Cultivated Plants from Ḥorvat Beter (Beersheba)," *ᶜAtiqot* 2, 1959, pp. 48–52; S. Angress, "Mammal Remains from Horvat Beter (Beersheba)," *ᶜAtiqot* 2, 1959, pp. 53–71, pls. 8–9; J. Perrot, "The Dawn of History in Southern Palestine," *Archaeology* 12, 1959, pp. 8–15, figs.; *id.*, "Statuettes en ivoire et autres objets en ivoire et en as provenent des gisements préhistoriques de la région de Beershéba," *Syria* 36, 1959, pp. 8–19, figs. 1–9, pls. 2–3; *id.*, "Beershéba: Bir es-Safadi," *IEJ* 10, 1960, pp. 120–121; A. Biran, "A Unique Beersheba Figurine," *CNI* 11:2, 1960, pp. 17–18, pl. 2; J. Perrot, "Safadi," *RB* 67, 1960, pp. 253–255, pl. 17a; *id.*, "The Underground Communities of Beersheba," *ILN*, July 23, 1960, pp. 144–147, figs. 1–22; *id.*, "The Ivory Art of the Mysterious Troglodytes of the Beersheba of 5000 Years Ago," *ILN*, July 30, 1960, pp. 183–185, figs. 1–15; R. Gophna, "Beersheba," *IEJ* 13, 1963, pp. 145–146; J. Perrot, "Beersheba and the Negev 5000 Years Ago," *Ariel* 11, 1965, pp. 69–78, figs.; A. Biran, "Beersheba," *CNI* 17:2–3, 1966, p. 26; *id.*, "Beersheba," *CNI* 18:1–2, 1967, pp. 42–43, pl. 8:2; Y. Israeli, "Beersheba," *RB* 75, 1968, pp. 415–416; N. Glueck, *The River Jordan*, 1968, pp. 151, 154, figs.

Excavated by Mme. Y. Israeli for the Department of Antiquities, Israel, 1968.

A. Biran, "Beersheba," *CNI* 19:3–4, 1968, pp. 44–45; J. Perrot, "La 'Venus' de Beersheva," *EI* 9, 1969, pp. 100–101, pl. 13; A. Biran, "Beersheba," *CNI* 20:3–4, 1969, p. 51; J. B. Pritchard, ed., *ANEP*, 1969, nos. 823, 824.

Excavated by Y. Aharoni for the University of Tel Aviv, 1969–1971.

Y. Aharoni, "Tel Beersheba," *IEJ* 19, 1969, pp. 245–247; *id.*, "Tel Béershéva," *RB* 77, 1970, pp. 404–405, pls. 26b, 27, 28; *id.*, "Tel Beersheba," *IEJ* 20, 1970, pp. 227–229; J. Perrot, "Bᶜer Shevaᶜ," *EAEHL*, 1970, pp. 28–32, figs. (Hebrew); R. Gofna, "Bᶜer Shevaᶜ," *EAEHL*, 1970, p. 33, figs. (Hebrew); B. Boyd, "Excavations at Tell Beer-Sheba, Israel, 1969–70," *AJA* 75, 1971, p. 196.

Beidha, see Petra

Beisamoun, see ʿEinan

Beisan, see Beth-shan

Beit Jibrin, see Tell Sandahannah

Beit Sahur, see Bethlehem

Belvoir, Kokhav Hayarden

Excavations conducted by M. Ben Dov and Y. Mintzker, for the Department of Antiquities and the National Parks Authority, Israel, 1963, 1966–1967.

A. Biran, "Kokhav Hayarden," *CNI* 18:1–2, 1967, pp. 25–26, pl. 2; M. Ben Dov, Y. Mintzker, "Kokhab ha-Yarden," *RB* 75, 1968, pp. 419–420, pl. 51; A. Biran, "Kokhav Hayarden," *CNI* 19:3–4, 1968, p. 39, pl. 1; M. Ben Dov, "The Excavations at the Crusader Fortress of Kokhav-Hayarden," *Qadmoniot* 2, 1969, pp. 22–27, figs. (Hebrew); M. Benvenisti, *The Crusaders in the Holy Land*, 1970, pp. 294–300, figs.

Bene Beraq

Caves excavated by J. Ory for the Department of Antiquities, Palestine, 1942.

J. Ory, "A Chalcolithic Necropolis at Benei Beraq," *QDAP* 12, 1946, pp. 43–57, figs. 1–5, pls. 15–18.

Cave excavated by J. Kaplan for the Department of Antiquities, Israel, 1951.

J. Kaplan, "Excavations at Benei Beraq, 1951," *IEJ* 13, 1963, pp. 300–312, figs. 1–9, pls. 32–34a, b; *id.*, "Bne Braq," *EAEHL*, 1970, pp. 98–99, figs. (Hebrew).

Benot Yaʿaqov, see Jisr Banāt Yaʿqūb

Ben Shemen

J. Perrot, "Hazoréa, Tell Turmus, Ben Shemen," *IEJ* 13, 1963, pp. 140–141.

Excavations conducted by J. Perrot and P. Ladiray for the Department of Antiquities, Israel and the Centre de Recherches Préhistoriques, 1968.

J. Perrot, "Les Ossuaires de Ben Shemen," *EI* 8, 1967, pp. 46–49, pls. 11–13; *id.*, "Ben Shemen," *IEJ* 19, 1969, pp. 117–118; P. Ladiray, "Ben Shemen," *RB* 77, 1970, p. 380.

Besara, see Beth-Sheʿarim

Beth Alpha

Excavations conducted by E. L. Sukenik for the Hebrew University, 1929.

E. L. Sukenik, *The Ancient Synagogue at Beth Alpha*, 1932; *id.*, *Ancient Synagogues in Palestine and Greece*, 1934, pp. 31–35, 56–57, 76, 77; *id.*, "A New Discovery at Beth Alpha," *Bulletin Rabinowitz* 2, 1951, p. 26, pl. 11; E. R. Goodenough, *Symbols* 1, 1953, pp. 241–253; E. Kitzinger, *Israeli Mosaics of the Byzantine Period*, 1965, pp. 9–15, pls. 8–14; N. Avigad, "Bet Alfa," *EAEHL*, 1970, pp. 37–39, figs. (Hebrew).

Bethany

Excavated for the Custody of the Holy Land by S. Saller, 1949–1953, S. Loffreda, 1969.

S. Saller, "Bethany," *ADAJ* 1, 1951, p. 44; *id.*, "Bethany," *ADAJ* 2, 1953, pp. 82–83; *id.*, *Excavations at Bethany (1949–53)*, 1957; S. Loffreda, "Due Tombe a Betania presso le suore della Nigrizia," *LA* 19, 1969, pp. 349–366, figs. 1–6; J. Finegan, *The Archeology of the New Testament*, 1969, pp. 89–94, figs.

Bethel, Beitin

Soundings made by W. F. Albright for the American Schools of Oriental Research, 1927.

W. F. Albright, "A Trial Excavation in the Mound of Bethel," *BASOR* 29, 1928, pp. 9–11.

Excavated by W. F. Albright for the American Schools of Oriental Research and Pittsburgh-Xenia Theological Seminary, 1934.

W. F. Albright, "The First Month of Excavation of Bethel," *BASOR* 55, 1934, pp. 23–25; *id.*, "The Kyle Memorial Excavation at Bethel," *BASOR* 56, 1934, pp. 2–15, figs. 1–9; *id.*, "Observations on the Bethel Report," *BASOR* 57, 1935, pp. 27–30; *id.*, "Archaeology and the Date of the Hebrew Conquest of Palestine," *BASOR* 58, 1935, pp. 10–17.

Excavated by J. L. Kelso, 1954, 1957, 1960 for the American Schools of Oriental Research and Pittsburgh Theological Seminary.

J. L. Kelso, "The Second Campaign at Bethel," *BASOR* 137, 1955, pp. 5–10, figs. 1–3; *id.*, "Excavations at Bethel," *BA* 19, 1956, pp. 37–43, figs. 7–9; *id.*, "The Third Campaign at Bethel," *BASOR* 151, 1958, pp. 3–8, figs. 1–2; G. W. Van Beek, A. Jamme, "An Inscribed South Arabian Clay Stamp from Bethel," *BASOR* 151, 1958, pp. 9–16, figs. 1–4; J. L. Kelso, "The Fourth Campaign at Bethel," *BASOR* 164, 1961, pp. 5–19, figs. 1–8; *id.*, "Condensed Report of the 1960 Beitin Expedition," *ADAJ* 6–7, 1962, pp. 122–123; *id.*, *IDB*, 1962, pp. 391–393, figs.; *id.*, *The Excavation of Bethel 1934–1960*, *AASOR* 39, 1968; Y. Yadin, "An Inscribed South Arabian Clay Stamp from Bethel?" *BASOR* 196, 1969, pp. 37–45, figs. 1–8; J. B. Pritchard, ed., *ANEP*, 1969, no. 468; P. W. Lapp, *NEATC*, 1970, p. 115, n. 108 on p. 129; G. W. Van Beek, A. Jamme, "The Authenticity of the Bethel Stamp Seal," *BASOR* 199, 1970, pp. 59–65, figs. 1–2; J. L. Kelso, "A Reply to Yadin's Article on the Finding of the Bethel Seal," *BASOR* 199, 1970, p. 65; *id.*, "Bet-El," *EAEHL*, 1970, pp. 36–37, figs. (Hebrew).

Beth-haccherem, see Ramat Raḥel

Bethlehem, Beit Sahur

Excavated by R. W. Hamilton for the Department of Antiquities of Palestine, 1932, 1935.

R. W. Hamilton, "Excavations in the Atrium, Church of the Nativity, Bethlehem," *QDAP* 3, 1934, pp. 1–8, fig. 1, pls. 1–7; E. T. Richmond, "Basilica of the Nativity," *QDAP* 5, 1936, pp. 75–81, pls. 35–48; *id.*, "The Church of the Nativity," *QDAP* 6, 1937, pp. 63–66, fig. 1; pp. 67–72, figs. 1–3, pls. 13–17; R. W. Hamilton, "Note on a Mosaic Inscription in the Church of the Nativity," *QDAP* 6, 1937, pp. 210–211, fig. 1, pl. 72; J. W. Crowfoot, *Early Churches in Palestine*, 1941, pp. 18–20, 22–30, 77–85, 119–120, pls. 3, 6b, 11, 28.

Beit Sahur tomb excavated by Y. Labadi for the Department of Antiquities, Jordan, 1962.

J. B. Hennessy, "An Early Bronze-Age Tomb Group from Beit Sahur," *ADAJ* 11, 1966, pp. 19–40, pls. 22–26; L. Vetrali, "Le Iscrizioni dell'acquedotto Romano presso Betlemme," *LA* 17, 1967, pp. 149–161, figs. 1–5; E. D. Stockton, "The Stone Age of Bethlehem," *LA* 17, 1967, pp. 129–148, map; S. Saller, "Iron Age Remains from the Site of a New School at Bethlehem," *LA* 18, 1968, pp. 153–180, figs. 1–9; B. Bagatti, "Recenti Scavi a Betlemme," *LA* 18, 1968, pp. 181–237, figs. 1–45, plan; J. Finegan, *The Archeology of the New Testament*, 1969, pp. 18–26, figs.; S. Gutman, A. Berman, "Bethléem," *RB* 77, 1970, pp. 583–585, fig. 3; M. Stekelis, "Bet Leḥem," *EAEHL*, 1970, p. 48, fig. (Hebrew); M. Avi-Yonah, "Bet Leḥem," *EAEHL*, 1970, pp. 48–53, figs. (Hebrew).

Beth-pelet, see Tell el-Far'ah (S)

Beth-shan, Tell el-Husn, Beisan, Scythopolis.

Excavated by C. S. Fisher, A. Rowe, G. M. FitzGerald, for The University Museum, University of Pennsylvania, 1921–23, 1925–28, 1930, 1931, 1933.

G. J. H. Ovenden, "Notes on the Excavations at Beisan," *PEFQS* 1923, pp. 147–149; W. F. Albright, *AASOR* 6, 1926, pp. 32–38; S. A. Cook, "The American Excavations at Beisān," *PEFQS* 1926, pp. 29–30; A. Rowe, "The New Discoveries at Beth-shan," *PEFQS* 1927, pp. 67–84, 1 pl.; pp. 148–149; G. M. FitzGerald, "Two Inscriptions from Beisan," *PEFQS* 1927, pp. 150–154, pls. 6–7; A. Rowe, "Excavations at Beisan during the 1927 Season," *PEFQS* 1928, pp. 73–90, fig. 1, pls. 1–5; W. F. Albright, "A Visit to Beth-shan," *BASOR* 29, 1928, pp. 7–8; A. Rowe, "Beisan — Third Report 1928 Season," *PEFQS* 1929, pp. 78–94, pls. 2–16; *id.*, *The Topography and History of Beth-shan*, Beth-shan I, 1930; G. M. FitzGerald, *The Four Canaanite Temples of Beth-shan, the Pottery*, Beth-shan II:2, 1930; *id.*, *Beth-shan Excavations 1921–23, The Arab and Byzantine Levels*, Beth-shan III, 1931; A. Rowe, L. H. Vincent, "New Light on the Evolution of Canaanite Temples as Exemplified by Restorations of the Sanctuaries Found at Beth-shan," *PEFQS* 1931, pp. 12–21, pls. 1–4; G. M. FitzGerald, "Excavations at Beth-shan in 1930," *PEFQS* 1931, pp. 59–70, pls. 1–6; *id.*, "Excavations at Beth-shan in 1931," *PEFQS* 1932, pp. 138–148, pls. 1–5; *id.*, "Excavations at Beth-shan in 1933," *PEFQS* 1934, pp. 123–134, pls. 1–7; *id.*, "The Earliest Pottery of Beth-shan," *The Museum Journal* 24, 1935, pp. 5–22, pls. 1–10; H. Comfort, F. O. Waage, "Selected Pottery from Beth Shan," *PEFQS* 1936, pp. 221–224, pls. 1–2; M. Avi-Yonah, "Mosaic Pavements at el-Hammam, Beisān," *QDAP* 5, 1936, pp. 11–30, pls. 13–17; G. M. FitzGerald, *A Sixth Century Monastery at Beth-shan*, Beth-shan IV, 1939; A. Rowe, *The Four Canaanite Temples of Beth-shan*, Beth-shan II:1, 1940; S. Ben-Dor, "Concerning the Era of Nysa-Scythopolis," *PEQ* 1944, pp. 152–156, pl. 5; M. Avi-Yonah, "Greek Inscriptions from Ascalon, Jerusalem, Beisan, and Hebron," *QDAP* 10, 1944, pp. 160–169, pl. 35; J. Leibovitch, "Beth-shan," *CNI* 4:2–3, 1953, p. 30, pl. 3:3; A. Rowe, "A Provisional Chronological Table of the Prehistoric and Historic Ages of Palestine," I, *PEQ* 1954, pp. 76–82; *id.*, "Chronological Table," II, *PEQ* 1955, pp. 176–179; N. Zori, "Neolithic and Chalcolithic Sites in the Valley of Beth-shan," *PEQ* 1958, pp. 44–51, figs. 1–4, pls. 2–5; J. Černý, "Stela of Ramesses from Beisan," *EI* 5, 1958, pp. 75–82, 2 figs.

Excavation by N. Zori and S. Applebaum in 1959–60, 1964, for the Department of Antiquities, Israel.

N. Zori, "Beth Shean," *IEJ* 9, 1959, p. 276; L. Y. Rahmani, "A Lion-faced Figurine from Bet Sheᶜan," *ᶜAtiqot* 2, 1959, pp. 184–185, pl. 24:1–3; S. Applebaum, "Beth Shean," *IEJ* 10, 1960, pp. 126–127; *id.*, "Beth Shean," *IEJ* 10, 1960, pp. 263–264; N. Zori, "On Two Rare Coins from Scythopolis (Beth-shan)," *PEQ* 1960, p. 70, pl. 5; *id.*, "Beth Shean," *RB* 67, 1960, pp. 400–401, pl. 27b; W. F. Albright, *The Archaeology of Palestine*, 1960, pp. 40–41, 75, 120, pl. 6; G. E. Wright, *Biblical Archaeology*, 1962, pp. 26, 73, figs. 58–59 on pp. 95–96, p. 115, fig. 71 on p. 117, p. 125; R. W. Hamilton, "Beth-shan," *IDB*, 1962, pp. 397–401, figs.; A. Biran, "Beth Shean Theatre," *CNI* 13:1, 1962, pp. 19–20, pls. 1, 3:1; M. Avi-Yonah, "Scythopolis," *IEJ* 12, 1962, pp. 123–134; A. Negev, "Beth Shean," *IEJ* 12, 1962, p. 151; S. Applebaum, "Beth Shean," *RB* 69, 1962, pp. 408–410, pl. 45; B. Lifshitz, "Beiträge zur palästinischen Epigraphik, III: Inschriften aus Beisan," *ZDPV* 78, 1962, pp. 80–81, pls. 7b, 8; A. Biran, "Beth Shean," *CNI* 14:1, 1963, pp. 18–19, pls. 1:2, 2:1, 3:3; N. Zori, "Beth Shean," *IEJ* 13, 1963, pp. 148–149; A. Negev, "Beth Shean," *RB* 70, 1963, p. 585, pl. 25a; M. Avi-Yonah, "The Bath of the Lepers at Scythopolis," *IEJ* 13, 1963, pp. 325–326, pl. 34e; S. Applebaum, "Where Saul and Jonathan Perished: Beth Shean in Israel," *ILN*, March 16, 1963, pp. 380–383, figs. 1–23; N. Zori, "Beth Shean," *RB* 71, 1964, pp. 410–411, pl. 22; *id.*, "The House of Kyrios Leontis at Beth Shean," *IEJ* 16, 1966, pp. 123–134, figs. 1–4, pls. 9–13; A. Biran, "Beth-shan," *CNI* 16:4, 1965, p. 20, pl. 4:1,2; N. Zori, "The Lid of a Sarcophagus from Beth-Shean," *ᶜAtiqot* 3, 1966, p. 65, pl. 16:1 (Hebrew); *id.*, "A Zoomorphic Vessel from Beth-Shean," *ᶜAtiqot* 3, 1966, p. 64, pl. 15; F. James, *The Iron Age at Beth Shan: A Study of Levels VI–IV*, 1966; N. Zori, "Beth Shean," *RB* 74, 1967, pp. 92–93, pl. 15b; H. O. Thompson, "Tell el-Husn — Biblical Beth-shan," *BA* 30, 1967, pp. 110–135, figs. 1–10; N. Zori, "On Two Pithoi from the Beth-shean Region and the Jordan Valley," *PEQ* 1967, pp. 101–103, figs. 1–2, pls. 26–28; *id.*, "The Ancient Synagogue at Beth-shean," *EI* 8, 1967, pp. 149–167, figs. 1–12, pls. 27–34 (Hebrew); G. M. FitzGerald, "Beth-shean," *AOTS*, 1967, pp. 185–196, pl. 7; T. C. Mitchell, "Philistia," *AOTS*, 1967, p. 414, pl. 18; N. Glueck, *The River Jordan*, 1968, pp. 172–175, figs. on pp. 145–147, 158–160, 166; J. B. Pritchard, ed., *ANEP*, 1969, nos. 228, 320, 321, 338, 469:5, 475, 478, 487, 585, 590, 641, 732, 736–738; G. E. Wright, *NEATC*, 1970, pp. 21–22, 27; R. Amiran, *NEATC*, 1970, p. 84; Y. Aharoni, *NEATC*, 1970, pp. 257–259, figs. 1, 2 on p. 258; N. Zori, "Bronze Utensils from Byzantine Beth Sheᵓan," *Qadmoniot* 3, 1970, pp. pp. 67–68, figs. (Hebrew); N. Glueck, *The Other Side of the Jordan*, 1970, fig. 93b on p. 186, p. 188; K. M. Kenyon, *Archaeology in the Holy Land*, 1970, pp. 112–113, 218–219, pp. 307–308, 323, 340; H. O. Thompson, *Mekal. The God of Beth-shan*, 1970, 3 plans, 1 map, 2 pls.; F. James, "Bet Shᶜan," *EAEHL*, 1970, pp. 63–65, figs. (Hebrew); A. Kempinski, "Bet Shᶜan," *EAEHL*, 1970, pp. 65–70, figs. (Hebrew); F. James, "Bet Shᶜan," *EAEHL*, 1970, pp. 71–76, figs. (Hebrew); N. Zori, "Bet Shᶜan," *EAEHL*, 1970, pp. 76–77, figs. (Hebrew); S. Applebaum, "Bet Shᶜan," *EAEHL*, 1970, p. 78, fig. (Hebrew).

Beth-She'arim, Sheikh Abreiq, Besara.

Excavated by B. Maisler (Mazar) 1936–40, 1956, N. Avigad 1953–1960, for the (Jewish Palestine) Israel Exploration Society and the Hebrew University.

B. Maisler, "Sheikh Abreiq," *QDAP* 6, 1937, pp. 222–223; *id.*, "The Second Campaign of Excavation at Beth Sheᶜarim (Sheikh Abreiq) 1937," *BJPES* 5:3, 1937, pp. 49–76, figs. 1–10, pls. 1–16 (Hebrew); *id.*, "The Excavations at Sheikh Ibreiq (Beth Sheᶜarim)," *JPOS* 18, 1938, pp. 41–49, figs. 1–2, pls. 4–11; *id.*, "Sheikh Abreiq," *QDAP* 7, 1938, pp. 51–53; *id.*, "The Second Campaign of Excavations at Beth Sheᶜarim (Sheikh Abreiq)," *BJPES* 5:3, 1938, pp. 49–76, figs. 1–10, pls. 1–16 (Hebrew); D. Schwabe, "Greek Inscriptions from Beth Sheᶜarim," *BJPES* 5:3, 1938, pp. 77–97, figs. 1–4 (Hebrew); *id.*, "The Greek Inscriptions Discovered at Beth Sheᶜarim during the Third Season," *BJPES* 6:2, 1939, p. 104; B. Maisler, pp. 101–103 (Hebrew); *id.*, "The Fourth Campaign at Beth Sheᶜarim 1940," *BJPES* 9:1, 1941, pp. 5–19, figs. 1–4, pl. 4 (Hebrew); M. Schwabe, "Two Inscriptions from the Synagogue Area, Beth Sheᶜarim," *BJPES* 9:1, 1941, pp. 21–30 (Hebrew); S. Yeivin, "Notes on the Report of the *JPES* Excavations at Beth Sheᶜarim," *BJPES* 9:2–3, 1942, pp. 69–76, fig. 1 (Hebrew); B. Maisler, "Sheikh Abreiq," *QDAP* 9, 1942, pp. 212–215; *id.*, *Beth Sheᶜarim: Vol. I, Report on the Excavations during 1936–40, Catacombs 1–4*, 1944, 1957 (Hebrew); *id.*, "Sheikh Abreiq," *QDAP* 10, 1944, pp. 196–198; E. R. Goodenough, *Jewish Symbols in the Greco-Roman Period*, I, 1953, pp. 89–102, 138–139, 208–211; III, 1953, nos. 50–56, 58–78, 80–86, 89, 92–94, 278, 369, 373, 456, 545, 980–982; N. Avigad, "Excavations at Beth Sheᶜarim, 1953," *IEJ* 4, 1954, pp. 88–107, figs. 1–7, pls. 8:b, 9–12; M. Schwabe, "Greek Inscriptions Found at Beth Sheᶜarim in the Fifth Excavation Season, 1953," *IEJ* 4, 1954, pp. 249–261, pls. 22–24; N. Avigad, "The Necropolis of Beth Sheᶜarim," *Archaeology* 8, 1955, pp. 236–244, figs.; *id.*, "Excavations at Beth Sheᶜarim, 1954," *IEJ* 5, 1955, pp. 205–239, figs. 1–12, pls. 25–36; *id.*, "The Discovery of a Huge Catacomb Full of Sarcophagi in the Necropolis of Beth Shearim," *ILN*, Jan. 7, 1956, pp. 20–23, figs.; M. Schwabe, B. Lifshitz, "A Graeco-Jewish Epigram from Beth Sheᶜarim," *IEJ* 6, 1956, pp. 78–88, pl. 9a; B. Mazar, "Beth Sheᶜarim," *IEJ* 6, 1956, pp. 261–262; N. Avigad, "The Sixth Season of Excavations at Beth Sheᶜarim 1954," *EI* 4, 1956, pp. 85–103, figs. 1–12, pls. 9–18 (Hebrew); M. Schwabe, B. Lifshitz, "A Graeco-Jewish Epigram from Beth Sheᶜarim," *EI* 4, 1956, pp. 104–110, pl. 17:1 (Hebrew); N. Avigad, "The Beth-Sheᶜarim Necropolis," *A and S* 2, 1957, pp. 244–261, figs. 1–20; *id.*, "Excavations at Beth Sheᶜarim, 1955," *IEJ* 7, 1957, pp. 73–92, figs. 1–4, pls. 17–24; *id.*, "Sarcophagi at Beth Sheᶜarim," *Archaeology* 10, 1957, pp. 266–269; M. Avi-Yonah, "Beth Sheᶜarim," *CNI* 8:1–2, 1957, pp. 25–26, pls. 3, 4:3; U. Ben-Horin, "An Arabic Inscription Found at Beth Sheᶜarim," *IEJ* 7, 1957, pp. 163–167, pl. 33c; N. Avigad, "Excavations at Beth Sheᶜarim, 1955," *IEJ* 7, 1957, pp. 239–255, figs. 5–11; *id.*, "Excavations at Beth-Sheᶜarim, 1955," *EI* 5, 1958, pp. 171–188, figs. 1–11, pls. 13–20 (Hebrew); *id.*, "Beth Sheᶜarim," *IEJ* 8, 1958, pp. 276–277; *id.*, "Excavations at Beth Sheᶜarim, 1958," *IEJ* 9, 1959, pp. 205–220, figs. 1–4, pls. 21–24; *id.*, "Excavations at Beth Sheᶜarim, 1958," *EI* 6, 1960, pp. 61–67, figs. 1–4, pls. 11–14; B. Mazar, "Beth Sheᶜarim," *IEJ* 10, 1960, p. 264; M. Avi-Yonah, *Oriental Art in Roman Palestine*, 1961, pp. 36–38, 40, 41, pls. 5, 6; B. Mazar, "Beth Sheᶜarim," *BTS* 46, 1962, pp. 6–19, pls.; N. Avigad, "Relics of Ancient Art in Galilee," *EI* 7, 1964, pp. 19–20, pl. 1:2 (Hebrew); *id.*, "The Necropolis of Beth Sheᶜarim," *ADHL*, 1967, pp. 175–186, figs.; M. Schwabe, B. Lifshitz, *Beth Sheᶜarim, Vol. II: The Greek Inscriptions*, 1967 (Hebrew); M. Avi-Yonah, "The Leda Coffin from Beth-Sheᶜarim," *EI* 8, 1967, pp. 143–148, pls. 25–26 (Hebrew); J. Finegan, *The Archeology of the New Tes-*

tament, 1969, pp. 203–208, figs. 236–241; N. Avigad, B. Mazar, "Bet-Seᶜarim," *EAEHL*, 1970, pp. 83–97, figs. (Hebrew).

Beth-shemesh, ᶜAin Shems, Rumeileh.

Excavated by D. Mackenzie for the Palestine Exploration Fund in 1911–1912.

D. Mackenzie, "Excavations at ᶜAin Shems (Beth-shemesh)," *PEFA* 1, 1911, pp. 41–94, figs. 1–28, pls. 7–14; *id.*, "The Ancient Site of ᶜAin Shems," *PEFQS* 1911, pp. 69–79, figs. 1–3, pl. 1; *id.*, "The Fund's Excavations at ᶜAin Shems," *PEFQS* 1911, pp. 139–142, 169–172, pl. 1; H. Vincent, "The Archaeological Invocation of a Biblical Site — Beth-shemesh (ᶜAin Shems)," *PEFQS* 1911, pp. 143–151, figs. 1–4; D. Mackenzie, "The Excavations at ᶜAin Shems, June-July, 1912," *PEFQS* 1912, pp. 171–178; *id.*, "Excavations at ᶜAin Shems (Beth-shemesh)," *PEFA* 2, 1912–13, pp. 1–100, figs. 1–11, pls. 1–61; C. Watson, "Beth-shemesh," *PEFQS* 1913, pp. 113–118.

Excavated by Elihu Grant for Haverford College in 1928–1931, 1933.

E. Grant, "Work at Beth Shemesh in 1928," *PEFQS* 1928, pp. 179–181; *id.*, "The Haverford College Excavations at Ancient Beth Shemesh, 1928," *PEFQS* 1929, pp. 201–210, pls. 1–3; *id.*, *Beth Shemesh*, 1929; *id.*, "Beth-shemesh, 1930," *PEFQS* 1930, pp. 133–134; *id.*, *ᶜAin Shems Excavations*, I, 1931, II, 1932; *id.*, *Rumeileh being ᶜAin Shems Excavations*, 1934; T. H. Gaster, "The Beth-shemesh Tablet and the Origins of Ras-Shamra Culture," *PEFQS* 1934, pp. 94–96; S. Yeivin, "The Palestino-Sinaitic Inscriptions," *PEFQS* 1937, pp. 180–193, esp. pp. 187–193, pl. 5; E. Grant, G. E. Wright, *ᶜAin Shems Excavations*, IV, 1938, V, 1939; G. E. Wright, *Biblical Archaeology*, 1962, fig. 52 on p. 89, fig. 55 on p. 91, fig. 142 on p. 199; J. A. Emerton, "Beth-shemesh," *AOTS*, 1967, pp. 197–206; K. M. Kenyon, *Archaeology in the Holy Land*, 1970, pp. 230, 238, 252–4, 273–4, 308; G. E. Wright, "Bet-Shemesh," *EAEHL*, 1970, pp. 79–82, figs. (Hebrew).

Beth-Yeraḥ, Khirbet el-Kerak, Philoteria, aṣ-Ṣinnabra

E. L. Sukenik, "The Ancient City of Philoteria (Beth-Yeraḥ)," *JPOS* 2, 1922, pp. 101–109; D. C. Baramki, "Coin Hoards from Palestine," *QDAP* 11, 1945, pp. 30–36, 86–90.

Excavations carried out by B. Maisler, M. Stekelis, M. Avi-Yonah for the Jewish Palestine Exploration Society, 1944–1946.

B. Maisler, "Beth-Yeraḥ," *QDAP* 13, 1948, pp. 168–170; L. A. Mayer, "Aṣ-Ṣinnabra," *IEJ* 2, 1952, pp. 183–187; B. Maisler, M. Stekelis, M. Avi-Yonah, "The Excavations at Beth Yerah (Khirbet el-Kerak) 1944–46," *IEJ* 2, 1952, pp. 165–173, fig. 1, pls. 9–11, pp. 218–229, figs. 1–3, pls. 17–19, pp. 251–252.

Excavated by P. Bar-Adon for the Department of Antiquities, Israel, 1953–1955.

P. Bar-Adon, "Beth-Yeraḥ," *IEJ* 3, 1953, p. 132; J. Leibovitch, "Beth-Yerah," *CNI* 4:2–3, 1953, p. 30, pl. 4:1,2; P. Bar-Adon, "Beth-Yeraḥ," *IEJ* 4, 1954, pp. 128–129; J. Leibovitch, "Beth-Yerah," *CNI* 5:1–2, 1954, p. 26, pl. 2; Y. Aharoni, "Beth-Yeraḥ," *IEJ* 5, 1955, p. 273; J. Leibovitch, "Beth-Yerah," *CNI* 6:3–4, 1955, p. 34, pl. 2; P. Bar-Adon, "Sinnabra and Beth Yerah in the Light of the Sources and Archaeological Finds," *EI* 4, 1956, pp. 50–55 (Hebrew); P. Delougaz, R. C. Haines, *A Byzantine Church at Khirbat al-Karak*, 1960; P. Bar-Adon, "Another Ivory Bull's Head from Palestine," *BASOR* 165, 1962, pp. 46–47, fig.; R. L. Cleveland, "Acknowledgment of the Bull's Head from Khirbet Kerak," *BASOR* 165, 1962, p. 47; E. Anati,

Palestine Before the Hebrews, 1963, pp. 330–332, 337–339, 348–351, 353, 357, 359, figs.; A. Biran, "Beth-Yerah," *CNI* 16:3, 1965, p. 14.

Excavated by D. Ussishkin for the Department of Antiquities, Israel, 1968.

D. Ussishkin, "Beth Yeraḥ," *RB* 75, 1968, pp. 266–268; A. Biran, "Beit Yerah," *CNI* 19:3–4, 1968, p. 37; N. Glueck, *The River Jordan*, 1968, pp. 75, 155–156, figs.; K. M. Kenyon, *Archaeology in the Holy Land*, 1970, pp. 124–127, figs.; R. Hestrin, "Bet-Yeraḥ," *EAEHL*, 1970, pp. 42–47, figs. (Hebrew).

Beth-zur, Khirbet et-Tubeiqah

Excavated by O. R. Sellers, for McCormick Theological Seminary and American Schools of Oriental Research, 1931, 1957.

O. R. Sellers, W. F. Albright, "The First Campaign of Excavation at Beth-zur," *BASOR* 43, 1931, pp. 2–13, figs.; O. R. Sellers, *The Citadel of Beth-zur*, 1933; R. W. Funk, "The 1957 Campaign at Beth-zur," *BASOR* 150, 1958, pp. 8–20, figs. 1–4; P. Lapp, N. Lapp, "A Comparative Study of a Hellenistic Pottery Group from Beth-zur," *BASOR* 151, 1958, pp. 16–27, figs. 1–4; O. R. Sellers, *et al.*, *The 1957 Excavation at Beth-zur*, *AASOR* 38, 1968; J. B. Pritchard, ed., *ANEP*, 1969, no. 227; R. W. Funk, "Bet-Tsur," *EAEHL*, 1970, pp. 60–63, figs. (Hebrew).

Bir Abu Matar (Tell Abu Matar), see Beersheba

Bireh, el-, see Khirbet Ruddana

Bir eṣ-Ṣafadi, see Beersheba

Bozrah, see Buseirah

Buqêʻah

E. W. G. Masterman, "Notes on Some Ruins and a Rock-cut Aqueduct in the Wâdy Ḳumrân," *PEFQS* 1903, pp. 264–267, figs. 1–2.

Explorations carried out by J. T. Milik, F. M. Cross, Jr., for the American Schools of Oriental Research, Drew University, Department of Antiquities, Jordan, 1954–55.

F. M. Cross, Jr., J. T. Milik, "Explorations in the Judean Buqêʿah," *BASOR* 142, 1956, pp. 5–17, figs. 1–6; F. M. Cross, Jr., "ʿel-Buqêʿa," *EAEHL*, 1970, pp. 99–100, fig. (Hebrew).

Buseirah, Bozrah

W. J. Phythian-Adams, "Israel in the Arabah," *PEFQS* 1934, pp. 181–188; N. Glueck, *AASOR* 14, 1934, fig. 6 on p. 23, p. 78, fig. 29 on p. 79; *id.*, *AASOR* 15, 1935, pp. 83, 97–98; G. L. Harding, "Some Objects from Transjordan," *PEQ* 1937, pp. 253–255, figs. 11–12, pls. 9–10; N. Glueck, "Surface Finds in Edom and Moab," *PEQ* 1939, pp. 188–192, pls. 30–32; *id.*, *AASOR* 18–19, 1939, pp. 36–37, fig. 19; V. R. Gold, "Bozrah," *IDB*, 1962, pp. 459–460, fig. 45; N. Glueck, *The Other Side of the Jordan*, 1970, pp. 184–191, 197, figs. 90–96.

Excavated by C. M. Bennett and G. L. Harding for the British School of Archaeology, 1971.

C. M. Bennett, "An Archaeological Survey of Biblical Edom," *Perspective* 12:1–2, 1971, pp. 35–44, esp. 43.

Caesarea Maritima

O. H. Knight, "Notes on Caesarea and Neighbourhood," *PEFQS* 1920, pp. 79–81; Z. Vilnay, "A New Inscription from the Neighbourhood of Caesarea," *PEFQS* 1928, pp. 45–47, pl. 8; *id.*, "Another Roman Inscription from the Neighbourhood of Caesarea," *PEFQS* 1928, pp. 108–109, pl. 6; J. H. Iliffe, "A Portrait of Vitellius (?) in Rock Crystal," *QDAP* 1, 1932, pp. 153–154, pl. 58.

Soundings made by J. Ory for the Department of Antiquities, Palestine, 1948.

E. L. Sukenik, *Bulletin Rabinowitz* 1, 1949, p. 17, pls. 10, 11; A. Reifenberg, "Caesarea: A Study in the Decline of a Town," *IEJ* 1, 1950–1951, pp. 20–32, fig. 1, pls. 8–16; M. Schwabe, "A Jewish Sepulchral Inscription from Caesarea Palestinae," *IEJ* 1, 1950–1951, pp. 49–53, pl. 15; E. L. Sukenik, *Bulletin Rabinowitz* 2, 1951, pp. 28–30, pls. 13–16; M. Schwabe, "Two Jewish-Greek Inscriptions Recently Discovered at Caesarea," *IEJ* 3, 1953, pp. 127–130; 233–236, pl. 6; J. Leibovitch, "Caesarea," *CNI* 4:2–3, 1953, p. 29, pl. 1:2; Department of Antiquities, *Short Guide to the Ruins of Caesarea*, 1955; S. Yeivin, "Excavations at Caesarea Maritima," *Archaeology* 8, 1955, pp. 122–129, figs. 1–12; H. Hamburger, "Minute Coins from Caesarea," *ᶜAtiqot* 1, 1955, pp. 115–138, pls. 10–12; J. Leibovitch, "Caesarea," *CNI* 6:3–4, 1955, pp. 31–32, pl. 1.

Excavations conducted by M. Avi-Yonah for the Hebrew University on behalf of the Louis M. Rabinowitz Fund, 1956–1957.

M. Avi-Yonah, "Caesarea," *IEJ* 6, 1956, pp. 260–261; *id.*, "Caesarea," *CNI* 8:1–2, 1957, p. 26, pl. 4:1,2; A. Kindler, "A Seventh Century Lamp with Coin Decoration," *IEJ* 8, 1958, pp. 106–109, fig. 1, pl. 24c,d; J. Leibovitz, "Caesarea," *CNI* 9:1–2, 1958, pp. 22–23, pl. 2:2.

Excavated by A. Frova, for the Missione Archaeologica Italiana, Milan, 1959–1963.

A. Hamburger, "A Graeco-Samaritan Amulet from Caesarea," *IEJ* 9, 1959, pp. 43–45, pl. 4a,b; *id.*, "A New Inscription from the Caesarea Aqueduct," *IEJ* 9, 1959, pp. 188–190, fig. 1, pl. 17c.

Excavations conducted by M. Avi-Yonah, A. Negev, J. Vardaman, 1959, 1960–1962, for the Hebrew University, Department of Landscape, Israel, and Southern Baptist Theological Seminary, Louisville.

M. Avi-Yonah, "The Synagogue at Caesarea," *Bulletin Rabinowitz* 3, 1960, pp. 44–48, pls. 9:3–4, 10, 11:1–2.

Underwater Archaeological Expedition, directed by Edwin A. Link, 1960, for the America-Israel Society and Princeton Theological Seminary, Charles T. Fritsch and Immanuel Ben-Dor, archaeological advisors.

A. Negev, "Caesarea Maritima," *CNI* 11:4, 1960, pp. 17–22, pls. 1–4; *id.*, "Caesarea: Clearing of the Fortifications of the Medieval Town of Caesarea, 1960," *IEJ* 10, 1960, p. 127; *id.*, "Caesarea," *IEJ* 10, 1960, pp. 264–265; I. Ben-Dor, "A Marine Expedition to the Holy Land, Summer 1960," *AJA* 65, 1961, p. 186; C. T. Fritsch, I. Ben-Dor, "The Link Expedition to Israel, 1960," *BA* 24, 1961, pp. 50–59, figs. 8–10; A. Negev, "Caesarea," *IEJ* 11, 1961, pp. 81–83; I. Ben-Zvi, "A Lamp with a Samaritan Inscription," *IEJ* 11, 1961, pp. 139–142, fig. 1, pl. 32; A. Biran, "Caesarea," *CNI* 12:2, 1961, pp. 14–15; A. Negev, "Césarée Maritime, ville des procurateurs romains," *BTS* 41, 1961, pp. 6–10, figs.; A. Biran, "Caesarea," *CNI* 13:1, 1962, pp. 18–19, pl. 3:2; J. Vardaman, "A New Inscription which Mentions Pontius Pilate as Prefect," *JBL* 81, 1962, pp. 70–71; M. Avi-Yonah, "A List of Priestly Courses from Caesarea," *IEJ* 12, 1962, pp. 137–139, fig. 1, pl. 13; M. Avi-

Yonah, A. Negev, "Caesarea," *IEJ* 13, 1963, pp. 146–148; M. A. Calderini, "L'Inscription de Ponce Pilate à Césarée," *BTS* 57, 1963, pp. 8–10, figs.; A. Negev, "Caesarea Maritima," *ILN*, Oct. 26, 1963, pp. 684–686, figs. 1–14; A. Frova, "Italian Excavations at Caesarea," *CNI* 14:3–4, 1963, pp. 20–24, pls. 1–4; A. Negev, "Caesarea Maritima," *ILN*, Nov. 2, 1963, pp. 728–731, figs. 1–16; A. Frova, "Excavating the Theatre of Caesarea Maritima," *ILN*, April 4, 1964, pp. 524–526, figs. 1–15; A. Biran, "Caesarea," *CNI* 15:2–3, 1964, pp. 28–29, pl. 1; D. Barag, "An Inscription from the High Level Aqueduct of Caesarea — Reconsidered," *IEJ* 14, 1964, pp. 250–252, figs. 1–2, pls. 49–55; A. Negev, "A High Level Aqueduct at Caesarea," *IEJ* 14, 1964, pp. 237–249, figs. 1–7, pls. 49–64; M. Avi-Yonah, "The Caesarea Inscription of the 24 Priestly Courses," *EI* 7, 1964, pp. 24–28, pl. 2:4–5 (Hebrew); S. Levy, "A Hoard of Abbasid Coins from Caesarea," *EI* 7, 1964, pp. 47–68, pls. 10–14 (Hebrew); A. Frova, *et al.*, *Scavi di Caesarea Maritima*, 1965; E. Kitzinger, *Israeli Mosaics of the Byzantine Period*, 1965, p. 20, pls. 26, 27; M. Avi-Yonah, "Lucius Valerius Valerianus, Governor of Syria-Palaestina," *IEJ* 16, 1966, pp. 135–141, pl. 16; A. Biran, "Caesarea," *CNI* 17:2–3, 1966, pp. 25–26; B. Lifshitz, "Inscriptions de Césarée," *RB* 74, 1967, pp. 45–59, pl. 4; A. Hamburger, "Gems from Caesarea Maritima," *ʿAtiqot* 8, 1968, pp. 1–38, pls. 1–8; J. D. Brierman, "Chinese Ceramics from Ashkelon and Caesarea," *IEJ* 19, 1969, pp. 44–45, pl. 6b; J. Finegan, *The Archeology of the New Testament*, 1969, pp. 70–80, figs.; H. Hamburger, "The Coin Issues of the Roman Administration from the Mint of Caesarea Maritima," *IEJ* 20, 1970, pp. 81–91, fig. 1; M. Avi-Yonah, "The Caesarea Porphyry Statue," *IEJ* 20, 1970, pp. 203–208, pls. 44–46; M. Benvenisti, *The Crusaders in the Holy Land*, 1970, pp. 135–145, figs.; A. Negev, "Qesari," *EAEHL*, 1970, pp. 500–502, figs. (Hebrew); A. Frova, "Qesari," *EAEHL*, 1970, p. 503, fig. (Hebrew); M. Avi-Yonah, "Qesari," *EAEHL*, 1970, pp. 504–505, figs. (Hebrew); A. Negev, "Qesari," *EAEHL*, 1970, pp. 505–509, figs. (Hebrew); P. R. Diplock, "The Date of Askalon's Sculptured Panels and an Identification of the Caesarea Statues," *PEQ* 1971, pp. 11–16, pls. 5–10.

Capernaum, Tell Hum, Kfar-Naḥum

C. W. Wilson, "Notes on Jewish Synagogues in Galilee," *PEFQS* 1869, pp. 37–41, plans; H. Kohl, C. Watzinger, *Antike Synagogen in Galilaea*, 1916, pp. 4–40, figs. 2–76, pls. 1–6; J. G. Duncan, "The Sea of Tiberias and Its Environs," *PEFQS* 1926, pp. 15–22, pl. 1; pp. 65–74, pl. 1.

Excavated by the Custody of the Holy Land, 1921–

G. Orfali, *Capharnaüm et ses ruines d'apres les fouilles accomplies à Tell-Houm par la Custodie Franciscaine de Terre Sainte (1905–1921)*, 1922; E. L. Sukenik, *Ancient Synagogues in Palestine and Greece*, 1934, pp. 7–21, 71–72, pls. 1–7, 13a,b, 17; H. G. May, "Synagogues in Palestine," *BA* 7, 1944, pp. 1–20, figs. 1–14; E. L. Sukenik, *Bulletin Rabinowitz* 1, 1949, pp. 18–19, fig. 5; E. R. Goodenough, *Symbols* 1, 1953, pp. 181–192; A. Spijkerman, "A Hoard of Syrian Tetradrachms and Eastern Antoniniani from Capharnaum," *LA* 9, 1959, pp. 283–327, figs., pls. 1–2; B. Bagatti, "Oggetti inediti di Cafarnao," *LA* 14, 1964, pp. 261–272, figs. 1–6.

Excavated by V. C. Corbo for the Custody of the Holy Land, 1968.

V. C. Corbo, "La Casa di S. Pietro à Cafarnao," *LA* 18, 1968, pp. 5–54, figs. 1–23, 3 plans; *id.*, "St. Peter's House in Capernaum Rediscovered," *CNI* 20:1–2, 1969, pp. 39–50, figs. 1–7; A. Biran, "Capernaum," *CNI* 20:3–4, 1969, p. 40; V. C. Corbo, "Capharnaum," *RB* 76, 1969, pp. 557–563, pl. 26; S. Loffreda, "Evoluzione d'un piattotegame secondo gli scavi de Cafarnao," *LA* 19, 1969, pp. 237–263, figs. 1–9; V. C. Corbo, *The House of St. Peter at Capharnaum, 1968*; J. Finegan, *The*

Archeology of the New Testament, 1969, pp. 50–56, figs.; N. Avigad, "Kfar Naḥum," *EAEHL*, 1970, pp. 277–279, figs.

Chorazin, Korazin, Kerazeh

C. W. Wilson, "Notes on Jewish Synagogues in Galilee," *PEFQS* 1869, pp. 37–41; L. Oliphant, "Explorations North-East of Lake Tiberias and in Jaulan," *PEFQS* 1885, pp. 82–92, figs.; H. Kohl, C. Watzinger, *Antike Synagogen in Galilaea*, 1916, pp. 41–58, figs. 77–111, pl. 7; J. Ory, "An Inscription Newly Found in the Synagogue of Kerazeh," *PEFQS* 1927, pp. 51–52, pl. 3; A. Marmorstein, "About the Inscription of Judah ben Ishmael," *PEFQS* 1927, pp. 101–102; E. L. Sukenik, *Ancient Synagogues in Palestine and Greece*, 1934, pp. 21–24, fig. 2, pls. 8, 15; H. G. May, "Synagogues in Palestine," *BA* 7, 1944, pp. 1–20, figs. 1–14; E. R. Goodenough, *Symbols* 1, 1953, pp. 193–199; M. Avi-Yonah, *Oriental Art in Roman Palestine*, 1961, pp. 34, 36, pl. 4.

Excavated by Z. Yeivin for the Department of Antiquities, Israel, 1962.

Z. Yeivin, "Chorazin," *IEJ* 12, 1962, pp. 152–153; A. Biran, "Chorazin," *CNI* 14:1, 1963, p. 15, pl. 3:1,4; Z. Yeivin, "Two Ancient Oil Presses," *ʿAtiqot* 3, 1966, pp. 52–63, 10 figs., pls. 12–14 (Hebrew); *id.*, "Carved Menorahs at Chorazin," *Qadmoniot* 2, 1969, pp. 98–99, figs. (Hebrew); J. Finegan, *The Archeology of the New Testament*, 1969, pp. 57–58, figs.; Z. Yeivin, "Korazi," *EAEHL*, 1970, pp. 261–262, figs. (Hebrew).

Damiya

C. L. Irby, J. Mangles, *Travels in Egypt and Nubia, Syria and Asia Minor during the Years 1817 and 1818*, 1823, p. 325; M. Stekelis, *Les Monuments Mégalithiques de Palestine*, 1935; E. C. Broome, Jr., "The Dolmens of Palestine and Transjordania," *JBL* 59, 1940, pp. 479–497; J. A. d'Waechter, "The Excavations at Ala Safat, Transjordan," *JPOS* 21, 1948, pp. 98–103, 2 figs.; N. Glueck, *AASOR* 25–28, 1951, pp. 356–359, figs. 107–108; M. Stekelis, *La necropólis megalítica de Ala-Safat, Transjordania*, 1961; J. L. Swauger, "1962 Study of Three Dolmen Sites in Jordan," *ADAJ* 10, 1965, pp. 5–36, figs., pls. 1–15; M. Stekelis, "Megaliths," *EAEHL*, 1970, pp. 316–318, figs. (Hebrew).

Dan, Tell el-Qadi, Laish

B. Mazar, "The Cities of the Territory of Dan," *IEJ* 10, 1960, pp. 65–77, figs. 1–5; R. Giveon, "Two New Hebrew Seals and Their Iconographic Background," *PEQ* 1961, pp. 40–42, pl. 3b; O. Negbi, "A Canaanite Bronze Figurine from Tel Dan," *IEJ* 14, 1964, pp. 270–271, pl. 56a,b; A. Negev, "Soundings at Tel Dan," *Ariel* 16, 1966, pp. 71–75.

Excavated by A. Biran in 1966– , for the Department of Antiquities, Israel.

A. Biran, "Tel Dan," *IEJ* 16, 1966, pp. 144–145; N. Avigad, "An Inscribed Bowl from Dan," *PEQ* 1968, pp. 42–44, fig. 1, pl. 18; A. Biran, "Tel Dan," *CNI* 19:3–4, 1968, pp. 36–37; *id.*, "Tel Dan," *CNI* 20:3–4, 1969, pp. 36–39, pl. 3; *id.*, "Tel Dan," *IEJ* 19, 1969, pp. 239–241; *id.*, "Tel Dan," *RB* 76, 1969, pp. 402–404, pl. 13b; *id.*, "Tell Dan," *RB* 77, 1970, pp. 383–385, pls. 14, 15; A. Malamat, *NEATC*, 1970, pp. 168–169, 171–172; A. Biran, "Tel Dan," *BTS* 125, 1970, pp. 8–15, figs.; *id.*, "A Mycenean Charioteer Vase from Tel Dan," *IEJ* 20, 1970, pp. 92–94, fig. 1, pl. 25; *id.*, "Tel Dan," *IEJ* 20, 1970, pp. 118–119.

Dead Sea Scrolls, see Khirbet Qumran

Dhahrat el-Humraiya

Excavated by J. Ory for the Department of Antiquities, Palestine, 1942.

J. Ory, "A Bronze Age Cemetery at Dhahrat el-Humraiya," *QDAP* 13, 1948, pp. 75–89, figs. 1–44, pls. 29–33.

Dhahr Mirzbâneh

K. M. Kenyon, "Tombs of the Intermediate Early Bronze-Middle Bronze Age at Tell Ajjul," *ADAJ* 3, 1956, pp. 41–55, figs. 1–10, esp. 47; R. Amiran, "MB I Pottery in Palestine," *IEJ* 10, 1960, pp. 204–225, figs. 1–10, pls. 25–26, esp. 208, 213, fig. 2:7–9; S. Saller, "Jerusalem and its Surroundings in the Bronze Age," *LA* 12, 1962, pp. 147–176, figs. 1–3, esp. 167; P. W. Lapp, "Palestine Known but Mostly Unknown," *BA* 26, 1963, pp. 121–134, esp. 123, 130.

Excavated by P. W. Lapp for the American Schools of Oriental Research, 1963–1964.

P. W. Lapp, *The Dhahr Mirzbâneh Tombs: Three Intermediate Bronze Age Cemeteries in Jordan*, 1966; W. F. Albright, *Yahweh and the Gods of Canaan*, 1968, p. 63; P. W. Lapp, *Biblical Archaeology and History*, 1969, pp. 99, 119, 128, pls. 27–28; K. M. Kenyon, *Archaeology in the Holy Land*, 1970, pp. 323–324, 338–339; W. G. Dever, "Vestigial Features in MB I," *BASOR* 200, 1970, pp. 19–30, figs. 1–3, esp. 20, n. 5, 22, n. 7, 22–23, n. 11.

Dhat Ras

N. Glueck, *AASOR* 18–19, 1939, pp. 63–65, fig. 32; G. L. Harding, *The Antiquities of Jordan*, 1967, p. 112, pl. 12:b.

Tomb excavated in 1968 by F. Zayadine, for the Department of Antiquities, Jordan.

F. Zayadine, "Une Tombé Nabatéene près de Dhat-Râs (Jordanie)," *Syria* 47:1–2, 1970, pp. 117–135, figs. 1–11, pl. 10.

Dhībân, see Dībôn

Dibôn, Dhībân

C. Warren, *et al.*, "The Moabite Stone," *PEFQS* 1870, pp. 169–182, fig. 1; F. A. Klein, "The Original Discovery of the Moabite Stone," *PEFQS* 1870, pp. 281–283; C. W. Wilson, C. Warren, "The Moabite Stone," *Recovery of Jerusalem*, 1871, pp. 496–512; D. Mackenzie, "Dibon, the City of King Mesha and of the Moabite Stone," *PEFQS* 1913, pp. 57–79, plan; N. Glueck, *AASOR* 18–19, 1939, pp. 115, 243, 250.

Excavated by F. V. Winnett, A. D. Tushingham, W. L. Reed, W. H. Morton, for the American Schools of Oriental Research, 1950–1953, 1955–1956.

F. V. Winnett, "Excavations at Dībôn in Moab, 1950–51," *BASOR* 125, 1952, pp. 7–20, figs. 1–6; R. E. Murphy, "A Fragment of an Early Moabite Inscription from Dībôn," *BASOR* 125, 1952, pp. 20–23, 1 fig.; W. L. Reed, "Dībôn," *BASOR* 128, 1952, p. 7; G. L. Harding, "Dhībân," *ADAJ* 2, 1953, pp. 86–87; A. D. Tushingham, "Excavations at Dībôn in Moab, 1952–53," *BASOR* 133, 1954, pp. 6–26, figs. 1–10; *id.*, "An Inscription of the Roman Imperial Period from Dhībân," *BASOR* 138, 1955, pp. 29–33, 1 fig.; W. H. Morton, "Dhībân," *BASOR* 140, 1955, pp. 5–6; W. L. Reed, "A Recent Analysis of Grain from Ancient Dībôn in Moab," *BASOR*

146, 1957, pp. 6–10, figs. 1–2; A. H. Van Zyl, *The Moabites*, 1960, pp. 77–80; G. R. H. Wright, "The Nabataean-Roman Temple at Dhībân: A Suggested Reinterpretation," *BASOR* 163, 1961, pp. 26–30, fig. 1; F. V. Winnett, W. L. Reed, *The Excavations at Dībôn (Dhībân) in Moab, AASOR* 36–37, 1964; G. L. Harding, *The Antiquities of Jordan*, 1967, pp. 42–43, pl. 8b; J. B. Pritchard, ed., *ANEP*, 1969, nos. 274, 851–852; O. D. Tushingham, "Divon," *EAEHL*, 1970, pp. 133–134, figs. (Hebrew).

Diocaesarea, see Sepphoris

Dor, Dora, Tanturah.

S. A. Cook, Review of *The Materials for the History of Dor*, by G. Dahl, 1915, *PEFQS* 1915, pp. 205–206.

Excavations by J. Garstang, W. J. Phythian-Adams for the British School of Archaeology, 1923–1924.

S. A. Cook, "Tantura," *PEFQS* 1925, p. 99; J. Garstang, "Tantura," *PEFQS* 1930, p. 80; Bibliography, "Tantūra," *QDAP* 1, 1932, p. 148; J. Leibovitch, "Dor," *IEJ* 1, 1950–51, p. 249.

Excavations by J. Leibovitch for the Department of Antiquities, Israel, 1951–1952.

J. Leibovitch, "The Reliquary Column of Dor," *CNI* 5:1–2, 1954, pp. 22–23, fig. 1.

Ḥorvat Tafat explored by G. A. Larue for the University of Southern California, 1968.

A. Biran, "Ḥorvat Tafat," *CNI* 20:3–4, 1969, p. 43; A. Siegelman, "Herodian Columbarium near Maᶜagan Michael," *ᶜAtiqot* 6, 1970, pp. 70–73, pls. 20–21 (Hebrew); M. Benvenisti, *The Crusaders in the Holy Land*, 1970, p. 189; G. Foerster, "Dor," *EAEHL*, 1970, pp. 130–132, figs. (Hebrew).

Dothan, Tell Dotha

Excavated by J. P. Free for Wheaton College, 1953–1956, 1958–1960.

J. P. Free, "The First Season of Excavation at Dothan," *BASOR* 131, 1953, pp. 16–20, figs. 1–2; *id.*, "The Second Season at Dothan," *BASOR* 135, 1954, pp. 14–20, figs. 1–2; *id.*, "The Third Season at Dothan," *BASOR* 139, 1955, pp. 3–9, figs. 1–2; *id.*, "Dothan, 1954," *ADAJ* 3, 1956, pp. 79–80; *id.*, "The Excavation of Dothan," *BA* 19, 1956, pp. 43–48, figs. 10–11; *id.*, "The Fourth Season at Dothan," *BASOR* 143, 1956, pp. 11–17, figs. 1–2; *id.*, "Radiocarbon Date of Iron Age Level at Dothan," *BASOR* 147, 1957, pp. 36–37; *id.*, "The Fifth Season at Dothan," *BASOR* 152, 1958, pp. 10–18, figs. 1–3; *id.*, "The Sixth Season at Dothan," *BASOR* 156, 1959, pp. 22–29, figs. 1–3; *id.*, "The Seventh Season at Dothan," *BASOR* 160, 1960, pp. 6–15, figs. 1–3; *id.*, "The Seventh Season at Dothan," *ADAJ* 6–7, 1962, pp. 117–120; D. Ussishkin, "Dothan," *EAEHL*, 1970, pp. 135–136 (Hebrew).

Eboda, see ʿAbdah

ʿEinan, Mallaḥa

Excavated by J. Perrot for the Centre National de la Recherche Scientifique, Department of Antiquities, Israel, American Philosophical Society, Wenner-Gren Foundation for Anthropological Research, 1955–1961.

J. Perrot, "ᶜEynan," *IEJ* 7, 1957, pp. 125–127; *id.*, "Le Mésolithique de Palestine et les récentes découvertes à Eynan (Ain Mallaha)," *A and S* 2, 1957, pp. 91–110, figs. 1–10, pls. 1–6; *id.*, "Excavations at ᶜEynan (ᶜEin Mallaḥa), Preliminary Report on the 1959 Season," *IEJ* 10, 1960, pp. 14–22, figs. 1–6, pls. 1–2; *id.*, "Einan," *RB* 67, 1960, pp. 257–260; *id.*, "ᶜEynan," *IEJ* 10, 1960, pp. 257–258; A. Biran, "Einan," *CNI* 12:2, 1961, p. 17; *id.*, "ᶜEynan," *CNI* 13:1, 1962, p. 17, pl. 2a,c; J. Perrot, "Beisamoun," *IEJ* 16, 1966, pp. 271–272; J. B. Pritchard, ed., *ANEP*, 1969, no. 802; G. A. Wright, A. A. Gordus, "Source Areas for Obsidian Recovered at Munḥata, Beisamoun, Hazorea and el-Kheàm," *IEJ* 19, 1969, pp. 79–88, figs.; A. LeBrun, "Beisamoun," *IEJ* 19, 1969, pp. 116–117; *id.*, "Beisamun," *RB* 77, 1970, pp. 378–380; J. Perrot, "ᶜEnan," *EAEHL*, 1970, pp. 451–454, figs. (Hebrew).

ʻEin Gev

Excavated by B. Mazar, A. Biran, M. Dothan, I. Dunayevsky for the Department of Antiquities, Israel and Avshalom Institute for Homeland Studies, 1961.

B. Mazar, A. Biran, M. Dothan, I. Dunayevsky, "ᶜEin-Gev," *IEJ* 11, 1961, pp. 192–193; A. Biran, "ᶜEin Gev," *CNI* 13:1, 1962, pp. 20–22, pl. 3:2–3; M. Stekelis, O. Yosef, "Un habitat du Paléolithique Supérierur à Ein Gev (Israel) note préliminaire," *L'Anthropologie* 69, 1965, pp. 176–183, figs. 1–4; B. Mazar, A. Biran, M. Dothan, I. Dunayevsky, "ᶜEin Gev: Excavations in 1961," *IEJ* 14, 1964, pp. 1–49, figs. 1–11, pls. 1–14; B. Mazar, "ᶜEn-Gev," *EAEHL*, 1970, pp. 438–440, figs. (Hebrew).

ʻEin Ha-Shivʻah, see ʻAin eṭ-Ṭabgha

ʻEin Mallaḥa, see ʻEinan

Elath, see Tell el-Kheleifeh

el-Jib, see Gibeon

el-Jish, see Giscala

el-Makr, see Acre

Elusa, see Khalasa

ʻEmmaus, ʻAmwās, Nicopolis.

Bibliography, *QDAP* 1, 1932, "ᶜImwās," p. 93; J. W. Crowfoot, Review of *Emmäus, sa basilique et son Histoire*, by L. H. Vincent, F. M. Abel, 1932, *PEFQS*, 1935, pp. 40–47; R. de Vaux, "Une Mosaïque Byzantine a Maᶜin," *RB* 47, 1938, pp. 227–258, figs. 1–4, pls. 11–16, esp. pp. 244–245, pl. 12; J. W. Crowfoot, *Early Churches in Palestine*, 1941, pp. 71, 145, pl. 26; M. Avi-Yonah, *The Madaba Mosaic Map*, 1954, "Nicopolis," no. 74 on p. 64, pl. 7; D. Buzy, "ᶜEmmaüs," *BTS* 36, 1961, pp. 4–13, figs.; J. Finegan, *The Archeology of the New Testament*, 1969, pp. 177–180, figs.; M. Benvenisti, *The Crusaders in the Holy Land*, 1970, pp. 226, 227, 347–351, figs.; M. Avi-Yonah, "Emmaus," *EAEHL*, 1970, pp. 11–12, figs. (Hebrew).

ʻEn-Gedi, Tell el-Jurn

Excavations by B. Mazar, I. Dunayevsky, T. Dothan, for the Israel Exploration Society, Hebrew University, 1949–1965.

B. Maisler (Mazar), "A Sounding at En Gedi," *BJPES* 15, 1949, pp. 25–28, pl. 8 (Hebrew); J. Naveh, "ᶜEin Gedi," *IEJ* 7, 1957, p. 264; B. Mazar, "En-gedi,"

IEJ 11, 1961, pp. 76–77; A. Biran, "Cave of the Letters," *CNI* 12:1, 1961, pp. 19–20; B. Mazar, I. Dunayevsky, T. Dothan, "Engedi," *IEJ* 12, 1962, pp. 145–146; B. Mazar, "Excavations at the Oasis of Engedi," *Archaeology* 16, 1963, pp. 99–107, figs.; *id.*, "Engedi," *ILN*, April 13, 1963, pp. 546–547, figs. 1–8; B. Mazar, I. Dunayevsky, "En-Gedi, Third Season of Excavations," *IEJ* 14, 1964, pp. 121–130, figs. 1–3, pls. 25–30; *id.*, "Engeddi," *IEJ* 15, 1965, pp. 258–259; A. Biran, "ᶜEn-Gedi," *CNI* 16:4, 1965, p. 18; *id.*, "ᶜEn-Gedi," *CNI* 17:1, 1966, pp. 18–19, pl. 4:1; B. Mazar, T. Dothan, I. Dunayevsky, "En-Gedi, The First and Second Seasons of Excavations, 1961–1962," *ᶜAtiqot* 5, 1966, pp. 1–100, figs. 1–33, pls. 1–36; B. Mazar, "En Gedi," *RB* 74, 1967, pp. 85–86, pl. 13; *id.*, "En-gedi," *AOTS*, 1967, pp. 222–230, pl. 8; *id.*, "Excavations at the Oasis of Engedi," *Archaeological Discoveries in the Holy Land*, 1967, pp. 67–76; B. Mazar, I. Dunayevsky, "En-Gedi, Fourth and Fifth Seasons of Excavations," *IEJ* 17, 1967, pp. 133–143, frontispiece, figs. 1–3, pls. 29–34; E. Stern, "Eretz-Israel in the Persian Period," *Qadmoniot* 2, 1969, pp. 110–124, figs. (Hebrew); D. Barag, Y. Porat, "The Synagogue at En-Gedi," *Qadmoniot* 3, 1970, pp. 97–100, figs. (Hebrew); B. Mazar, "ᶜEn-Gedi," *EAEHL*, 1970, pp. 440–447, figs. (Hebrew); D. Ussishkin, "The 'Ghassulian' Temple in Ein Gedi and the Origin of the Hoard from Nahal Mishmar," *BA* 34, 1971, pp. 23–39, figs. 10–23.

Eriḥa, see Jericho

'Esfia, see 'Isfiyā

Eshtemo'a, es-Samū

Excavated by L. A. Mayer, A. Reifenberg, for the Hebrew University, 1936.

L. A. Mayer, A. Reifenberg, "es Samū," *QDAP* 6, 1937, pp. 221–222; *id.*, "The Synagogue of Eshtemoa," *JPOS* 19, 1939–40, pp. 314–326; E. L. Sukenik, *Bulletin Rabinowitz* 1, 1949, p. 16; E. R. Goodenough, *Symbols* 1, 1953, pp. 232–236; Z. Yeivin, "Eshtemoᶜa," *RB* 77, 1970, pp. 401–402, pl. 24; S. J. Saller, *A Revised Catalogue of the Ancient Synagogues of the Holy Land*, 1969, pp. 59–60; J. Finegan, *The Archaeology of the New Testament*, 1969, p. 52; D. Barag, "Eshtmoaᶜ," *EAEHL*, 1970, pp. 26–27, figs. (Hebrew).

et-Tell, see 'Ai

Ezion-geber, see Tell el-Kheleifeh

Gadara, see Ḥammat-Gader

Gath, see Tell esh-Sheikh Aḥmed el-'Areini

Gaza, see Tell el-'Ajjul

Bibliography, *QDAP* 1, 1932, "Gaza," p. 92; R. W. Hamilton, "Two Churches at Gaza, as Described by Choricus of Gaza," *PEFQS* 1930, pp. 178–191, fig. 1; J. W. Crowfoot, *Early Churches in Palestine*, 1941, pp. 105, 107, 108, 112–113, 159; E. R. Goodenough, *Symbols* 1, 1953, p. 223.

Excavation by A. Ovadiah, for the Department of Antiquities, Israel, 1967.

A. Ovadiah, "The Synagogue at Gaza," *Qadmoniot* 1, 1968, pp. 124–127, figs. (Hebrew); A. Biran, "Gaza," *CNI* 19:3–4, 1968, pp. 43–44; S. J. Saller, *A Revised Catalogue of the Ancient Synagogues of the Holy Land*, 1969, pp. 25–26; A. Ovadiah,

"Excavations in the Area of the Ancient Synagogue at Gaza," *IEJ* 19, 1969, pp. 193–198, fig. 1, pls. 15–18; U. Rappaport, "Gaza and Ascalon in the Persian and Hellenistic Periods in Relation to their Coins," *IEJ* 20, 1970, pp. 75–80; L. Y. Rahmani, "A Eulogia Stamp from the Gaza Region," *IEJ* 20, 1970, pp. 105–108, fig. 1, pl. 28a–c; M. Benvenisti, *The Crusaders in the Holy Land*, 1970, pp. 189–194, figs.

Georgiopolis, see Lod

Gerar, see Tell Jemmeh

Gerasa, see Jerash

Gerizim, see Mount Gerizim

Gesher, see Jisr Banāt Ya'qūb

Gezer

C. Clermont-Ganneau, *Archaeological Researches in Palestine* 2, 1896, pp. 224–275, figs.

Excavations by R. A. S. Macalister for the Palestine Exploration Fund, 1902–1905, 1907–1909.

R. A. S. Macalister, "History and Site of Gezer," *PEFQS* 1902, pp. 227–232; *id.*, 'First Quarterly Report of the Excavation of Gezer," *PEFQS* 1902, pp. 317–364, figs. 1–23, pls. 1–11; W. M. F. Petrie, "Description of the Scarabs and Weights," *PEFQS* 1902, p. 365; R. A. S. Macalister, "Second Quarterly Report on the Excavation of Gezer," *PEFQS* 1903, pp. 7–50, figs. 1–5, pls. 1–10; A. Macalister, "The Bodies of the Second Burial Cave," *PEFQS* 1903, pp. 50–51; R. A. S. Macalister, "Third Quarterly Report of the Excavation of Gezer," *PEFQS* 1903, pp. 107–125, figs. 1–6, pls. 1–3; *id.*, "Fourth Quarterly Report of the Excavation of Gezer," *PEFQS* 1903, pp. 195–231, figs. 1–16, pls. 1–4; *id.*, "Fifth Quarterly Report of the Excavation of Gezer," *PEFQS* 1903, pp. 299–322, figs. 1–7, pls. 1–6; *id.*, "Report on the Human Remains Found at Gezer," *PEFQS* 1903, pp. 322–326; *id.*, "Sixth Quarterly Report on the Excavation of Gezer," *PEFQS* 1904, pp. 9–26, figs. 1–8, pls. 1–3; *id.*, "Seventh Quarterly Report on the Excavation of Gezer," *PEFQS* 1904, pp. 107–127, figs. 1–4; *id.*, "Eighth Quarterly Report on the Excavation of Gezer," *PEFQS* 1904, pp. 194–228, figs. 1–9, pls. 1–6; T. G. Pinches, "The Fragment of an Assyrian Tablet Found at Gezer," *PEFQS* 1904, pp. 229–236, figs., pls. 1–2; A. H. Sayce, "Note on the Assyrian Tablet," *PEFQS* 1904, pp. 236–237; C. H. W. Johns, "Note on the Gezer Contract Tablet," *PEFQS* 1904, pp. 237–244; W. M. F. Petrie, "Notes on Objects from Gezer," *PEFQS* 1904, pp. 244–245; R. A. S. Macalister, "Ninth Quarterly Report on the Excavation of Gezer," *PEFQS* 1904, pp. 320–354, figs. 1–8, pls. 1–4; *id.*, "Supplementary Notes on the Eighth Report," *PEFQS* 1904, pp. 355–357; *id.*, "Tenth Quarterly Report on the Excavation of Gezer," *PEFQS* 1905, pp. 16–33, figs. 1–3, pl. 1; *id.*, "Eleventh Quarterly Report on the Excavation of Gezer," *PEFQS* 1905, pp. 97–115, figs. 1–2, pls. 1–4; *id.*, "Twelfth Quarterly Report on the Excavation of Gezer," *PEFQS* 1905, pp. 183–199, figs. 1–4, pls. 1–2; C. H. W. Johns, "The New Cuneiform Tablet from Gezer," *PEFQS* 1905, pp. 206–219, figs. 1–2; R. A. S. Macalister, "Thirteenth Quarterly Report on the Excavation of Gezer," *PEFQS* 1905, pp. 309–327, figs. 1–5, pls. 1–6; *id.*, "Gezer and Megiddo," *PEFQS* 1906, pp. 62–66; *id.*, "Gezer and Taanach," *PEFQS* 1906, pp. 115–120; F. L. Griffith, "The

Egyptian Statuette from Gezer," *PEFQS* 1906, pp. 121–122, figs.; R. A. S. Macalister, "Three Ossuary Inscriptions from Gezer," *PEFQS* 1906, pp. 123–124, figs. 1–3; *id.*, "Fourteenth Quarterly Report on the Excavation of Gezer," *PEFQS* 1907, pp. 184–204, figs. 1–8, pl. 1; J. L. Myres, "The 'Philistine' Graves Found at Gezer," *PEFQS* 1907, pp. 240–243; R. A. S. Macalister, "Fifteenth Quarterly Report on the Excavation of Gezer," *PEFQS* 1907, pp. 254–268, figs. 1–9; *id.*, *Bible Sidelights from the Mound of Gezer*, 1907; *id.*, "Sixteenth Quarterly Report on the Excavation of Gezer," *PEFQS* 1908, pp. 13–25, figs. 1–6, pl. 1; C. J. Ball *et al.*, "Communications on the 'Zodiac-Tablet' from Gezer," *PEFQS* 1908, pp. 26–30, pl. 1; R. A. S. Macalister, "Seventeenth Quarterly Report on the Excavation of Gezer," *PEFQS* 1908, pp. 96–111, figs. 1–8; *id.*, "Eighteenth Quarterly Report on the Excavation of Gezer," *PEFQS* 1908, pp. 200–218, figs. 1–4, pls. 1–3; H. Vincent, "The Gezer Tunnel," *PEFQS* 1908, pp. 218–229; R. A. S. Macalister, "Nineteenth Quarterly Report on the Excavation of Gezer," *PEFQS* 1908, pp. 272–290, figs. 1–4, pls. 1–4; *id.*, "Twentieth Quarterly Report on the Excavation of Gezer," *PEFQS* 1909, pp. 13–25, figs. 1–7; M. Lidzbarski *et al.*, "An Old Hebrew Calendar-Inscription from Gezer," *PEFQS* 1909, pp. 26–34, pls. 1–2; R. A. S. Macalister, "Twenty-first Quarterly Report on the Excavation of Gezer," *PEFQS* 1909, pp. 87–105, figs. 1–7, pls. 1–3; P. Dhorme, "A Note on the New Cuneiform Tablet from Gezer," *PEFQS* 1909, p. 106; S. Ronzevalle, "The Gezer Hebrew Inscription," *PEFQS* 1909, pp. 107–112; S. Daiches, "Notes on the Gezer Calendar and Some Babylonian Parallels," *PEFQS* 1909, pp. 113–118; G. Dalman, "Notes on the Old Hebrew Calendar-Inscription from Gezer," *PEFQS* 1909, pp. 118–119; R. A. S. Macalister, "The Excavation of Gezer: Supplementary Details," *PEFQS* 1909, pp. 183–189, figs. 1–3; G. B. Gray, "The Gezer Inscription," *PEFQS* 1909, pp. 189–193; M. Lidzbarski, "The Old Hebrew Calendar-Inscription from Gezer," *PEFQS* 1909, pp. 194–195; S. A. Cook, "The Old Hebrew Alphabet and the Gezer Tablet," *PEFQS* 1909, pp. 284–309; R. A. S. Macalister, *The Excavations of Gezer, 1902–1905 and 1907–1909*, 1–3, 1912; E. W. G. Masterman, "Gezer," *PEFQS* 1934, pp. 135–140.

Excavations by A. Rowe for the Palestine Exploration Fund, 1934.

A. Rowe, "The 1934 Excavations at Gezer," *PEFQS* 1935, pp. 19–33, 2 plans, pls. 1–6; *id.*, "Gezer," *QDAP* 4, 1935, pp. 198–201; G. E. Wright, "The Troglodytes of Gezer," *PEQ* 1937, pp. 67–78, fig. 1; W. F. Albright, "The Gezer Calendar," *BASOR* 92, 1943, pp. 16–26, figs. 1–2; L. Finkelstein, "A Talmudic Note on the Word for Cutting Flax in the Gezer Calendar," *BASOR* 94, 1944, pp. 28–29; N. Avigad, "Epigraphical Gleanings from Gezer," *PEQ* 1950, pp. 43–47, figs. 1–3; F. M. Cross, Jr., D. N. Freedman, *Early Hebrew Orthography*, 1952, pp. 46–47; R. Amiran, "The 'Cream Ware' of Gezer and the Beersheba Late Chalcolithic," *IEJ* 5, 1955, pp. 240–245, figs. 1–2, pl. 34; Y. Yadin, "Solomon's City Wall and Gate at Gezer," *IEJ* 8, 1958, pp. 80–86, figs. 1–4; G. E. Wright, "A Solomonic City Gate at Gezer," *BA* 21, 1958, pp. 103–104; W. F. Albright, *The Archaeology of Palestine*, 1960, pp. 31, 104, 132, 152, 191, 220, 227–228, pl. 29; B. D. Rahtjen, "A Note Concerning the Form of the Gezer Tablet," *PEQ* 1961, pp. 70–72; R. W. Hamilton, "Gezer," *IDB* 2, 1962, pp. 388–389, fig.; J. A. Callaway, "The Gezer Crematorium Re-Examined," *PEQ* 1962, pp. 104–117, figs. 1–4, pl. 26; S. Talmon, "The Gezer Calendar and the Seasonal Cycle of Ancient Canaan," *JAOS* 83, 1963, pp. 177–187.

Excavations conducted for the Harvard Semitic Museum and the Hebrew Union College Biblical and Archaeological School, G. E. Wright and N. Glueck, Executive Committee, directed by G. E. Wright, W. G. Dever, H. D. Lance, J. D. Seger, 1964–71.

A. R. Millard, "A Letter from the Ruler of Gezer," *PEQ* 1965, pp. 140–143, pl. 25; G. E. Wright, "Gezer," *IEJ* 15, 1965, pp. 252–253; A. Biran, "Gezer," *CNI* 17:1,

1966, p. 20; W. G. Dever, "Gezer," *IEJ* 16, 1966, pp. 277–278; J. F. Ross, "Gezer in the Tell el-Amarna Letters," *Bulletin Museum Haaretz* 8, 1966, pp. 45–54; G. A. Smith, *The Historical Geography of the Holy Land*, 1966, pp. 151–154; W. G. Dever, "Gezer," *IEJ* 17, 1967, pp. 274–275; A. Biran, "Gezer," *CNI* 18:1–2, 1967, pp. 30–31; G. E. Wright, "Gezer," *RB* 74, 1967, pp. 72–73, pls. 9–10; N. Glueck, "Fouilles de Gezer," *Syria* 44, 1967, p. 450; H. D. Lance, "Gezer in the Land and in History," *BA* 30, 1967, pp. 34–47, figs. 1–6; W. G. Dever, "Excavations at Gezer," *BA* 30, 1967, pp. 47–62, figs. 7–12; J. F. Ross, "Gezer in the Tell el-Amarna Letters," *BA* 30, 1967, pp. 62–70, figs. 13–16; W. G. Dever, "Excavations at Gezer, 1964–1967," *Jerusalem Through the Ages*, 1968, pp. 26–32; *id.*, "Gezer," *RB* 75, 1968, pp. 381–387, pls. 38b, 39; *id.*, "Gezer — A Palestinian Mound Re-excavated," *Raggi* 8, 1968, pp. 65–74, figs. 1–6; A. Biran, "Gezer," *CNI* 19:3–4, 1968, pp. 42–43, pl. 2; N. Glueck, "Fouilles de Gezer," *Syria* 46, 1969, pp. 186–187; A. Biran, "Gezer," *CNI* 20:3–4, 1969, pp. 46–48; W. G. Dever, "Gezer," *IEJ* 19, 1969, pp. 241–243; *id.*, "Gezer," *RB* 76, 1969, pp. 563–567, pls. 27–28a; J. B. Pritchard, ed., *ANEP*, 1969, nos. 272, 286, 369, 469; P. W. Lapp, *Biblical Archaeology and History*, 1969, pp. 74, 118, pl. 20; R. Giveon, "Thutmosis IV and Asia," *JNES* 28, 1969, pp. 54–59; O. Tufnell, "The Pottery from Royal Tombs I-III at Byblos," *Berytus* 18, 1969, pp. 5–33, figs. 1–7, esp. pp. 7, 11, 13; W. G. Dever, "Gezer," *RB* 76, 1969, pp. 563–567, pls. 27, 28a; *id.*, "The Water Systems at Hazor and Gezer," *BA* 32, 1969, pp. 71–78, figs. 8–9; J. B. Pritchard, ed., *ANET*, 1969, pp. 242, 248, 320, 378, 485–490; W. G. Dever, "Gezer," *BTS* 116, 1969, pp. 8–16, figs.; N. Glueck, *The Other Side of the Jordan*, 1970, p. 151; J. D. Seger, "Tel Gezer," *IEJ* 20, 1970, p. 117; W. G. Dever, "Tel Gezer," *IEJ* 20, 1970, pp. 226–227; *id.*, "Gezer — A City Coming to Life," *Qadmoniot* 3, 1970, pp. 57–62, figs. (Hebrew); *id.*, "Gezer," *RB* 77, 1970, pp. 394–398, pls. 18–19; R. G. Bullard, "Geological Studies in Field Archaeology," *BA* 33, 1970, pp. 97–132, figs. 1–24; G. E. Wright, *NEATC*, 1970, pp. 34–35; J. Naveh, *NEATC*, 1970, p. 277; W. G. Dever, H. D. Lance, G. E. Wright, *Gezer I: Preliminary Report of the 1964–66 Seasons*, 1970; K. M. Kenyon, *Archaeology in the Holy Land*, 1970, pp. 310–311, 324; D. Ussiskin, G. E. Wright, "Gezer," *EAEHL*, 1970, pp. 111–117, figs. (Hebrew); A. Furshpan, "1970 Excavations of Hebrew Union College at Tell Gezer, Israel," *AJA* 75, 1971, p. 202.

Ghrubba, el-

Excavated by J. Mellaart for the Department of Antiquities, Jordan, 1953.

J. Mellaart, "The Neolithic Site of Ghrubba," *ADAJ* 3, 1956, pp. 24–40, figs. 3–6, pl. 5; R. Amiran, *Ancient Pottery of the Holy Land*, 1970, pp. 20–21.

Gibeah, Tell el-Fûl

Excavated by W. F. Albright for the American Schools of Oriental Research, 1922–23, 1933.

W. F. Albright, *Excavations and Results at Tell el-Fûl (Gibeah of Saul)*, *AASOR* 4, 1924; *id.*, "A New Campaign of Excavation at Gibeah of Saul," *BASOR* 52, 1933, pp. 6–12, figs. 1–4; J. Simons, *The Geographical and Topographical Texts of the Old Testament*, 1959, nos. 669–70, 893; L. A. Sinclair, "An Archaeological Study of Gibeah (Tell el-Fûl)," *AASOR* 34–35, 1960, pp. 5–52, pls. 1–35.

Excavated by P. W. Lapp for the American Schools of Oriental Research and Pittsburgh Theological Seminary, 1964.

L. A. Sinclair, "An Archaeological Study of Gibeah (Tell el-Fûl)," *BA* 27, 1964, pp. 52–64, figs. 13–17; P. W. Lapp, "Tell el-Fûl," *BA* 28, 1965, pp. 2–10, figs. 2–4;

J. B. Pritchard, ed., *ANEP*, 1969, no. 719; K. M. Kenyon, *Archaeology in the Holy Land*, 1970, pp. 237–238, 311; G. E. Wright, *NEATC*, 1970, p. 25; L. A. Sinclair, "Givᶜat Shaul," *EAEHL*, 1970, pp. 109–111, figs. (Hebrew).

Gibeon, el-Jib.

C. Schick, "The Waters of Gibeon," *PEFQS* 1890, p. 23, 2 plans; J. Muilenberg in C. C. McCown, *Tell en-Naṣbeh* 1, 1947, pp. 40–43.

Excavations of caves carried out by A. K. Dajani for the Department of Antiquities, Jordan, 1950.

A. Dajani, "An Iron Age Tomb at al-Jib," *ADAJ* 2, 1953, pp. 66–74, pls. 9–11.

Excavated by J. B. Pritchard for the American Schools of Oriental Research, The University Museum, Church Divinity School of the Pacific, Department of Antiquities, Jordan, 1956, 1957, 1959, 1960. 1962.

J. B. Pritchard, "Gibeon," *ILN*, October 27, 1956, pp. 695–697, figs. 1–10; *id.*, "The Water System at Gibeon," *BA* 19, 1956, pp. 65–75, figs. 1–5; *id.*, "The Underground Spring-Room of the Biblical Pool of Gibeon Discovered," *ILN*, March 29, 1958, pp. 505–507, figs. 1–14; *id.*, "The Wine Industry at Gibeon: 1959 Discoveries," *Expedition* 2, 1959, pp. 17–25, figs.; *id.*, *Hebrew Inscriptions and Stamps from Gibeon*, 1959; N. Avigad, "Some Notes on Hebrew Inscriptions from Gibeon," *IEJ* 9, 1959, pp. 130–133; J. B. Pritchard, "Industry and Trade at Biblical Gibeon," *BA* 23, 1960, pp. 23–29, figs. 8–11; *id.*, "Gabaon," *RB* 67, 1960, pp. 248–249, pl. 15b; *id.*, "Wine Making in Biblical Gibeon," *ILN*, September 10, 1960, pp. 433–435, figs. 1–10; *id.*, "Gibeon," *ILN*, September 24, 1960, pp. 518–519, figs. 1–10; *id.*, "More Inscribed Jar Handles from el-Jib," *BASOR* 160, 1960, pp. 2–6, figs. 1–2; *id.*, "The Bible Reports on Gibeon," *Expedition* 3, 1961, pp. 2–9, figs.; *id.*, "A Bronze Age Necropolis at Gibeon," *BA* 24, 1961, pp. 19–24, figs. 4–7; *id.*, *The Water System of Gibeon*, 1961; *id.*, "Two Thousand Years of Gibeon," *ILN*, September 22, 1962, pp. 440–443, figs. 1–18; *id.*, "Gibeon," *IDB* 2, 1962, pp. 391–393, figs.; F. M. Cross, Jr., "Epigraphical Notes on Hebrew Documents of the Eighth-Sixth Centuries B.C.: III. The Inscribed Jar Handles from Gibeon," *BASOR* 168, 1962, pp. 18–23; J. B. Pritchard, *Gibeon: Where the Sun Stood Still*, 1962; *id.*, "Excavations at el-Jib, 1960," *ADAJ* 6–7, 1962, pp. 121–122; *id.*, "Civil Defense at Gibeon," *Expedition* 5, 1962, pp. 10–17, figs.; *id.*, *The Bronze Age Cemetery at Gibeon*, 1963; F. F. Bruce, Review of J. B. Pritchard, *Gibeon*, *PEQ* 1963, pp. 144–146; J. B. Pritchard *et al.*, *Winery, Defenses and Soundings at Gibeon*, 1964; J. B. Pritchard, "El-Jib Excavations 1962," *ADAJ* 8–9, 1964, pp. 86–87; *id.*, "Gibeon: Where the Sun Stood Still," *Archaeological Discoveries in the Holy Land*, 1967, pp. 139–146, figs.; W. L. Reed, "Gibeon," *AOTS*, 1967, pp. 231–243, pl. 9; J. B. Pritchard, ed., *ANEP*, 1969, nos. 787, 809, 810, 875, 878, 879; K. M. Kenyon, *Archaeology in the Holy Land*, 1970, pp. 324–325; J. B. Pritchard, "Givᶜon," *EAEHL*, 1970, pp. 107–109, figs. (Hebrew); A. Demsky, "The Genealogy of Gibeon (I Chronicles 9:35–44): Biblical and Epigraphic Considerations," *BASOR* 202, 1971, pp. 16–23, fig. 1.

Giscala, el-Jish, Gush Ḥalav

H. Kohl, C. Watzinger, *Antike Synagogen in Galilaea*, 1916, pp. 107–111, figs. 204–217, pl. 15.

Tombs excavated by N. Makhouly for the Department of Antiquities, Palestine, 1937.

N. Makhouly, "Rock-cut Tombs at el-Jish," *QDAP* 8, 1939, pp. 45–50, figs. 1–4, pls. 30–33; E. R. Goodenough, *Symbols* 1, 1953, p. 205; H. Hamburger, "A

Hoard of Syrian Tetradrachms and Tyrian Bronze Coins from Gush Ḥalav," *IEJ* 4, 1954, pp. 201–226, fig., pls. 18–21a; S. J. Saller, *A Revised Catalogue of the Ancient Synagogues of the Holy Land*, 1969, pp. 34, 36; M. Avi-Yonah, "Synagogues," *EAEHL*, 1970, pp. 100–106, figs. (Hebrew); *BTS* 130, 1971, p. 14, fig.

Giv'at ha-Mivtar, see Jerusalem, Tombs off Nablus Rd.

Gush Ḥalav, see Giscala

Ḥammat-Gader, Amatha, Gadara (Umm Qeis), Tell el-Ḥammeh

Soundings made at Tell el-Ḥammeh by N. Glueck and C. S. Fisher for the American Schools of Oriental Research, 1932.

N. Glueck, "The Archaeological Exploration of el-Ḥammeh on the Yarmuk," *BASOR* 49, 1933, pp. 22–23.

Excavations conducted at el-Ḥammeh by E. L. Sukenik for the Department of Antiquities, Palestine, and the Hebrew University, 1932.

E. L. Sukenik, *Ancient Synagogues in Palestine and Greece*, 1934, pp. 81–82; *id.*, "el-Hammeh: the Synagogue," *QDAP* 3, 1934, p. 175; *id.*, *The Ancient Synagogue of El Ḥammeh (Hammath by Gadara)*, 1935; *id.*, "The Ancient Synagogue of el-Hammeh," *JPOS* 15, 1935, pp. 101–180; N. Glueck, "Tell el-Ḥammeh," *AJA* 39, 1935, pp. 321–330, figs. 1–8; N. Makhouly, "el-Hamme," *QDAP* 6, 1937, pp. 59–62, figs. 1–3, pls. 11–12; H. G. May, "Synagogues in Palestine," *BA* 7, 1944, pp. 1–20, figs. 1–14; E. L. Sukenik, *Bulletin Rabinowitz* 1, 1949, pp. 13–14, pl. 4; N. Glueck, *AASOR* 25–28, 1951, pp. 137–140, fig. 59; E. R. Goodenough, *Symbols* 1, 1953, pp. 239–241; M. Avi-Yonah, "Ḥammat-Gader," *EAEHL*, 1970, pp. 154–157, figs. (Hebrew).

Ḥammath-Tiberias

H. Kohl, C. Watzinger, *Antike Synagogen in Galilaea*, 1916, pp. 140, 143, 181–182, pl. 18:1–5.

Excavations conducted by N. Slousch for the Jewish Palestine Exploration Society, 1921.

G. M. FitzGerald, *PEFQS* 1921, pp. 183–185; E. L. Sukenik, *Ancient Synagogues in Palestine and Greece*, 1934, pp. 55, 58–59, fig. 18, pl. 12; *id.*, *The Ancient Synagogue of El-Ḥammeh (Ḥammath by-Gadara)*, 1935, pp. 33, 60, pls. 13–14; *id.*, *Bulletin Rabinowitz* 1, 1949, p. 12; E. R. Goodenough, *Symbols* 1, 1953, pp. 214–216.

Excavated by M. Dothan for the Department of Antiquities, Israel, 1961.

M. Dothan, "Ḥammath-Tiberias," *IEJ* 12, 1962, pp. 153–154; A. Biran, "Ḥammath-Tiberias," *CNI* 14:1, 1963, pp. 16–17, pl. 4:2; E. Kitzinger, *Israeli Mosaics of the Byzantine Period*, 1965, p. 24, pls. 19–21; M. Dothan, "The Synagogues at Hammath-Tiberias," *Qadmoniot* 1, 1968, pp. 116–123, figs. (Hebrew); J. Finegan, *The Archeology of the New Testament*, 1969, pp. 44–45, figs.; M. Dothan, "Ḥammat-Tverya," *EAEHL*, 1970, pp. 196–200, figs. (Hebrew); E. D. Oren, "Early Islamic Material from Ganei-Hamat (Tiberias)," *Archaeology* 24, 1971, pp. 274–277, figs.

Ḥanita

Excavations of cave-tombs carried out by D. Barag for the Department of Antiquities, Israel, 1957.

A. Biran, "Ḥanita," *CNI* 16:4, 1965, p. 19, pl. 3:1,2; A. Ronen, *The Flint Implements in the Ḥanita Museum*, 1968 (Hebrew); O. Negbi, *Canaanite Cave-Tombs at Ḥanita*, 1969 (Hebrew).

Har ha-Qefiṣah, see Jebel Qafze

Har Yeruḥam, see Yeruḥam

Hayonim Cave

Excavated by O. Bar-Yosef and E. Tchernov for the Hebrew University, 1965–1970.

O. Bar-Yosef, E. Tchernov, "Archaeological Finds and the Fossil Faunas of the Natufian and Microlithic Industries at Hayonim Cave (Western Galilee) Israel," *Israel Journal of Zoology* 15, 1967, pp. 104–140; *id.*, "The Natufian Bone Industry of ha-Yonim Cave," *IEJ* 20, 1970, pp. 141–150, figs. 1–4, pl. 35.

Hazor, Tell el-Qedah.

J. Garstang, "Hazor," *PEFQS* 1927, pp. 111, 224–225.

Soundings by J. Garstang for the Palestine Exploration Fund, 1928.

J. Garstang, *The Foundations of Bible History: Joshua, Judges*, 1931, pp. 381–383, fig., pl. 72.

Excavations directed by Y. Yadin, for the J. A. deRothschild Expedition and the Hebrew University, 1955–1958, 1968–1969.

Y. Yadin, "Excavations at Hazor," *BA* 19, 1956, pp. 1–12, figs. 1–7; *id.*, "Excavations at Hazor, 1955," *IEJ* 6, 1956, pp. 120–125, fig. 1, pls. 15–20; *id.*, "Excavating the Great Canaanite City of Hazor which Joshua Overthrew," *ILN*, April 14, 1956, pp. 298–301, figs. 1–23; *id.*, "Archaeological Excavations at Hazor," *CNI* 7:1–2, 1956, pp. 23–30, pls. 1–4; *id.*, "Further Light on Biblical Hazor," *CNI* 7:3–4, 1956, pp. 18–26, pls. 1–4; *id.*, "Hazor," *ILN*, December 1, 1956, pp. 951–953, figs. 1–15; *id.*, "Hazor," *ILN*, December 8, 1956, pp. 990–993, figs. 1–22; *id.*, "Excavations at Hazor, 1956," *IEJ* 7, 1957, pp. 118–123, pls. 27–32; *id.*, "Some Aspects of the Material Culture of Northern Israel during the Canaanite and Israelite Periods, in the Light of Excavations at Hazor," *A and S* 2, 1957, pp. 165–186, figs. 1–30; M. Avi-Yonah, "Places of Worship in the Roman and Byzantine Periods," *A and S* 2, 1957, pp. 262–272, figs. 1–14, esp. fig. 11; Y. Yadin, "The Rise and Fall of Hazor," *Archaeology* 10, 1957, pp. 83–92, figs.; *id.*, "Further Light on Biblical Hazor, the City Which Joshua Destroyed and Solomon Rebuilt," *CNI* 8:3–4, 1957, pp. 22–31, pls. 1–4; *id.*, "Excavations at Hazor, 1957," *IEJ* 8, 1958, pp. 1–14, fig. on p. 68, pls. 1–10:1; *id.*, "Hazor," *ILN*, April 19, 1958, pp. 633–635, figs. 1–17; *id.*, "Hazor," *ILN*, May 3, 1958, pp. 730–733, figs. 1–17; *id.*, "The Fourth Season of Excavations at Hazor," *CNI* 9:3–4, 1958, pp. 21–32, pls. 1–4; Y. Yadin *et al.*, *Hazor I: An Account of the First Season of Excavations, 1955*, 1958; Y. Yadin, "Hazor and the Idolatrous Israelites," *ILN*, March 21, 1959, pp. 479–481, figs.; *id.*, "Hazor and the Idolatrous Israelites," *ILN*, March 28, 1959, pp. 527–529, figs. 1–16; *id.*, "Excavations at Hazor, 1958," *IEJ* 9, 1959, pp. 74–88, fig. 1, pls. 6–13; O. Tufnell, "Hazor, Samaria and Lachish," *PEQ* 1959, pp. 90–105, 2 charts; G. E. Wright, "Philistine Coffins and Mercenaries," *BA* 22, 1959, pp. 54–66, figs. 1–10; Y. Yadin, "Hazor," *RB* 67, 1960, pp. 371–375, pls. 18–19; Y. Yadin *et al.*, *Hazor II: An Account of the Second Season of Excavations, 1956*, 1960; *id.*, *Hazor III-IV: An Account of the Third and Fourth Seasons of Excavations, 1957–1958*, 1961; Y. Yadin, *The Art of Warfare in Biblical Lands*, 1963, pp. 287–290, 378–379, figs.; *id.*, "Excavations at Hazor (1955–1958)," *The Biblical Archaeologist Reader* 2, 1964, pp. 191–224, pls. 15–18; R. D. Barnett, *Illustrations of Old Testament History*, 1966, pp. 16–23, figs. 4–9; J. Gray, "Hazor," *VT* 16, 1966, pp. 26–52; Y. Aharoni, *The Land of the Bible*, 1967, pp. 206–208, 219–220, 295; Y. Yadin, "Hazor," *AOTS*, 1967, pp. 244–263, fig. 6, pl. 10; *id.*, "The Rise and Fall of Hazor," *Archaeological Discoveries in the Holy Land*, 1967, pp. 57–66, figs.; *id.*, "Excavations at Hazor, 1968–1969," *IEJ* 19, 1969, pp. 1–19, fig. 1, pls. 1–5; A. Biran, "Hazor," *CNI* 20:3–4, 1969, p. 39; *id.*, "Haṣor," *RB* 76, 1969, pp. 550–557, pls. 24, 25; P. W. Lapp, *Biblical Archaeology and History*, 1969, pp. 107–111; J. B. Pritchard, ed., *ANEP*, 1969, nos. 831–836, 843, 844, 854, 856, 861, 862, 869–871, 874; Y. Yadin, "The Fifth Season of Excavations at Hazor, 1968–1969," *BA* 32, 1969, pp. 49–71, figs. 1–7; W. G. Dever, "The Water Systems at Hazor and Gezer," *BA* 32, 1969, pp. 71–78, figs. 8–9; Y. Yadin, "The Fifth Season of Excavations at Hazor, 1968," *Qadmoniot* 2, 1969, pp. 127–131, figs. (Hebrew); S. Yeivin, "Ostracon A1/382 from Hazor and its Implications," *EI* 9, 1969, pp. 86–87, pl. 34b (Hebrew); A. Malamat, "Hazor and its Northern Neighbours in New Mari Documents," *EI* 9, 1969, pp. 102–108 (Hebrew); Y. Yadin, "Symbols of Deities at Zinjirli, Carthage and Hazor," *NEATC*, 1970, pp. 200–231, figs. 1–15, pls. 17–26; K. M. Kenyon, *Archaeology in the Holy Land*, 1970, pp. 212, 342–343, 348; Y. Yadin, "Ḥatsor," *EAEHL*, 1970, pp. 158–170, figs. (Hebrew).

Hazorea, el-Jarba

E. Anati, *Palestine Before the Hebrews*, 1963, pp. 292, 321, 368–370, figs.

Excavated by J. Kaplan for the Museum of Antiquities of Tel Aviv-Yafo, 1967.

E. Anati, N. Haas, "A Palaeolithic Site with Pithecanthropian Remains in the Plain of Esdraelon, near Kibbutz Hazorea," *IEJ* 17, 1967, pp. 114–118, figs. 1–4; J. Kaplan, "el-Jarba," *IEJ* 17, 1967, pp. 269–270; *id.*, "el-Jarba," *RB* 25, 1968, p. 266; G. A. Wright, A. A. Gordus, "Source Areas for Obsidian Recovered at Munhata, Beisamoun, Hazorea, and el-Khiam," *IEJ* 19, 1969, pp. 79–89, figs. 1–3.

Hebron

M. Avi-Yonah, "Greek Inscriptions from Ascalon, Jerusalem, Beisan and Hebron," *QDAP* 10, 1944, pp. 160–169, pl. 35.

Excavations conducted by P. C. Hammond for the Department of Antiquities, Jordan, Princeton Theological Seminary et al., 1964–1966.

P. C. Hammond, "Hebron," *RB* 73, 1966, pp. 566–569, pl. 39a; *id.*, "Hebron," *BTS* 80, 1966, pp. 6–8, figs.; *id.*, "Hebron," *RB* 75, 1968, pp. 253–258, fig. 6, pl. 30;

Tombs excavated west of Hebron, Jebel Qaᶜaqir, Khalit el-Fûl, Khirbet el-Kôm, by W. G. Dever for the Hebrew Union College Biblical and Archaeological School and the Department of Antiquities, Israel, 1967, 1968, 1971.

A. Biran, "Khalit el-Fûl," *CNI* 20:3–4, 1969, pp. 51–53; W. G. Dever, "Khalit el-Fûl," *RB* 76, 1969, pp. 572–576, pl. 30; *id.*, "Iron Age Epigraphic Material from the Area of Khirbet el-Kôm," *HUCA*, 40–41, 1970, pp. 139–204, figs. 1–22, pls. 1–9; *id.*, "The Middle Bronze I Period in Syria and Palestine," *NEATC*, 1970, pp. 132–163, figs. 1–4, pls. 13–16; *id.*, "Vestigial Features in MB I: An Illustration of Some Principles of Ceramic Typology," *BASOR* 200, 1970, pp. 19–30, figs. 1–3; D. Barag, "Note on an Inscription from Khirbet el-Qôm," *IEJ* 20, 1970, pp. 216–218, figs. 1–2, pl. 48b.

Ḥederah

Excavated by E. L. Sukenik for the Hebrew University and the Department of Antiquities, Palestine, 1934.

E. L. Sukenik, "A Chalcolithic Necropolis at Ḥederah," *JPOS* 17, 1937, pp. 15–30, figs. 1–10, pls. 1–4; E. Anati, *Palestine Before the Hebrews*, 1963, pp. 288, 290,

292, fig.; B. A. Mastin, "Chalcolithic Ossuaries and 'Houses for the Dead'," *PEQ* 1965, pp. 153–160; K. M. Kenyon, *Archaeology in the Holy Land*, 1970, pp. 77, 312; Y. Yadin, "Ḥedera," *EAEHL*, 1970, p. 150, figs. (Hebrew).

Heptapegon, see 'Ain eṭ-Ṭabgha

Herodium, Jebel Fureidis

C. R. Conder, "Herodium," *PEFQS* 1877, p. 27; P. Benoit, J. T. Milik, R. deVaux, *Discoveries in the Judaean Desert, 2, Les Grottes de Murabbaʿat*, 1961, pp. 124–132, pl. 1; Y. Yadin, "Expedition D," *IEJ* 11, 1961, pp. 36–52, esp. pp. 51–52.

Excavated by V. C. Corbo for the Department of Cultural Relations in the Italian Foreign Ministry, 1962–1967.

V. C. Corbo, "L'Herodion di Gebel Fureidis," *LA* 13, 1963, pp. 219–277, figs. 1–27; *id.*, "L'Hérodium," *BTS* 60, 1963, pp. 6–10, figs.; E. M. Lapperrousaz, "L'Hérodium, Quartier Général de Bar Kokhba?" *Syria* 41, 1964, pp. 347–358; V. C. Corbo, "L'Herodion di Gebal Fureidis," *LA* 17, 1967, pp. 65–121, figs. 1–24; *id.*, "Herodium (Gebel Fureidis)," *CNI* 18:3–4, 1967, pp. 33–36, pls. 1–4; *id.*, "Gebel Fureidis (Hérodium)," *RB* 75, 1968, pp. 424–428, pls. 53–54; *id.*, "The Excavations at Herodium," *Qadmoniot* 1, 1968, pp. 132–136, figs. (Hebrew).

Excavation and clearing carried out by G. Foerster for the Department of Antiquities and National Parks Authority, Israel, 1969.

G. Foerster, "Herodium," *IEJ* 19, 1969, pp. 123–124; *id.*, "Herodium," *RB* 77, 1970, pp. 400–401, pls. 20–23; V. Corbo, "Herodion," *EAEHL*, 1970, pp. 141–144, figs. (Hebrew).

Heshbon, Ḥesbân

Excavated by S. H. Horn for Andrews University, American Schools of Oriental Research, Department of Antiquities, Jordan, 1968.

S. H. Horn, "Discoveries at Ancient Heshbon," *ADAJ* 12–13, 1968, pp. 51–52; *id.*, "The 1968 Heshbon Expedition," *BA* 32, 1969, pp. 26–41, figs. 1–7; R. S. Boraas, S. H. Horn *et al.*, "Heshbon 1968," *Andrews University Seminary Studies* 7, 1969, pp. 97–239, figs. 1–12, pls. 10–25; S. H. Horn, "Heshbon," *RB* 76, 1969, pp. 395–398, pls. 10, 11a.

Herzliya

Excavated by M. W. Prausnitz et al. for the Department of Antiquities and Museums, Israel and the Centre de Récherches Préhistoriques en Israël, 1969.

M. W. Prausnitz *et al.*, "Herzliya," *IEJ* 19, 1969, p. 236.

Hippos, see Sûsîtâ

Ḥolon, see Tel Aviv

Ḥorvat Minḥa, see Munḥata

Ḥorvat Tafat, see Dor

Hulda

Excavated by J. Ory for the Department of Antiquities, Israel, 1953.

J. Ory, "Hulda," *IEJ* 3, 1953, pp. 133–134; M. Avi-Yonah, "Places of Worship in the Roman and Byzantine Periods," *A and S* 2, 1957, pp. 262–276, esp. fig. 8 and p. 269; *id.*, "Ḥuldah," *Bulletin Rabinowitz* 3, 1960, pp. 57–60, fig. 1, pls. 11:3, 12.

Husn, el-, Ḥusn el-Ajlun

Excavated by G. L. Harding for the Department of Antiquities, Jordan, 1946.

N. Glueck, "Band-slip Ware in the Jordan Valley and North Gilead," *BASOR* 101, 1946, pp. 3–20, pls. 15–31; *id.*, *AASOR* 25–28, 1951, pp. 161–164; G. L. Harding, "An Early Bronze Cave from Jordan," *PEFA* 6, 1953, pp. 1–4, figs. 1–5, pl. 1; B. S. J. Isserlin, "Notes and Comparisons," *PEFA* 6, 1953, pp. 5–8; R. Amiran, "The Pottery of the Middle Bronze Age I in Palestine," *IEJ* 10, 1960, pp. 204–225, figs. 1–10, pls. 25–26, esp. pp. 209–213, 215, 217; K. M. Kenyon, *Amorites and Canaanites*, 1966, pp. 32–33; G. L. Harding, *The Antiquities of Jordan*, 1967, p. 57; M. Kochavi, "El-Ḥusn," *EAEHL*, 1970, pp. 170–171, figs. (Hebrew).

ʻIrâq el-Barûd, see Mount Carmel Caves

Irbid, (Galilee)

C. W. Wilson, "Notes on Jewish Synagogues in Palestine," *PEFQS* 1869, pp. 37–42, plans, esp. 40–42; L. Oliphant, "Explorations North-East of Lake Tiberias, and in Jaulan," *PEFQS* 1885, pp. 82–92, figs.; H. Kohl, C. Watzinger, *Antike Synagogen in Galilaea*, 1916, pp. 59–70, figs. 112–134, pls. 8–9; E. R. Goodenough, *Symbols* 1, 1953, p. 199; M. Avi-Yonah, "Synagogues," *EAEHL*, 1970, pp. 100–106, figs. (Hebrew).

Irbid, (Jordan)

Excavation of tombs by R. W. Dajani, for the Department of Antiquities, Jordan, 1958–1959.

F. S. Maʿayeh, "Irbed," *ADAJ* 4–5, 1960, p. 116, pl. 6:1; R. W. Dajani, "Iron Age Tombs from Irbed," *ADAJ* 8–9, 1964, pp. 99–101, pls. 38–40; *id.*, "Four Iron Age Tombs from Irbed," *ADAJ* 11, 1966, pp. 88–101, pls. 32–40.

Isbeiṭa, Shivta

E. H. Palmer, "The Desert of the Tíh and the Country of Moab," *PEFQS* 1871, pp. 3–80, figs., esp. pp. 29–30; C. L. Woolley, "The Desert of the Wanderings," *PEFQS* 1914, pp. 58–66, figs. 1–3; C. L. Woolley, T. E. Lawrence, "The Wilderness of Zin," *PEFA* 3, 1914–1915, pp. 72–91, figs. 9–22, pls. 16–22.

Excavations conducted by the H. D. Colt Archaeological Expedition, for the British School of Archaeology, 1935–1936.

H. D. Colt, "Isbeiṭa," *PEFQS* 1935, pp. 9–11; C. Baly, "S'baita," *PEFQS* 1935, pp. 171–181, pls. 1–6; H. D. Colt, "Isbeiṭa," *QDAP* 4, 1935, pp. 201–202; G. Crowfoot, "The Nabataean Ware of Sbaita," *PEFQS* 1936, pp. 14–27, fig. 1, pls. 1–4; H. C. Youtie, "Ostraca from Sbeitah," *AJA* 40, 1936, pp. 452–459; H. D. Colt, "Isbeiṭa," *QDAP* 5, 1936, pp. 198–199; J. W. Crowfoot, *Early Churches in Palestine*, 1941, pp. 70–71, pls. 4a, 6a, 29b, 30a,b; C. J. Kraemer, Jr., *Excavations at Nessana*,

3, *Non-Literary Papyri,* 1958, pp. 227–233; P. Mayerson, "Ancient Agricultural Remains in the Central Negeb: The Teleilat el-ᶜAnab," *BASOR* 153, 1959, pp. 19–31, figs. 1–6; *id.*, "The Desert of Southern Palestine According to Byzantine Sources," *Proceedings of the American Philosophical Society* 107, 1963, pp. 160–172; N. Glueck, *Deities and Dolphins,* 1965, pp. 71, 519–525, pls. 216a, 217, 218b, 219a; *id., Rivers in the Desert,* 1968, pp. 264–269, figs. 45–46; A. Negev, "Shivta," *EAEHL,* 1970, pp. 523–526, figs. (Hebrew); M. Evenari, L. Shanan, N. Tadmor, *The Negev,* 1971, pp. 161, 168–171, figs.

'Isfiya, 'Esfia

Cleared by N. Makhouly and M. Avi-Yonah, for the Department of Antiquities, Palestine, 1933.

N. Makhouly, "A Sixth-Century Synagogue at ᶜIsfiyā, I. Excavation Report," *QDAP* 3, 1934, pp. 118–120, fig. 1; M. Avi-Yonah, "A Sixth-Century Synagogue at ᶜIsfiyā, II. The Mosaic Pavement, the Inscriptions," *QDAP* 3, 1934, pp. 120–131, fig. 2, pls. 41–44; E. L. Sukenik, *Ancient Synagogues in Palestine and Greece,* 1934, pp. 85–86; *id., Bulletin Rabinowitz* 1, 1949, p. 14; E. R. Goodenough, *Symbols* 1, 1953, pp. 257–259; S. J. Saller, *A Revised Catalog of the Ancient Synagogues of the Holy Land,* 1969, p. 31; M. Avi-Yonah, "ᶜIsfiyā," *EAEHL,* 1970, pp. 151–152, figs. (Hebrew); *BTS* 130, 1971, fig. on p. 17.

Jaffa, Jafo

Sounding by P. L. O. Guy for the Department of Antiquities, Israel, 1950.

B. S. J. Isserlin, "Jaffa," *PEQ* 1950, p. 101; J. Bowman, B. S. J. Isserlin, K. R. Rowe, "Archaeological Expedition to Jaffa 1952," *Proceedings of the Leeds Philosophical Society* 7, 1955, pp. 231–250, 4 plans, 3 figs., 4 pls.; A. Kindler, "The Jaffa Hoard of Alexander Jannaeus," *IEJ* 4, 1954, pp. 170–185, figs. 1–4, pls. 13, 16.

Excavated by J. Kaplan for the Museum of Antiquities, Tel-Aviv-Jaffa, 1955–1966.

J. Pinkerfeld, "Two Fragments of a Marble Door from Jaffa," *ᶜAtiqot* 1, 1955, pp. 89–94, figs. 1–2, pl. 7; J. Kaplan, "Jaffa," *IEJ* 6, 1956, pp. 259–260; A. Biran, "Jaffa," *CNI* 10:1–2, 1959, pp. 30–31, pl. 4:1; J. H. Landau, "A Stamped Jar Handle from Jaffa," *ᶜAtiqot* 2, 1959, pp. 186–187, pl. 23:4; J. Kaplan, "Jaffa," *IEJ* 10, 1960, pp. 121–22; *id.*, "Jaffa," *RB* 67, 1960, pp. 376–377, pl. 20; *id.*, "Jaffa," *IEJ* 11, 1961, pp. 191–192; *id.*, "Jaffa," *IEJ* 12, 1962, pp. 149–50; *id.*, "Jaffa's History Revealed by the Spade," *Archaeology* 17, 1964, pp. 270–276, figs.; *id.*, "Jaffa," *IEJ* 14, 1964, pp. 285–286; A. Biran, "Jaffa," *CNI* 16:4, 1965, p. 16, pl. 1:1; J. Kaplan, "Jaffa," *RB* 72, 1965, pp. 553–554; *id.*, "Jaffa," *IEJ* 16, 1966, p. 282; N. Doudayi, "Jaffa Resurgent," *Ariel* 20, 1967, pp. 17–19, figs.; J. Kaplan, "Jaffa," *RB* 74, 1967, pp. 87–88, pl. 14b; *id.*, "Jaffa's History Revealed by the Spade," *Archaeological Discoveries in the Holy Land,* 1967, pp. 113–118, figs.; *id.*, "Yafo," *EAEHL,* 1970, pp. 201–204, figs. (Hebrew).

Jalamet el-'Asafna

Excavated by G. D. Weinberg for the Museum of Art and Archaeology, University of Missouri-Columbia, and P. N. Perrot, for the Corning Museum of Glass, 1964–1967.

G. D. Weinberg, "Glass Factories in Western Galilee," *IEJ* 14, 1964, pp. 286–288; *id.*, "Search for Glass Factories," *Archaeology* 17, 1964, pp. 283–284, fig.; A. Engle, "Does Western Galilee Contain the Secrets of Glass-Blowing?" *CNI* 15:4, 1964, pp. 13–18, pls. 2–4; *id.*, *Janus* 51, 1964, pp. 125–135; A. Biran, "Jalamet el-ᶜAsafna," *CNI* 16:4, 1965, pp. 18–19; *id.*, "Jalamet el-ᶜAsafna," *CNI* 17:2–3, 1966, pp. 22–23; G. D. Weinberg, "Jelemiye, Beth-Sheᶜarim, Kafr Yasif," *IEJ* 16, 1966, pp. 283–284; *id.*, "Jalamet el-ᶜAsafna," *RB* 74, 1967, pp. 88–90, pl. 14a; A. Biran, "Jalamet el-ᶜAsafna," *CNI* 18:1–2, 1967, pp. 27–28; G. D. Weinberg, "Excavations at Jalame 1964–1967," *Muse* 2, 1968, p. 13, fig.; *id.*, "Roman Glass Factories in Galilee," *BMH* 10, 1968, pp. 49–50, pl. 7.

Japhia, Yafa

G. M. FitzGerald, "Remains of an Ancient Synagogue at Yafa in Galilee," *PEFQS* 1921, pp. 182–183.

Excavated by E. L. Sukenik for the Department of Antiquities, Israel, 1950.

E. L. Sukenik, "The Ancient Synagogue at Yafa, near Nazareth," *Bulletin Rabinowitz* 2, 1951, pp. 6–24, fig. 1–6, pls. 1–10; E. R. Goodenough, *Symbols* 1, 1953, pp. 216–218; M. Avi-Yonah, "Places of Worship in the Roman and Byzantine Periods," *A and S* 2, 1957, pp. 262–272, figs. 1–14, esp. p. 264, fig. 1; D. Barag, "Yafiᶜa," *EAEHL*, 1970, pp. 205–206, figs. (Hebrew).

Jarba, el-, see Hazorea

Jebel Fureidis, see Herodium

Jebel Qaʿaqir, see Hebron

Jebel Qafze, Har ha-Qefiṣah, Qedumim

Excavated by M. R. Neuville and M. M. Stekelis for the Institut de Paléontologie Humaine, 1933–1935.

M. R. Neuville, "Jabal Qafze," *QDAP* 3, 1934, p. 175; *id.*, "Jabal Qafze," *QDAP* 4, 1935, p. 202; *id.*, "Jabal Qafze," *QDAP* 5, 1936, p. 199; R. Neuville, "La Grotte du Djebel Qafzeh," *Le Paléolithique et le Mésolithique du Désert de Judée*, 1951, pp. 179–184.

Excavated by B. Vandermeersch for the Centre National de la Recherche Scientifique Français, Laboratoire de Paléontologie de la Sorbonne, and the Department of Antiquities, Israel, 1965–1969.

B. Vandermeersch, "Har ha-Qefiṣah (Jebel Qafzeh)," *IEJ* 15, 1965, pp. 247–248; A. Biran, "Kafzeh," *CNI* 17:2–3, 1966, p. 24; B. Vandermeersch, "Har ha-Qefiṣeh (Jebel Qafzeh)," *IEJ* 16, 1966, pp. 267–269; *id.*, "Kafzeh," *RB* 74, 1967, pp. 60–63; A. Biran, "Kafzeh (Meᶜarat Qedumim)," *CNI* 18:1–2, 1967, p. 34; B. Vandermeersch, "Jebel Qafzeh," *IEJ* 17, 1967, pp. 264–266; *id.*, "Kafzeh," *RB* 75, 1968, pp. 258–261; A. Biran, "Meᶜarat Qedumim," *CNI* 19:3–4, 1968, p. 40; B. Vandermeersch, "Har ha-Qefiṣeh," *IEJ* 20, 1970, p. 115; *id.*, "Qafzeh," *RB* 77, 1970, pp. 561–564, pl. 32; M. Stekelis, "Cave of Qafze," *EAEHL*, 1970, pp. 370–371, figs. (Hebrew).

Jerash, Gerasa

J. L. Burckhardt, *Travels in Syria and the Holy Land, 1812*, 1822, pp. 251–264, plan; C. Warren, "Expedition to East of Jordan, July and August, 1867," *PEFQS* 1870, pp. 284–306, esp. 301–302; A. E. Northey, "Expedition to the East of Jordan," *PEFQS* 1872, pp. 57–72, esp. 69–70; C. R. Conder, "Tour of Their Royal Highnesses

Princes Albert Victor and George of Wales in Palestine," *PEFQS* 1882, p. 197–234, esp. 218–221, map.

Reconstruction and restoration carried out by J. Garstang, G. Horsfield, P. A. Ricci, for the British School of Archaeology in Jerusalem, and the Department of Antiquities of Palestine and of Transjordan, 1925–1928.

A. H. M. Jones, "Some Inscriptions from Jerash," *PEFQS* 1928, pp. 186–197, pls. 2–3.

Excavated by J. W. Crowfoot, B. W. Bacon, C. S. Fisher, for the British School of Archaeology in Jerusalem and Yale University, 1928–1929; C. S. Fisher, C. C. McCown, for the American Schools of Oriental Research, 1930–1931; C. C. McCown, C. S. Fisher, A. H. Detweiler, C. H. Kraeling, for Yale University and the American Schools of Oriental Research, 1933–1934.

J. W. Crowfoot, "The Church of S. Theodore at Jerash," *PEFQS* 1929, pp. 17–35, pls. 5–8; *id.*, "Jerash, 1929," *PEFQS* 1929, pp. 179–182; J. W. Crowfoot, R. W. Hamilton, "The Discovery of a Synagogue at Jerash," *PEFQS* 1929, pp. 211–219, pls. 1–5; J. W. Crowfoot, "The Churches of Gerasa, 1928, 1929," *PEFQS* 1930, pp. 32–42, fig.; C. S. Fisher, "Yale University-Jerusalem School Expedition at Jerash: First Campaign," *BASOR* 40, 1930, pp. 2–11, figs. 1–9; E. L. Sukenik, "Note on the Aramaic Inscription at the Synagogue at Gerasa," *PEFQS* 1930, pp. 48–49; C. C. McCown, "Jerash," *BASOR* 41, 1931, pp. 10–12, fig. 5; *id.*, "The Yale University-American School Excavation at Jerash, Autumn, 1930," *BASOR* 43, 1931, pp. 13–19, 4 figs.; J. W. Crowfoot, *Churches at Jerash*, 1931, pp. 1–48, pls. 1–13, plans; C. S. Fisher, C. C. McCown, "Jerash-Gerasa, 1930," *AASOR* 11, 1931, pp. 1–59, figs. 1–6, pls. 1–16, 3 plans; C. S. Fisher, "The Campaign at Jerash in September and October, 1931," *AASOR* 11, 1931, pp. 131–169, pls. 1–19, 1 plan; J. W. Crowfoot, "Recent Work Round the Fountain Court at Jerash," *PEFQS* 1931, pp. 143–154, pls. 1–6; C. S. Fisher, "Excavations at Jerash, 1931," *BASOR* 45, 1932, pp. 3–20, figs. 1–13; J. P. Naish, "The Excavations at Jerash," *PEFQS* 1933, pp. 90–96; C. C. McCown, "The Goddesses of Gerasa," *AASOR* 13, 1933, pp. 129–166; *id.*, "New Inscriptions from Jerash," *BASOR* 49, 1933, pp. 3–8, 2 figs.; N. Glueck, "Jerash in the Spring of 1933," *BASOR* 53, 1934, pp. 2–13, figs. 1–6; E. L. Sukenik, *Ancient Synagogues in Palestine and Greece*, 1934, pp. 35–37, pl. 9; C. S. Fisher, "Jerash in the Autumn of 1933," *BASOR* 54, 1934, pp. 5–13, figs. 1–8; W. F. Stinespring, "The Inscription of the Triumphal Arch at Jerash," *BASOR* 56, 1934, pp. 15–16; *id.*, "Jerash in the Spring of 1934," *BASOR* 57, 1935, pp. 3–5, figs. 1–5; J. W. Crowfoot, "The Propylaea Church at Jerash," *BASOR* 57, 1935, pp. 9–12, figs. 6–7; C. H. Kraeling, ed., *Gerasa: City of the Decapolis*, 1938; N. Glueck, "The Earliest History of Jerash," *BASOR* 75, 1939, pp. 22–30, fig.; C. H. Kraeling, "The Nabataean Sanctuary at Gerasa," *BASOR* 83, 1941, pp. 7–14, figs. 1–2; J. W. Crowfoot, *Early Churches in Palestine*, 1941, pp. 39–42, 44–55, 58–65, 68–70, 85–89, 96–98, 124–125, 128–134, 139–140, figs. 1–4, pls. 4b, 5, 7, 14, 15, 16, 17, 18, 22; A. H. Detweiler, "Some Early Jewish Architectural Vestiges from Jerash," *BASOR* 87, 1942, pp. 10–17, figs. 1–2; C. C. McCown, *The Ladder of Progress in Palestine*, 1943, pp. 280–282, 309–325, 4 pls.; H. G. May, "Synagogues in Palestine," *BA* 7, 1944, pp. 1–20, figs. 1–14; J. H. Iliffe, "Imperial Art in Trans-Jordan: Figurines and Lamps from a Potter's Store at Jerash," *QDAP* 11, 1945, pp. 1–26, pls. 1–9; G. L. Harding, "Recent Work on the Jerash Forum," *PEQ* 1949, pp. 12–20, pls. 1–3; S. J. Saller, B. Bagatti. *The Town of Nebo*, 1949, pp. 269–289, pls. 45–51; E. L. Sukenik, "Jerash," *Bulletin Rabinowitz* 1, 1949, p. 11; R. Amy, "Temples à escaliers," *Syria* 27, 1950, pp. 82–136, figs. 1–38, pls. 1–2; E. R. Goodenough, *Symbols* 1, 1953, pp. 180, 192, 259–260.

Excavation of tombs by F. S. Maʿayeh for the Department of Antiquities, Jordan, 1959.
F. S. Maʿayeh, "Jerash," *ADAJ* 4–5, 1960, pp. 115–116, pl. 4:2; *id.*, "Jerash," *RB* 67, 1960, pp. 228–229, pls. 10a, 11.

Restoration of the South Theater by T. Canaan and D. Kirkbride for the Department of Antiquities, Jordan, 1953–1956.
D. Kirkbride, "A Brief Outline of the Restoration of the South Theatre at Jerash," *ADAJ* 4–5, 1960, pp. 123–127, pls. 10–11; K. W. Clark, "Gerasa," *IDB*, 1962, pp. 382–384, figs.; E. Hoade, *East of the Jordan*, 1966, pp. 240–258, figs.; S. Mittmann, "The Roman Road from Gerasa to Adraa," *ADAJ* 11, 1966, pp. 65–87, figs.; G. L. Harding, *The Antiquities of Jordan*, 1967, pp. 79–105, 178, pls. 9–10; N. Glueck, *The River Jordan*, 1968, pp. 52–57, 98–101, 168, figs.; J. Finegan, *The Archeology of the New Testament*, 1969, pp. 61–70, figs.; N. Glueck, *The Other Side of the Jordan*, 1970, pp. 154–157, 183, figs.; S. Applebaum, "Geresh," *EAEHL*, 1970, pp. 120–128, figs. (Hebrew).

Jericho, Tell es-Sultan, Eriha

Excavations carried out by C. Warren for the Palestine Exploration Fund, 1868.
C. Warren, "Mounds at ʿAin es-Sultan," *PEFQS* 1869, pp. 14–16; F. J. Bliss, "Notes on the Plain of Jericho," *PEFQS* 1894, pp. 175–183, esp. 175–176.

Excavated by E. Sellin, C. Watzinger for the Kaiserlichen Academie der Wissenschaften in Wien and the Deutsche Orient-Gesellschaft, 1907–1908.
E. Sellin, C. Watzinger, *Jericho, die Ergebnisse der Ausgrabungen*, 1913; J. Garstang, "The Date of the Destruction of Jericho," *PEFQS* 1927, pp. 96–100.

Excavated by J. Garstang for the Marston-Melchett Expedition, University of Liverpool, British School of Archaeology in Jerusalem, 1930–1936.
J. Garstang, "Jericho, Sir Charles Marston's Expedition of 1930," *PEFQS* 1930, pp. 123–132, pls. 1–10; L. H. Vincent, "The Chronology of Jericho," *PEFQS* 1931, pp. 104–105; J. Garstang, "Prof. Garstang's Reply," *PEFQS* 1931, pp. 105–107; *id.*, "The Walls of Jericho, The Marston-Melchett Expedition of 1931," *PEFQS* 1931, pp. 186–196, figs. 1–5, pls. 1–7; *id.*, "The Third Season at Jericho," *PEFQS* 1932, pp. 149–153; Bibliography, *QDAP* 1, 1932, pp. 93–94; J. Garstang, "Jericho: City and Necropolis," *Annals of Archaeology and Anthropology* 19, 1932, pp. 3–22, figs. 1–7, pls. 1–25; *id.*, "Jericho: City and Necropolis," *Annals of Archaeology and Anthropology* 20, 1933, pp. 3–42, figs. 1–11, pls. 1–34; *id.*, "Jericho," *QDAP* 3, 1934, pp. 176–177.

Church cleared by D. C. Baramki for the Department of Antiquities, Palestine, 1934.
J. Garstang, "The Fall of Bronze Age Jericho," *PEFQS* 1935, pp. 61–68, pls. 1–5; D. C. Baramki, "An Early Byzantine Basilica at Tell Ḥassān, Jericho," *QDAP* 5, 1936, pp. 82–89, figs. 1–3, pls. 49–58; J. Garstang, "Jericho: City and Necropolis," *Annals of Archaeology and Anthropology* 22, 1935, pp. 143–184, pls. 23–59; *id.*, "Jericho," *QDAP* 5, 1936, pp. 199–201; J. Garstang *et al.*, "Jericho: City and Necropolis," *Annals of Archaeology and Anthropology* 23, 1936, pp. 67–100, pls. 29–42, plan.

Synagogue cleared by D. C. Baramki for the Department of Antiquities, Palestine, 1936.
D. C. Baramki, "An Early Byzantine Synagogue near Tell es-Sultan," *QDAP* 6, 1937, pp. 73–77, fig. 1, pls. 18–23; J. Crowfoot, "Notes on the Flint Implements of

Jericho, 1936," *Annals of Archaeology and Anthropology* 24, 1937, pp. 35–51, pls. 6–10; J. Garstang, "Jericho," *QDAP* 6, 1937, p. 212; H. G. May, "Synagogues in Palestine," *BA* 7, 1944, pp. 1–20, figs. 1–14; J. Garstang, J. B. E. Garstang, *The Story of Jericho*, 1948; E. L. Sukenik, "Jericho," *Bulletin Rabinowitz* 1, 1949, pp. 14–15, pl. 7.

Excavated by K. M. Kenyon for the British School of Archaeology in Jerusalem, Palestine Exploration Fund, British Academy, American Schools of Oriental Research, Department of Antiquities, Jordan, 1952–1958.

K. M. Kenyon, "Some Notes on the History of Jericho in the Second Millennium B.C.," *PEQ* 1951, pp. 101–138, figs. 1–12; *id.*, "Excavations at Jericho 1952, Interim Report," *PEQ* 1952, pp. 4–6; *id.*, "Excavations at Jericho 1952," *PEQ* 1952, pp. 62–82, figs. 1–6, pls. 13–23; *id.*, "The 7000-year-old Plastered Skull Portraits of Neolithic Jericho," *ILN*, April 18, 1953, pp. iv, 627, figs. 1–9; *id.*, "Excavations at Jericho 1953," *PEQ* 1953, pp. 81–95, figs. 1–3, pls. 35–45; *id.*, "The Bronze Age Tombs of Jericho," *ILN*, October 3, 1953, pp. 520–523, figs. 1–21; *id.*, "Mankind's Earliest Walled Town," *ILN*, October 17, 1953, pp. 603–604, figs. 1–10; E. R. Goodenough, *Symbols* 1, 1953, pp. 260–262; K. M. Kenyon, "Excavations at Jericho 1954," *PEQ* 1954, pp. 45–63, figs. 1–5, pls. 7–17; F. E. Zeuner, "The Neolithic-Bronze Age Gap on the Tell of Jericho," *PEQ* 1954, pp. 64–68; K. M. Kenyon, "The Everyday Life of Jericho 3650 Years Ago," *ILN*, July 24, 1954, pp. 144–145, figs. 1–8; F. E. Zeuner, "The Goats of Early Jericho," *PEQ* 1955, pp. 70–86, pls. 7–9; K. M. Kenyon, "Excavations at Jericho, 1955," *PEQ* 1955, pp. 108–117, pls. 12–23; F. E. Zeuner, "Notes on the Bronze Age Tombs of Jericho I," *PEQ* 1955, pp. 118–128, figs. 1–2; K. Kenyon, "Excavating the Jericho of 7000 Years Ago, and Earlier," *ILN*, May 12, 1956, pp. 504–506, figs. 1–9; *id.*, "The Jericho of Abraham'sTime," *ILN*, May 19, 1956, pp. 552–555, figs. 1–10; *id.*, "Excavations at Jericho 1956," *PEQ* 1956, pp. 67–82, figs. 1–6, pls. 6–16; I. W. Cornwall, "The Pre-Pottery Neolithic Burials, Jericho," *PEQ* 1956, pp. 110–124, pls. 17–22; K. M. Kenyon, "Jericho — the World's Oldest Town," *ILN*, October 13, 1956, pp. 611–613, figs. 1–16; P. C. Hammond, "A Note on Two Seal Impressions from Tell es-Sultan," *PEQ* 1957, pp. 68–69, pls. 16–17, and p. 145; *id.*, "A Note on a Seal Impression from Tell es-Sultan," *BASOR* 147, 1957, pp. 37–39, fig.; K. M. Kenyon, "Excavations at Jericho 1957," *PEQ* 1957, pp. 101–107, fig. 1, pls. 21–23; *id.*, *Digging Up Jericho*, 1957; F. E. Zeuner, "Dog and Cat in the Neolithic of Jericho," *PEQ* 1958, pp. 52–55; K. M. Kenyon, "Excavations at Jericho," *PEQ* 1960, pp. 88–113, figs. 1–3, pls. 6–12; D. Kirkbride, "A Brief Report on the Pre-pottery Flint Cultures of Jericho," *PEQ* 1960, pp. 114–119, pls. 13–15; K. M. Kenyon, *Excavations at Jericho I, The Tombs Excavated in 1952–54*, 1960, R. L. Cleveland, "An Ivory Bull's Head from Ancient Jericho," *BASOR* 163, 1961, pp. 30–36, figs. 1–2; *id.*, "Acknowledgement of the Bull's Head from Khirbet Kerak," *BASOR* 165, 1962, p. 47; P. Bar-Adon, "Another Ivory Bull's Head from Palestine," *BASOR* 165, 1962, pp. 46–47, fig.; K. M. Kenyon, *Excavations at Jericho II, The Tombs Excavated in 1955–58*, 1965; J. A. Callaway, "Jericho (Old Testament)," *The Biblical World*, 1966, pp. 305–309, fig.; K. M. Kenyon, *Amorites and Canaanites*, 1966, pp. 6–35, figs. 2, 6–13, 26, 30–32, 34, 40, pls. 1–4, 22–23, 27–30; *id.*, "Jericho," *Archaeology* 20, 1967, pp. 268–275, figs.; I. M. Blake, "Jericho (Ain es-Sultan): Joshua's Curse and Elisha's Miracle — One Possible Explanation," *PEQ* 1967, pp. 86–97; K. M. Kenyon, "Jericho: Oldest Walled Town," *Archaeological Discoveries in the Holy Land*, 1967, pp. 19–28, figs.; K. Branigan, "A Unique Juglet from Jericho," *PEQ* 1967, pp. 99–100, fig. 1, pl. 25; K. M. Kenyon, "Jericho," *AOTS*, 1967, pp. 264–275, pl. 11; G. L. Harding, *The Antiquities of Jordan*, 1967, pp. 29–30, 166–176, 193, pls. 25–26.

Suwanet eth-Thaniya excavated by G. M. Landes for the American Schools of Oriental Research, 1969.

A. Biran, "Suwanet eth-Thaniya," *CNI* 20:3–4, 1969, p. 54; J. B. Pritchard, ed., *ANEP*, 1969, nos. 151, 221, 714, 715, 778, 780, 781, 801, 863; E. Mazor, "The Radio-Activity of Waters at Jericho — a Reply to Blake's Hypothesis," *PEQ* 1969, pp. 46–47; I. M. Blake, "Correspondence," *PEQ* 1969, pp. 131–132; O. Tufnell, "The Pottery from Royal Tombs I-III at Byblos," *Berytus* 18, 1969, pp. 5–33, figs. 1–7, esp. pp. 10–14; P. W. Lapp, *Biblical Archaeology and History*, 1969, pp. 68, 72, 115, pl. 1; J. Kaplan, "A Suggested Correlation between Stratum IX, Jericho and Stratum XXIV, Mersin," *JNES* 28, 1969, pp. 197–199; E. V. Hulse, "Joshua's Curse: Radio-activity or Schistosomiasis?" *PEQ* 1970, pp. 92–101; K. M. Kenyon, *The Archaeology of the Holy Land*, 1970, pp. 313–314, 330–334, figs., pls.; *id.*, "Yriḥo," *EAEHL*, 1970, pp. 243–252, figs. (Hebrew); A. C. Western, "The Ecological Interpretation of Ancient Charcoals from Jericho," *Levant* 3, 1971, pp. 31–40, figs. 1–2; J. Clutton-Brock, "The Primary Food Animals of the Jericho Tell from the Proto-Neolithic to the Byzantine Period," *Levant* 3, 1971, pp. 41–55, figs. 1–7, pls. 23–25; P. D. C. Brown, "Roman Pottery Kilns at Jericho," *Levant* 3, 1971, pp. 95–96, fig. 1, pl. 29b.

Jericho, Tulûl Abū el-ʿAlâyiq

Tulûl Abū el-ʿAlâyiq excavated by J. L. Kelso, A. H. Detweiler and J. B. Pritchard for Pittsburgh-Xenia Seminary and the American Schools of Oriental Research, 1950–1951.

J. L. Kelso, "The First Campaign of Excavation in New Testament Jericho," *BASOR* 120, 1950, pp. 11–22, figs. 1–6; *id.*, "New Testament Jericho," *BA* 14, 1951, pp. 34–43, figs. 1–6; J. B. Pritchard, "The 1951 Campaign at Herodian Jericho," *BASOR* 123, 1951, pp. 8–17, figs. 1–7; J. L. Kelso, D. C. Baramki, *Excavations at New Testament Jericho and Khirbet en-Nitla*, *AASOR* 29–30, 1955; J. B. Pritchard, *The Excavation at Herodian Jericho 1951*, *AASOR* 32–33, 1958; J. L. Kelso, "Jericho (New Testament)," C. F. Pfeiffer, ed., *The Biblical World*, 1966, pp. 303–305; J. Finegan, *The Archeology of the New Testament*, 1969, pp. 81–86, figs.; G. Foerster, G. Balci, "Yriho in Roman and Byzantine Times," *EAEHL*, 1970, pp. 253–259, figs. (Hebrew).

Jerusalem

Excavated by the Palestine Exploration Fund, 1864–1868, 1873–1874, 1894–1897, 1923–1928.

C. W. Wilson, *Ordnance Survey of Jerusalem*, 1865; H. B. Tristram, *The Land of Israel: A Journal of Travels in Palestine*, 1866, pp. 171–193; C. W. Wilson, C. Warren, *The Recovery of Jerusalem*, 1871; C. Clermont-Ganneau, *Archaeological Researches in Palestine 1873–74*, I, 1899.

Excavated by the École Biblique et Archéologique Française, 1881–1894, 1912, 1918.

C. Warren, C. R. Conder, *The Survey of Western Palestine: Jerusalem, 1884*.

Excavated by the Franciscan Custody of the Holy Land, 1889, 1901–1903, 1909–1920.

Tombs excavated, off Nablus Road, by C. Schick for the Palestine Exploration Fund, 1891.

C. Schick, "Letters from Baurath C. Schick," and "Remarkable Rock-Cut Tombs in the Wâdy el-Jôz," *PEFQS* 1892, pp. 9–16, 2 figs.; *id.*, "Gordon's Tomb," *PEFQS* 1892, pp. 120–124, 2 figs.; F. J. Bliss, A. C. Dickie, *Excavations at Jerusalem,*

1898; L. H. Vincent, *Jérusalem sous Terre*, 1911; R. Weill, *La Cité de David, Compte rendu des fouilles exécutées à Jérusalem, sur le site de la ville primitive. Campagne de 1913–14*, 1920, 2 vols.

Excavated by R. A. S. Macalister, J. G. Duncan, J. W. Crowfoot for the British School of Archaeology in Jerusalem and the Department of Antiquities, Palestine, 1923–1928.

R. A. S. Macalister, "First Quarterly Report on the Excavation of the Eastern Hill of Jerusalem," *PEFQS* 1924, pp. 9–23, figs. 1–9, pls. 1–2; *id.*, "Second Quarterly Report on the Excavation of the Eastern Hill of Jerusalem," *PEFQS* 1924, pp. 57–68, figs. 1–7; *id.*, "Jerusalem," *PEFQS* 1924, pp. 108–123; J. G. Duncan, "Third Quarterly Report on the Excavation of the Eastern Hill of Jerusalem," *PEFQS* 1924, pp. 124–136, figs. 1–13, pls. 1–3; R. A. S. Macalister, "On a Remarkable Group of Cult-Objects from the Ophel Excavation," *PEFQS* 1924, pp. 137–142, figs. 1–6; J. G. Duncan, "Fourth Quarterly Report on the Excavation of the Eastern Hill of Jerusalem," *PEFQS* 1924, pp. 163–180, figs. 1–6, pls. 1–4; S. A. Cook, "Inscribed Hebrew Objects from Ophel," *PEFQS* 1924, pp. 180–186, pls. 5–6; L. A. Mayer, "A Tomb in the Kedron Valley Containing Ossuaries with Hebrew Graffiti Names," *Palestine Museum Bulletin* 1, 1924, pp. 56–60, pls. 5–6.

"Third Wall" excavated by E. L. Sukenik, L. A. Mayer, C. S. Fisher for the Hebrew University and the American Schools of Oriental Research, 1925–1928.

J. G. Duncan, "Fifth Quarterly Report on the Excavation of the Eastern Hill of Jerusalem," *PEFQS* 1925, pp. 8–24, figs. 1–19, pls. 1–8; *id.*, "Sixth Quarterly Report on the Excavation of the Eastern Hill of Jerusalem," *PEFQS* 1925, pp. 134–139, pls. 1–2; *id.*, "The Excavation of the Foundations of the Supposed Third Wall of Jerusalem," *PEFQS* 1925, pp. 172–182, figs. 1–6; *id.*, "New Rock Chambers and Galleries on Ophel," *PEFQS* 1926, pp. 7–14, 1 plan; R. Weill, "The PEF Map of Ophel," *PEFQS* 1926, pp. 171–175, 1 fig.; R. A. S. Macalister, J. G. Duncan, "Excavations on the Hill of Ophel, Jerusalem, 1923–25," *PEFA* 4, 1926; J. W. Crowfoot, "First Report of the New Excavations on Ophel," *PEFQS* 1927, pp. 143–147, pls. 1–5; *id.*, "Second Report of the Excavations in the Tyropoeon Valley," *PEFQS* 1927, pp. 178–183, pls. 1–4; C. Lambert, "A Hoard of Jewish Bronze Coins from Ophel," *PEFQS* 1927, pp. 184–188; J. W. Crowfoot, "Excavations in the Tyropoeon Valley," *PEFQS* 1928, pp. 9–27, pls. 1–6, plan; J. W. Crowfoot, G. M. FitzGerald, "Excavations in the Tyropoeon Valley, Jerusalem 1927," *PEFA* 5, 1929; E. L. Sukenik, L. A. Mayer, *The Third Wall of Jerusalem*, 1930.

Cemeteries at Y.M.C.A. excavated by J. H. Iliffe for the Department of Antiquities, Palestine, 1932.

L. A. Mayer, M. Avi-Yonah, Bibliography for Jerusalem, *QDAP* 1, 1932, pp. 163–188, 192, map on p. 60; F. J. Hollis, "The Sun-Cult and the Temple of Jerusalem," in S. H. Hooke, ed., *Myth and Ritual*, 1933, pp. 87–110; E. L. Sukenik, *Ancient Synagogues in Palestine and Greece*, 1934, pp. 69–70, pl. 16a; R. W. Hamilton, "Note on Excavations at Bishop Gobat School 1933," *PEFQS* 1935, pp. 141–143, pls. 1–6; J. H. Iliffe, "Cemeteries and a 'Monastery' at the Y.M.C.A. Jerusalem," *QDAP* 4, 1935, pp. 70–80, figs. 1–6, pls. 40–51; D. C. Baramki, "An Ancient Cistern in the Grounds of Government House, Jerusalem," *QDAP* 4, 1935, pp. 165–167, fig. 1, pls. 76–78; R. W. Hamilton, S. A. S. Husseini, "Shaft Tombs on the Nablus Rd., Jerusalem," *QDAP* 4, 1935, pp. 170–174, fig. 1, pls. 81–83.

Citadel excavated by C. N. Johns for the Department of Antiquities, Palestine, 1934–1947.

C. N. Johns, "Excavations at the Citadel, Jerusalem," *QDAP* 5, 1936, pp. 127–131, fig. 1, pls. 68–73.

Excavations against the North Wall carried out by R. W. Hamilton for the Department of Antiquities, Palestine, 1937–1938.

R. W. Hamilton, "Note on Recent Discoveries Outside St. Stephen's Gate, Jerusalem," *QDAP* 6, 1937, pp. 153–156, fig. 1, pls. 40–42; C. N. Johns, "Excavations at the Citadel, Jerusalem," *PEQ* 1940, pp. 36–56, pls. 3–8.

Hablet el-Amud tomb excavated by Y. Saʿad for the Department of Antiquities, Palestine, 1941.

J. W. Crowfoot, *Early Churches in Palestine*, 1941, pp. 9–21, 30–34, fig. 5; M. Solomiac, "The Northwest Line of the Third Wall of Jerusalem," *BASOR* 89, 1943, pp. 18–21, figs. 1–2; E. L. Sukenik, L. A. Mayer, "A New Section of the Third Wall, Jerusalem," *PEQ* 1944, pp. 145–151, figs. 1–3, pls. 3–4; R. W. Hamilton, "Excavations Against the North Wall of Jerusalem, 1937–38," *QDAP* 10, 1944, pp. 1–54, figs. 1–23, pls. 1–11; M. Avi-Yonah, "Greek Inscriptions from Ascalon, Jerusalem, Beisan, and Hebron," *QDAP* 10, 1944, pp. 160–169, pl. 35; E. L. Sukenik, "The Third Wall," *QDAP* 10, 1944, p. 195; H. Kendall, *Jerusalem: The City Plan, Preservation and Development during the British Mandate 1918–1948*, 1948; M. Stekelis, P. Solomonica, "Rephaim Baqa, a Palaeolithic Station in the Vicinity of Jerusalem," *JPOS* 21, 1948, pp. 80–97, figs. 1–10, pl. 27.

Excavations at Bethphage conducted by E. Testa for the Franciscan Custody of the Holy Land, 1949–1953.

C. N. Johns, "The Citadel, Jerusalem," *QDAP* 14, 1950, pp. 121–190, figs. 1–35, pls. 47–64; J. J. Simons, *Jerusalem in the Old Testament*, 1952; J. J. Rothschild, "The Tombs of Sanhedria," *PEQ* 1952, pp. 23–28, pls. 6–12; S. Corbett, "Some Observations on the Gateways to the Herodian Temple in Jerusalem," *PEQ* 1952, pp. 7–14, figs. 2–5, pls. 1–5; R. W. Hamilton, "Jerusalem in the Fourth Century," *PEQ* 1952, pp. 83–90; J. J. Rothschild, "The Tombs of Sanhedria II," *PEQ* 1954, pp. 16–22, fig. 1, pls. 1–5; L. H. Vincent, A. M. Stève, *Jérusalem de l'Ancien Testament*, 2 vols., 1954.

Tomb on Mount of Olives excavated by the Franciscan Custody of the Holy Land, 1954.

P. Lemaire, "Une Tombe du Recent Bronze au Mont des Oliviers," *LA* 5, 1955, pp. 261–299, figs. 1–21.

Dominus Flevit excavated by B. Bagatti, J. T. Milik for the Franciscan Custody of the Holy Land, 1954–1957.

B. Bagatti, "Scavo di un Monastero al 'Dominus Flevit'," *LA* 6, 1956, pp. 240–270, figs. 1–16, plan; B. Bagatti, J. T. Milik, *The Excavations at Dominus Flevit (Mount Olivet, Jerusalem)*, I, *La Necropoli del Periodo Romano*, 1958; V. R. Gold, "The Mosaic Map of Madaba," *BA* 21, 1958, pp. 50–71, figs. 1–9; R. Amiran, "A Late Bronze Age II Pottery Group from a Tomb in Jerusalem," *EI* 6, 1960, pp. 25–37, 3 figs., pls. 3–4 (Hebrew); J. Pinkerfeld, "David's Tomb," *Bulletin Rabinowitz* 3, 1960, pp. 41–43, 1 fig., pl. 9:1–2; L. Y. Rahmani, "Roman Tombs in Shmuel ha- Navi Street, Jerusalem," *IEJ* 10, 1960, pp. 140–148, figs. 1–3, pls. 19–21; *id.*, "Jewish Rock-Cut Tombs in Jerusalem," *ʿAtiqot* 3, 1961, pp. 93–120, figs. 1–10, pls. 13–17; E. Testa, "The Archaeological Setting of the Shrine of Bethphage," *LA* 11, 1961, pp. 172–287, figs. 1–40; H. E. Stutchbury, "Excavations in the Kedron Valley," *PEQ* 1961, pp. 101–113, fig. a-c, pls. 11–15; R. D. Barnett, "Reminiscences of Herod's Temple," *CNI* 12:3, 1961, pp. 14–20, pls. 1–4; K. M. Kenyon, "In Search of Ancient Jerusalem," *ILN*, April 14, 1962, pp. 578–580, figs. 1–7; *id.*, "The Holy City from Today back to 1800 B.C.," *ILN*, April 21, 1962, pp. 619–621, figs. 1–9; *id.*, "Biblical Jerusalem," *Expedition* 5, 1962, pp. 32–35, figs.; M. Burrows, "Jerusalem," *IDB* 1962, pp. 843–866, figs.; K. M. Kenyon, "Excavations in Jerusalem 1961," *ADAJ*

6–7, 1962, pp. 114–117; *id.*, "Excavations in Jerusalem 1961," *PEQ* 1962, pp. 72–89, figs. 1–5, pls. 17–25; S. Saller, "Jerusalem and its Surroundings in the Bronze Age," *LA* 12, 1962, pp. 147–176, figs. 1–3; K. M. Kenyon, "Excavations in Jerusalem 1962," *PEQ* 1963, pp. 7–21, fig. 1, pls. 1–10.

Excavations carried out at the Damascus Gate by C. M. Bennett, J. B. Hennessy, for the British School of Archaeology in Jerusalem and the Department of Antiquities, Jordan, 1964–1966.

Y. Saᶜad, "A Bronze Age Tomb Group from Hablet el-Amud, Silwan Village Lands," *ADAJ* 8–9, 1964, pp. 77–80, pls. 31–36; S. J. Saller, *The Excavations at Dominus Flevit (Mount Olivet, Jerusalem)*, II, *The Jebusite Burial Place*, 1964; K. M. Kenyon, "Excavations in Jerusalem 1963," *PEQ* 1964, pp. 7–18, figs. 1–2, pls. 1–10; *id.*, "Excavations in Jerusalem 1961–1963," *BA* 27, 1964, pp. 34–52, figs. 1–12; A. Spijkerman, "Observations on the Coinage of Aelia Capitolina," *LA* 14, 1964, pp. 245–260, figs.; V. Corbo, "Nuove Scoperte archeologiche nella Basilica del S. Sepolcro," *LA* 14, 1964, pp. 293–338, figs. 1–18; *World of the Bible*, Centenary Booklet of the Palestine Exploration Fund, 1965; K. M. Kenyon, "Excavations in Jerusalem 1964," *PEQ* 1965, pp. 9–20, figs. 1–2, pls. 1–12; V. Corbo, "Scavo della Cappella dell' Invenzione della S. Croce e nuovi reperti archeologici nella Basilica del S. Sepolcro a Gerusalemme (1965)," *LA* 15, 1965, pp. 318–366, figs. 1–27; K. M. Kenyon, "Excavations in Jerusalem 1965," *PEQ* 1966, pp. 73–88, figs. 1–4, pls. 23–29; *id.*, *Amorites and Canaanites*, 1966, pp. 2, 25; E. W. Hamrick, "New Excavations at Sukenik's 'Third Wall'," *BASOR* 183, 1966, pp. 19–26; J. A. Callaway, "Jerusalem," in C. F. Pfeiffer, ed., *The Biblical World*, 1966, pp. 309–323, figs.; R. P. S. Hubbard, "The Topography of Ancient Jerusalem," *PEQ* 1966, pp. 130–154, figs. 1–9, pl. 31; S. Loffreda, "Il Monolita di Soloe," *LA* 16, 1966, pp. 85–126, figs. 1–18; W. F. Stinespring, "Wilson's Arch and the Masonic Hall, Summer 1966," *BA* 30, 1967, pp. 27–31, figs. 15–17; D. R. AP-Thomas, "Jerusalem," in D. W. Thomas, ed., *AOTS*, 1967, pp. 277–295, fig. 7, pl. 12; K. M. Kenyon, "Excavations in Jerusalem 1966," *PEQ* 1967, pp. 65–71, pls. 12–24; *id.*, *Jerusalem: Excavating 3000 Years of History*, 1967; M. Avi-Yonah, "Zion, the Perfection of Beauty," *Ariel* 18, 1967, pp. 25–44, figs.; L. Y. Rahmani, "Jason's Tomb," *IEJ* 17, 1967, pp. 61–100, figs. 1–18, pls. 13–24; N. Avigad, "Aramaic Inscriptions in the Tomb of Jason," *IEJ* 17, 1967, pp. 101–111, figs. 1–2, pls. 25–27; P. Benoit, "L'Inscription grecque du rombeau de Jason," *IEJ* 17, 1967, pp. 112–113, pl. 28; N. Avigad, "Jewish Rock-cut Tombs in Jerusalem and in the Judean Hill-country," *EI* 8, 1967, pp. 119–142, 35 figs., pls. 20–24 (Hebrew); L. Y. Rahmani, "Jewish Tombs in the Romema Quarter of Jerusalem," *EI* 8, 1967, pp. 186–192, 6 figs., pls. 37–39 (Hebrew); R. H. Smith, "The Tomb of Jesus," *BA* 30, 1967, pp. 74–89, figs. 1–8.

Excavated by K. M. Kenyon for the British School of Archaeology in Jerusalem, British Academy, Department of Antiquities, Jordan, Palestine Exploration Fund, Royal Ontario Museum, 1961–1967.

Excavations carried out by B. Mazar at the Temple Mount for the Hebrew University and the Israel Exploration Society, 1968–

B. Mazar, "Jerusalem in the Biblical Period," *Qadmoniot* 1, 1968, pp. 3–12, figs. (Hebrew); R. Amiran, "The Water Supply of Jerusalem," *Qadmoniot* 1, 1968, pp. 13–18, figs. (Hebrew); M. Avi-Yonah, "Jerusalem of the Second Temple Period," *Qadmoniot* 1, 1968, pp. 19–27, figs. (Hebrew); N. Avigad, "The Architecture of Jerusalem in the Second Temple Period," *Qadmoniot* 1, 1968, pp. 28–36, figs. (Hebrew); *id.*, "A Jewish Tomb-Cave on Mount Scopus," *Qadmoniot* 1, 1968, pp. 37–38, figs. (Hebrew); J. Prawer, "Jerusalem in Crusader Days," *Qadmoniot* 1, 1968, pp. 39–46.

figs. (Hebrew); H. Z. Hirschberg, "The Remains of Ancient Synagogues in Jerusalem," *Qadmoniot* 1, 1968, pp. 56–62, figs. (Hebrew); Y. Shiloh, "A Table of the Major Excavations in Jerusalem 1863–1968," *Qadmoniot* 1, 1968, pp. 71–78 (Hebrew).

Tombs excavated, near Nablus Rd., by V. Tsaferis and S. Gudowitz for the Department of Antiquities and Museums, 1968.

V. Tsaferis, "The Burial of Simeon the Temple Builder," *Qadmoniot* 1, 1968, pp. 137–138, figs. (Hebrew); J. B. Hennessy, "Jerusalem (Porte de Damas)," *RB* 75, 1968, pp. 250–253, pls. 28–29; M. Avi-Yonah, "The Third and Second Walls of Jerusalem," *IEJ* 18, 1968, pp. 98–125, figs. 1–6; Israel Exploration Society, *The Twenty-fifth Archaeological Convention: Jerusalem Through the Ages*, 1968; K. M. Kenyon, "Jerusalem," *RB* 75, 1968, pp. 422–424; E. W. Hamrick, "Further Notes on the 'Third Wall'," *BASOR* 192, 1968, pp. 21–25, figs. 1–2; K. M. Kenyon, "Excavations in Jerusalem 1967," *PEQ* 1968, pp. 97–109, figs. 1–5, pls. 29–40; M. Ita, "The Antonia Fortress," *PEQ* 1968, pp. 140–143, figs. 1–2, pls. 42–46; A. Biran, "Mt. Scopus Cave," *CNI* 19:3–4, 1968, p. 35, pl. 3b.

Citadel excavated by R. Amiran, A. Eitan, for the Hebrew University, Israel Museum, Israel Exploration Society, 1968–1969.

J. Gray, *A History of Jerusalem*, 1969; J. E. Jennings, "Excavations on the Mount of Olives 1965," *ADAJ* 14, 1969, pp. 11–22, pls. 11–20; L. E. Stager, "An Inscribed Potsherd from the Eleventh Century B.C.," *BASOR* 194, 1969, pp. 45–52, figs. 1–3; P. W. Lapp, *Biblical Archaeology and History*, 1969, pp. 68, 72, 115–116, 124, pls. 2, 5, 6; B. Mazar, "The Excavations in the Old City of Jerusalem," *EI* 9, 1969, pp. 161–174, figs., pls. 39–50 (Hebrew); M. Avi-Yonah, "A Fragment of a Latin Inscription from the Excavations in the Old City of Jerusalem," *EI* 9, 1969, pp. 175–176, pl. 47:6 (Hebrew); B. Bagatti, "Nuovi Apporti Archeologici al 'Dominus Flevit' (Oliveto)," *LA* 19, 1969, pp. 194–236, figs. 1–23, plan; S. Saller, "An Inscribed Tombstone from Gethsemane," *LA* 19, 1969, pp. 367–368, 1 fig.; J. Finegan, *The Archaeology of the New Testament*, 1969, pp. 88–180, figs.; C. Thubron, *Jerusalem*, 1969; M. Avi-Yonah, ed., *A History of the Holy Land*, 1969, *passim*; D. Ussiskin, "On the Shorter Inscription from the Tomb of the Royal Steward," *BASOR* 196, 1969, pp. 16–22, fig. 1; B. Mazar, "Jerusalem — Old City," *IEJ* 19, 1969, pp. 249–250; J. B. Pritchard, ed., *ANEP*, 1969, nos. 275, 744, 804; *id.*, *ANET*, 1969, pp. 258, 287, 288, 321, 322, 329, 487–489, 491, 492, 563–564.

Jewish Quarter excavated by N. Avigad for the Hebrew University, Department of Antiquities and Museums, Israel Exploration Society, Israel, 1967–1969.

N. Avigad, "Excavations in the Jewish Quarter of the Old City of Jerusalem 1967/70 (Preliminary Report)," *IEJ* 20, 1970, pp. 1–8, figs. 1–2, front., pls. 1–4; R. Amiran, A. Eitan, "Excavations in the Courtyard of the Citadel, Jerusalem, 1968–1969 (Preliminary Report)," *IEJ* 20, 1970, pp. 9–17, figs. 1–5, pls. 5–8; V. Tsaferis, "Jewish Tombs at and near Givᶜat ha-Mivtar, Jerusalem," *IEJ* 20, 1970, pp. 18–32, figs. 1–8, pls. 9–17; J. Naveh, "The Ossuary Inscriptions from Givᶜat ha-Mivtar," *IEJ* 20, 1970, pp. 33–37, pls. 11–13, 17b; N. Haas, "Anthropological Observations on the Skeletal Remains from Givᶜat ha-Mivtar," *IEJ* 20, 1970, pp. 38–59, figs. 1–6, pls. 18–24; R. Grafman, "Herod's Foot and Robinson's Arch," *IEJ* 20, 1970, pp. 60–66, figs. 1–5; I. Renov, "A View of Herod's Temple from Nicanor's Gate in a Mural Panel of the Dura-Europos Synagogue," *IEJ* 20, 1970, pp. 67–74, fig. 1; Y. Meshorer, "A Stone Weight from the Reign of Herod," *IEJ* 20, 1970, pp. 97–98, pl. 27a; Y. Israeli, "A Second Jewish Applied Glass Medallion," *IEJ* 20, 1970, p. 104, pl. 27b–c; C. Graesser, Jr., "Ras el-Jamiᶜ, ᶜIsawiye," *IEJ* 20, 1970, p. 120; N. Avigad, "Excavations in the Jewish Quarter of the Old City of Jerusalem, 1970,"

IEJ 20, 1970, pp. 129–140, figs. 1–3, pls. 29–34; M. Benvenisti, *The Crusaders in the Holy Land*, 1970, pp. 35–73, figs. J. B. Hennessy, "Preliminary Report on Excavations at the Damascus Gate, Jerusalem, 1964–66," *Levant* 2, 1970, pp. v–vi, 22–27, figs. 1–3, pls. 13–24; K. M. Kenyon, *Archaeology in the Holy Land*, 1970, pp. 314–317, 339, 343–344, 349–352; J. Prignaud, "Notes d'Epigraphie Hébraique," *RB* 77, 1970, pp. 50–67, 9 figs., pl. 1; B. Couroyer, "Menues trouvailles à Jérusalem," *RB* 77, 1970, pp. 248–252, pl. 10; D. Ussishkin, "The Necropolis from the Time of the Kingdom of Judah at Silwan, Jerusalem," *BA* 33, 1970, pp. 1–46, figs. 1–8; B. Mazar, "The Excavations South and West of the Temple Mount in Jerusalem: The Herodian Period," *BA* 33, 1970, pp. 47–60, figs. 9–17; D. Ussishkin, "A Recently Discovered Monolithic Tomb in Siloam," *Qadmoniot* 3, 1970, pp. 25–26, figs. (Hebrew); N. Avigad, "Remains of Jewish Art Found in the Upper City of Jerusalem," *Qadmoniot* 3, 1970, pp. 27–29, figs. (Hebrew); R. Amiran, A. Eitan, "Excavations in the Jerusalem Citadel," *Qadmoniot* 3, 1970, pp. 64–66, figs. (Hebrew).

Jewish Quarter of Old City excavated by N. Avigad for the Hebrew University, Department of Antiquities and Museums, Israel, Israel Exploration Society, 1970.

N. Avigad, "Excavations in the Jewish Quarter of the Old City of Jerusalem 1970," *IEJ* 20, 1970, pp. 129–140, figs. 1–3, pls. 29–34; R. Amiran, A. Eitan, "Jerusalem Citadel," *RB* 77, 1970, pp. 564–570, fig. 2, pls. 33–34; N. Avigad, "Jerusalem," *RB* 77, 1970, pp. 570–572, pl. 35; O. Negbi, "Jerusalem," *RB* 77, 1970, pp. 572–573; B. Mazar, "The Excavations South and West of the Temple Mount," *Ariel* 27, 1970, pp. 11–19, figs.; K. M. Kenyon, "Israelite Jerusalem," *NEATC*, 1970, pp. 232–253, figs. 1–5, pls. 27–29; J. A. Sanders, ed., "Jerusalem," in Index of *NEATC*, 1970, p. 401; A. Bar-Yosef, "Emeq Refaim," *EAEHL*, 1970, pp. 207–208, figs. (Hebrew); B. Mazar, "Biblical Jerusalem," *EAEHL*, 1970, pp. 209–211, figs. (Hebrew); K. M. Kenyon, "The Biblical City," *EAEHL*, 1970, pp. 212–218, figs. (Hebrew); M. Avi-Yonah, "In the Days of the Second Temple," *EAEHL*, 1970, pp. 219–232, figs. (Hebrew); Y. Aharoni, "A 40-Shekel Weight with a Hieratic Numeral," *BASOR* 201, 1971, pp. 35–36, figs. 1–2; M. H. Burgoyne, "Some Mameluke Doorways in the Old City of Jerusalem," *Levant* 3, 1971, pp. 1–30, figs. 1–20, pls. 3–22; J. Landgraf, "The Manaḥat Inscription," *Levant* 3, 1971, pp. 92–95, figs. 1–2, pl. 30; K. M. Kenyon, "Archaeology and the Old Testament," *Perspective* 12:1–2, 1971, pp. 11–22, *passim*; J. Briend, "La Sépulture d'un Crucifie," *BTS* 133, 1971, pp. 6–10, figs.

Jib, el-, see Gibeon

Jish, el-, see Giscala

Jisr, see Yavneh-Yam

Jisr Banāt Ya'qūb, Gesher, Benot Ya'aqov

Excavated by M. Stekelis and M. Picard for the Hebrew University, 1936–1937.

M. Stekelis, "Jisr Banāt Yacqūb," *QDAP* 6, 1937, pp. 214–215; M. Stekelis, L. Picard, "Jisr Banāt Yacqūb," *QDAP* 7, 1938, p. 45; E. Anati, *Palestine Before the Hebrews*, 1963, pp. 67, 69, 70, 92, 259, figs.; M. Stekelis, "The Palaeolithic Deposits of Jisr Banāt Yacqūb," *The Bulletin of the Research Council of Israel* 9G, 1960, pp. 61–90, figs. 1–32, pls. 1–2; E. deVaumas, "Chronologie des dépôts paléolithiques stratifiés du Liban et de la Galilée," *IEJ* 13, 1963, pp. 195–207; D. Gilead, "A Stone Age Site near Geshur Benot Yacaqov," *Qadmoniot* 3, 1970, pp. 88–89, figs. (Hebrew); *id.*, "Gesher-Bnot-Yacakov," *EAEHL*, 1970, pp. 129–130, figs. (Hebrew).

Kabri, 'Ain el-Fawara

Excavated by M. W. Prausnitz for the Department of Antiquities, Israel, 1958.
M. Stekelis, "An Obsidian Core Found at Kibbutz Kabri," *EI* 5, 1958, pp. 35–37, pl. 4:3 (Hebrew); A. Biran, "Kabri," *CNI* 10:1–2, 1959, pp. 26–27, pls. 1:3, 2:1; M. W. Prausnitz, "Kabri," *IEJ* 9, 1959, pp. 268–269; *id.*, "Kabri," *RB* 67, 1960, pp. 390–391, pl. 23b; *id.*, "The Excavations at Kabri," *EI* 9, 1969, pp. 122–129, pls. 36–37 (Hebrew).

Kadesh, see Petra

Kadesh-barnea, see 'Ain el-Qudeirat

Kalandia

Excavated by D. C. Baramki for the Department of Antiquities, Palestine, 1931.
D. C. Baramki, "A Byzantine Bath at Qalandia," *QDAP* 2, 1933, pp. 105–109, figs. 95–96, pls. 38–41.

Tomb excavated by A. K. Dajani for the Department of Antiquities, Jordan, 1951.
A. K. Dajani, "A Hyksos Tomb at Kalandia," *ADAJ* 2, 1953, pp. 75–77, pl. 11.

Kerazeh, see Chorazin

Kfar Bir'im, Bar'am

C. W. Wilson, "Notes on Jewish Synagogues in Palestine," *PEFQS* 1869, pp. 37–41; L. Oliphant, "Explorations North-East of Lake Tiberias and in Jaulan," *PEFQS* 1885, pp. 82–92, figs.; H. Kohl, C. Watzinger, *Antike Synagogen in Galilaea*, 1916, pp. 89–100, figs. 174–191, pls. 12–13; E. L. Sukenik, *Ancient Synagogues in Palestine and Greece*, 1934, pp. 24–26, fig. 3, pls. front., 13c, 16b; H. G. May, "Synagogues in Palestine," *BA* 7, 1944, pp. 1–20, figs. 1–14; E. R. Goodenough, *Symbols* 1, 1953, pp. 201–203; R. Amiran, "A Fragment of an Ornamental Relief from Kfar Barᶜam," *EI* 3, 1954, pp. 178–180, figs. 1–4, pl. 5 (Hebrew); *id.*, "A Fragment of an Ornamental Relief from Kfar Barᶜam," *IEJ* 6, 1956, pp. 239–245, figs. 1–2, pls. 31–32:1; A. S. Hiram, "A Votive Altar from Upper Galilee," *BASOR* 167, 1962, pp. 18–22, figs. 1–2; J. Finegan, *The Archeology of the New Testament*, 1969, pp. 58–59, figs.; S. Saller, *A Revised Catalogue of the Ancient Synagogues of the Holy Land*, 1969, pp. 36–37, fig. 8; N. Avigad, "Kfar Birim," *EAEHL*, 1970, pp. 272–274, figs. (Hebrew); G. Foerster, "Les Synagogues de Galilee," *BTS* 130, 1971, p. 8, fig. 3 on p. 9, p. 13, fig. 18 on p. 15.

Kfar Gil'adi

Excavated by J. Kaplan for the Israel Exploration Society, 1958, 1961.
J. Kaplan, "Kfar Gilᶜadi," *IEJ* 8, 1958, p. 274; *id.*, "Kfar Gilᶜadi," *IEJ* 12, 1962, pp. 154–155; A. Biran, "Kfar Gilᶜadi," *CNI* 13:2, 1962, p. 14, pl. 4; *id.*, "Kfar Gilᶜadi," *CNI* 14:1, 1963, p. 14, pl. 2:2; J. Kaplan, "A Mausoleum at Kfar Gilᶜadi," *EI* 8, 1967, pp. 104–113, pls. 14–17 (Hebrew); *id.*, "Kfar Gilᶜadi," *RB* 74, 1967, pp. 67–68; *id.*, "Kfar Giladi," *EAEHL*, 1970, p. 275, figs. (Hebrew).

Kfar Kama

Excavated by A. Saarisalo for the Finnish Oriental Society, 1961, 1963.

A. Saarisalo, "Kfar Kama," *IEJ* 11, 1961, p. 197; A. Biran, "Kafr Kama," *CNI* 13:1, 1962, p. 19; A. Saarisalo, "Kafr Kama," *IEJ* 13, 1963, pp. 149–150; A. Biran, "Kafr Kama," *CNI* 15:2–3, 1964, pp. 31–32.

Kfar Kanna

C. Clermont-Ganneau, "Archaeological and Epigraphic Notes on Palestine," *PEFQS* 1901, pp. 369–389, fig., esp. pp. 374–381; p. 251, fig.

Excavated by B. Bagatti and S. Loffreda for the Custody of the Holy Land, 1955–56, 1965, 1969.

B. Bagatti, "Le Antichita' di Khirbet Qana e di Kefr Kenna in Galilee," *LA* 15, 1965, pp. 251–292, figs. 1–25; S. Loffreda, "Scavi a Kafr Kanna," *LA* 19, 1969, pp. 328–348, figs. 1–14; S. Saller, *A Revised Catalogue of the Ancient Synagogues of the Holy Land*, 1969, pp. 38–39, figs. 9–10.

Kfar Monash

R. Hestrin, M. Tadmor, "A Hoard of Tools and Weapons from Kfar Monash," *IEJ* 13, 1963, pp. 265–288, figs. 1–15, pls. 23–30; C. A. Key, "Note on the Trace-Element Content of the Artifacts of the Kfar Monash Hoard," *IEJ* 13, 1963, pp. 289–290; R. Gophna, "A Crescentic Axehead from Kfar Monash," *IEJ* 18, 1968, pp. 47–49, pl. 3c; J. B. Pritchard, ed., *ANEP*, 1969, no. 783; R. Gofna, "Hasharon," *EAEHL*, 1970, pp. 558–559, figs. (Hebrew).

Kfar-Naḥum, see Capernaum

Kfar Niburaya, see Nabratein

Khalasa, Elusa

E. H. Palmer, "Letters," *PEFQS* 1870, pp. 311–324, esp. 315–316; *id.*, "The Desert of the Tíh and the Country of Moab," *PEFQS* 1871, pp. 3–73, figs., esp. 35; C. L. Woolley, T. E. Lawrence, "The Wilderness of Zin," *PEFA* 3, 1914–1915, pp. 4, 25, 28–31, 33, 35, 40, 97, 99, 108–112, 135, 138–142, pls. 1, 34–36.

Excavated by the H. D. Colt Archaeological Expedition for the British School of Archaeology in Jerusalem, 1934–1938.

J. H. Iliffe, "Nabataean Pottery from the Negeb," *QDAP* 3, 1934, pp. 132–135, pls. 45–48; H. D. Colt, "Discoveries at Auja Hafia," *PEFQS* 1936, pp. 216–220; T. J. C. Baly, "Khalasa," *QDAP* 8, 1939, p. 159; G. E. Kirk, "Early Christian Gravestone-Formulae of Southern Palestine," *PEQ* 1939, pp. 181–186, pl. 29; *id.*, "The Negev or Southern Desert of Palestine," *PEQ* 1941, pp. 57–71, esp. 61–62, pl. 5; M. Avi-Yonah, *The Madaba Mosaic Map*, 1954, no. 103 on p. 73, pl. 9; C. J. Kraemer, Jr., *Excavations at Nessana*, 3, 1958, *passim*; N. Glueck, *Deities and Dolphins*, 1965, p. 520, pl. 218a on p. 524; *id.*, *Rivers in the Desert*, 1968, pp. 257–260; A. Negev, "Khalasa," *EAEHL*, 1970, pp. 152–154, figs. (Hebrew).

Khalit el-Fûl, see Hebron

Khiam, el-

Excavated by R. Neuville for the Institut de Paléontologie Humaine, 1933.

R. Neuville, *Le Paléolithique et le Mésolithique du Désert de Judée*, 1951; J. Perrot, "La Terrasse d'el-Khiam," pp. 134–178, figs. 59–74, pls. 1:3, 16; R. Vaufrey, "el-Khiam," pp. 214–217.

Excavated by J. G. Echegary for the Casa de Santiago para Estudios Biblicos y Orientales in Jerusalem, Instituto Arqueologico Municipal de Madrid, and the Department of Antiquities, Jordan, 1962.

E. Anati, *Palestine Before the Hebrews*, 1963, pp. 124, 158, 237, 238, 240, 259; J. G. Echegary, "Nouvelles Fouilles à el-Khiam," *RB* 70, 1963, pp. 94–119, figs. 1–9, pls. 1–2; *id.*, "Excavations in el-Khiam," *ADAJ* 8–9, 1964, pp. 93–94, pl. 37; G. A. Wright, A. A. Gordus, "Source Areas for Obsidian Recovered at Munḥata, Beisamoun, Hazorea and el-Khiam," *IEJ* 19, 1969, pp. 79–89, figs. 1–3; D. Gilead, "el-Khiam," *EAEHL*, 1970, pp. 363–364, fig. (Hebrew).

Khirbet el-Bitar (Ḥorvat Beter), see Beersheba

Khirbet el-Kerak, see Beth-yeraḥ

Khirbet el-Kom, see Hebron

Khirbet el-Mefjer

F. J. Bliss, "Notes on the Plain of Jericho," *PEFQS* 1894, pp. 175–183, esp. 177–181, 2 figs.

Excavated by D. C. Baramki, R. W. Hamilton, for the Department of Antiquities, Palestine, 1935–1948.

D. C. Baramki, "Excavations at Khirbat al-Mafjar," *QDAP* 5, 1936, pp. 132–138, figs. 1–3, pls. 74–88; *id.*, "Excavations at Khirbat al Mafjar, II," *QDAP* 6, 1937, pp. 157–168, pls. 43–66; *id.*, "Excavations at Khirbat al Mafjar, III," *QDAP* 8, 1939, pp. 51–53, fig. 1, pls. 34–35; *id.*, "Excavations at Khirbat al Mafjar, IV," *QDAP* 10, 1944, pp. 153–159, fig. 1, pls. 30–34; R. W. Hamilton, "Khirbat Mafjar, Stone Sculpture I," *QDAP* 11, 1945, pp. 47–66, figs. 1–21, pls. 13–16; *id.*, "Khirbet Mafjar, Stone Sculpture II," *QDAP* 12, 1946, pp. 1–19, figs. 22–35, pls. 1–10; G. E. Kirk, "Archaeological Activities in Palestine and Transjordan since 1939," *PEQ* 1946, pp. 92–102, pls. 2–5; C. N. Johns, "Discoveries in Palestine since 1939," *PEQ* 1948, pp. 81–101, pls. 1–8, esp. 98–99; R. W. Hamilton, "Plaster Balustrades from Khirbat al-Mafjar," *QDAP* 13, 1948, pp. 1–58, figs. 1–68, pls. 1–23; *id.*, "The Baths at Khirbat Mafjar," *PEQ* 1949, pp. 40–51, fig. 1, pls. 4–5; *id.*, "The Sculpture of Living Forms at Khirbat al-Mafjar," *QDAP* 14, 1950, pp. 100–119, figs. 1–2, pls. 35–45; *id.*, "A Mosaic Carpet of Umayyad Date at Khirbat al Mafjar," *QDAP* 14, 1950, p. 120, fig. 1, pl. 46; O. Grabar, "The Umayyad Palace of Khirbat al-Mafjar," *Archaeology* 8, 1955, pp. 236–244, figs.; R. W. Hamilton, *Khirbat al Mafjar: An Arabian Mansion in the Jordan Valley*, 1959; N. Glueck, *The River Jordan*, 1968, pp. 60–62, 164–165, 167, figs.; O. Grabar, "The Umayyad Palace of Khirbat al-Mafjar," *Archaeological Discoveries in the Holy Land*, 1967, pp. 193–198, figs.; M. Avi-Yonah, *A History of the Holy Land*, 1969, pp. 201–213, pls.; R. W. Hamilton,. "Who Built Khirbat al Mafjar?" *Levant* 1, 1969, pp. 61–67, figs. 1–4, pls. 17–18; *id.*, "Khirbat al Mafjar," *EAEHL*, 1970, pp. 175–182, figs. (Hebrew).

Khirbet el-Mekkayyat, see Mount Nebo

Khirbet el-Minyeh

Excavated by A. E. Mader, A. M. Schneider, O. Puttrich-Reignard, for the Görres-Gesellschaft, Jerusalem and the Staatliche Museen, Berlin, 1932, 1936–1939.

A. E. Mader, "Khirbat Minya," *QDAP* 2, 1933, pp. 188–189; Bibliography, *QDAP* 3, 1934, p. 186; A. M. Schneider, "Khirbet Minya," *QDAP* 6, 1937, pp. 215–217; *id.*, "Khirbet Minya," *QDAP* 7, 1938, pp. 49–51; O. Puttrich-Reignard, "Khirbet Minya," *QDAP* 8, 1939, pp. 159–160, 177; *id.*, "Khirbet Minya," *QDAP* 9, 1942 pp. 209–210, 217.

Excavated by J. Perrot et al. for the University of Michigan and the Department of Antiquities, Israel, 1959.

O. Grabar, "Khirbet el-Minyeh," *RB* 67, 1960, pp. 387–388; O. Grabar, J. Perrot, B. Ravani, M. Rosen, "Sondages à Khirbet el-Minyeh," *IEJ* 10, 1960, pp. 226–243, figs. 1–8, pls. 27–30; E. Kitzinger, *Israeli Mosaics of the Byzantine Period*, 1965, pp. 8, 21, pl. 28; M. Avi-Yonah, *A History of the Holy Land*, 1969, p. 208, pl. opp. p. 202; J. Finegan, *The Archeology of the New Testament*, 1969, pp. 46–48, figs.; O. Grabar, "Khirbet el-Minye," *EAEHL*, 1970, p. 174, fig. (Hebrew).

Khirbet el-Musheyrife, see Rosh ha-Niqra

Khirbet es-Samiyeh, see Dhahr Mirzbaneh

Khirbet et-Tannur

Excavated by N. Glueck for the American Schools of Oriental Research and the Department of Antiquities, Transjordan, 1937.

N. Glueck, "Explorations in Eastern Palestine III," *BASOR* 65, 1937, pp. 8–29, figs. 1–2, esp. 15–19; *id.*, "The Nabataean Temple of Khirbet et-Tannûr," *BASOR* 67, 1937, pp. 6–16, figs. 1–8; R. Savignac, "Le Dieu Nabatéen de Laᶜaban et son Temple," *RB* 46, 1937, pp. 401–416, fig. 1, pls. 8–10; N. Glueck, "A Newly Discovered Temple of Atargatis and Hadad at Khirbet et-Tannûr, Transjordania," *AJA* 41, 1937, pp. 361–376, figs. 1–15; *id.*, "Syrian Gods in a Nabataean Temple, *ILN*, August 21, 1937, pp. 298–300, figs. 1–18; P. Thomsen, "Chirbet et-Tannur," *Archiv für Orientforschung* 12, 1937–1939, pp. 93, 184–185; N. Glueck, "The Early History of a Nabataean Temple (Khirbet et-Tannûr)," *BASOR* 69, 1938, pp.7–18 figs. 1–2; R. B. Freeman, "Nabataean Sculpture in the Cincinnati Art Museum," *AJA* 45, 1941, pp. 337–341; M. Avi-Yonah, "Oriental Elements in the Art of Palestine in the Roman and Byzantine Periods," *QDAP* 10, 1944, pp. 105–151, figs. 1–17, pls. 22–29, esp. 114–118, pl. 22; N. Glueck, "The Zodiac of Khirbet et-Tannur," *BASOR* 126, 1952, pp. 5–10, figs. 1–3; R. Savignac, J. Starcky, "Une inscription nabatéene provenant du Djof," *RB* 64, 1957, pp. 196–217, esp. 215–217, fig. 1, pl.5; M. Avi-Yonah, *Oriental Art in Roman Palestine*, 1961, pp. 47–50, 78, pls. 7:3, 8:1, 11:1; N. Glueck, "Nabataean Dolphins," *EI* 7, 1964, pp. 40–43, pl. 49:1; *id.*, *Deities and Dolphins*, 1965; G. L. Harding, *The Antiquities of Jordan*, 1967, pp. 112–113, pl. 13; N. Glueck, "Nabataean Symbols of Immortality," *EI* 8, 1967, pp. 37–41, fig. 1, pls. 9–10; J. Starcky, "Le Temple Nabatéen de Khirbet Tannur," *RB* 75, 1968, pp. 206–235, figs. 1–2, pls. 15–20; N. Glueck, "Die nabatäische Plastik von Khirbet et-Tannur," in H. J. Kellner, ed., *Die Nabataer*, 1970, pp. 31–34, pls. on pp. 57, 60, 66–68; *id.*, "Three Nabataean Zodiacal Symbols," in S. Avramsky, *et al.*, eds., *Samuel*

Yeivin Book, 1970, pp. 541–547, pls. 1–3; *id.*, *The Other Side of the Jordan*, 1970, pp. 192–243, figs. 99–144; R. D. Barnett, "Another Deity with Dolphins," *NEATC*, 1970, pp. 327–330, figs. 1–2; N. Glueck, "Khirbet et-Tannur," *EAEHL*, 1970, pp. 190–195, figs. (Hebrew).

Khirbet et-Tubeiqah, see Beth-zur

Khirbet Faḥil, see Pella

Khirbet Ḥaiyân, see 'Ai

Khirbet Iskander

N. Glueck, *AASOR* 18–19, 1939, pp. 124–130, figs. 47–48.

Excavated by P. J. Parr for the Ashmolean Museum, Oxford, and the Department of Antiquities, Jordan, 1955.

P. J. Parr, "Khirbet Iskander," *ADAJ* 3, 1956, p. 81; *id.*, "Excavations at Khirbet Iskander," *ADAJ* 4–5, 1960, pp. 128–133, fig. 1, pls. 12–14; N. Glueck, *The Other Side of the Jordan*, 1970, pp. 147–149, fig. 72; M. Kochavi, "Khirbet Iskander," *EAEHL*, 1970, p. 171 (Hebrew).

Khirbet Kerazeh, see Chorazin

Khirbet Qumran

C. Clermont-Ganneau, *Archaeological Researches in Palestine*, II, 1896, pp. 14–16, 1 fig.

Excavated by G. L. Harding, R. de Vaux, A. K. Dajani, for the Palestine Archaeological Museum, Department of Antiquities, Jordan and the École Biblique et Archéologique Française, 1949–1967.

R. J. Tournay, "Les anciens Manuscrits Hébreux, récemment découverts," *RB* 56, 1949, pp. 204–233; R. deVaux, "Post-scriptum: La Cachette des Manuscrits Hébreux," 56, 1949, pp. 234–237; G. L. Harding, "The Dead Sea Scrolls," *PEQ* 1949, pp. 112–116, pls. 17–21; R. deVaux, "La Grotte des Manuscrits Hébreux," *RB* 56, 1949, pp. 586–609, figs. 1–2, pls. 13–18; G. L. Harding, "Khirbet Qumran and Wady Murabaʿat," *PEQ* 1952, pp. 104–109, pls. 28–32; R. deVaux, "Fouille au Khirbet Qumrân," *RB* 60, 1953, pp. 83–106, figs. 1–5, pls. 2–7; *id.*, "Qumrân Caves," *ADAJ* 2, 1953, p. 82; *id.*, "Exploration de la Région de Qumrân," *RB* 60, 1953, pp. 540–561, figs. 1–4, pls. 20–24; *id.*, "Fouilles au Khirbet Qumrân," *RB* 61, 1954, pp. 206–236, figs. 1–6, pls. 5–12; pp. 567–568; M. Burrows, *The Dead Sea Scrolls*, 1955; D. Barthélemy, J. T. Milik, *et al.*, *Discoveries in the Judaean Desert*, I, 1955, II, 1961, III, 1962, IV, 1965, V, 1968; R. deVaux, "Fouilles de Khirbet Qumrân," *RB* 63, 1956, pp. 533–577, figs. 1–5, plan, pls. 3–13; G. L. Harding, "Khirbet Qumran," *ADAJ* 3, 1956, pp. 75–77, pls. 7–8; Y. Yadin, *The Message of the Scrolls*, 1957; M. Burrows, *More Light on the Dead Sea Scrolls*, 1958; G. L. Harding, "Recent Discoveries in Jordan," *PEQ* 1958, pp. 7–18; For bibliography see *Revue de Qumran*, issued since 1958; J. T. Milik, *Ten Years of Discovery in the Wilderness of Judaea*, 1959; *id.*, "The Copper Document from Cave III of Qumran: Translation and Commentary," *ADAJ* 4–5, 1960, pp. 137–155; F. E. Zeuner, "Notes on Qumran," *PEQ* 1960, pp. 27–36; F. M. Cross, Jr., *The Ancient Library of Qumran*, 1961; R. deVaux, *L'Archéologie et les Manuscrits de la Mer Morte*, 1961; J. C. Trever, *The Untold Story of Qumran*, 1965;

A. Y. Samuel, *Treasure of Qumran*, 1966; F. M. Cross, Jr., "The Scrolls from the Judaean Desert," *Archaeological Discoveries in the Holy Land*, 1967, pp. 157–167, figs.; J. A. Sanders, "Palestinian Manuscripts 1947–1967," *JBL* 86, 1967, pp. 431–440; D. N. Freedman, J. C. Greenfield, eds., *New Directions in Biblical Archaeology*, 1969; F. M. Cross, Jr., "The Early History of the Qumran Community," pp. 63–79; R. G. Boling, "Twenty Years of Discovery," pp. 81–88; P. W. Skehan, "The Scrolls and the Old Testament Text," pp. 89–100; J. A. Sanders, "Cave 11 Surprises and the Question of Canon," pp. 101–116; D. N. Freedman, "The Old Testament at Qumran," pp. 117–126; F. V. Filson, "The Dead Sea Scrolls and the New Testament," pp. 127–138; Y. Yadin, "The Temple Scroll," pp. 139–148, 1 pl.; E. F. Campbell, Jr., R. G. Boling, "A Qumran Bibliography," pp. 167–170; J. Finegan, *The Archeology of the New Testament*, 1969, pp. 6–7, figs.; P. W. Lapp, *Biblical Archaeology and History*, 1969, pp. 74, 95–96, 118, pl. 18; P. Bar-Adon, "Rivage de la Mer Morte. Un établissement essénien," *RB* 77, 1970, pp. 398–400; P. W. Skehan, "The Biblical Scrolls from Qumran and the Text of the Old Testament," in E. F. Campbell, Jr., D. N. Freedman, eds., *The Biblical Archaeologist Reader* 3, 1970, pp. 240–253; R. deVaux, "Khirbet Qumran," *EAEHL*, 1970, pp. 183–189, figs. (Hebrew).

Khirbet Ruddana, el-Bireh

Excavated by J. A. Callaway for the Department of Antiquities, Israel, 1969, 1970.

J. A. Callaway, "Khirbet Ruddana (el-Bireh)," *IEJ* 20, 1970, pp. 230–232.

Khirbet Shema

Excavated by R. J. Bull for the Albright Institute of Archaeological Research, Jerusalem, Luther College, Iowa, and the Universities of Drew, Dropsie, Duke, Harvard, Minnesota, 1970—1971.

R. J. Bull, "Khirbet Shema," *IEJ* 20, 1970, pp. 232–234; *id.*, "The 1970 Excavations at Khirbet Shema," *AJA* 75, 1971, pp. 196–197.

Kinneret, Tell el'Oreimeh

P. Karge, *Rephaim*, 1917, p. 172; W. F. Albright, *BASOR* 11, 1923, p. 14; *id.*, *AASOR* 2–3, 1923, p. 37; *id.*, "The Jordan Valley in the Bronze Age," *AASOR* 6, 1926, pp. 24–26.

Tomb excavated by B. Mazar for the Jewish Palestine Exploration Society, 1940.

B. Mazar, *BJPES* 10, 1942, pp. 1–9, fig. 1, pls. (Hebrew); W. F. Albright, *BASOR* 93, 1944, pp. 25–26; B. Mazar, "Kinneret," *QDAP* 12, 1946, p. 106; S. Yeivin, H. Z. Hirschberg, eds., *Erez Kinneroth*, 1950 (Hebrew); R. Amiran, "Connections between Anatolia and Palestine in the Early Bronze Age," *IEJ* 2, 1952, pp. 89–103, figs. 1–5, pls. 5–6; W. F. Albright, *The Archaeology of Palestine*, 1960, p. 103; R. W. Ehrich, ed., *Chronologies in Old World Archaeology*, 1965, pp. 29, 33, 36, fig.; R. Amiran, *Ancient Pottery of the Holy Land*, 1970, pp. 64–65, pl. 17; B. Mazar, "Kinnrot," *EAEHL*, 1970, p. 271, figs. (Hebrew); Y. Aharoni, "Tel Kinnrot," *EAEHL*, 1970, p. 272, fig. (Hebrew).

Kokhav Hayarden, see Belvoir

Korazin, see Chorazin

Kurnub, Mampsis

C. L. Woolley, T. E. Lawrence, "The Wilderness of Zin," *PEFA* 3, 1914–1915, pp. 121–128, figs. 55–58, pls. 30–31; J. H. Iliffe, "Nabataean Pottery from the Negeb," *QDAP* 3, 1934, pp. 132–135, pls. 45–48; G. E. Kirk, "Archaeological Exploration in the Southern Desert," *PEQ* 1938, pp. 211–235, figs. 1–4, pl. 16, esp. 216–221; J. W. Crowfoot, *Early Churches in Palestine*, 1941, pp. 71, 156, pl. 29c.

Excavated by A. Negev for the Hebrew University and National Parks Authority, Israel, 1956–1966.

S. Applebaum, "Mampsis," *IEJ* 6, 1956, pp. 262–263; A. Biran, "Kurnub," *CNI* 17:1, 1966, pp. 19–20, pl. 3; A. Negev, "Kurnub," *IEJ* 16, 1966, pp. 145–148; *id.*, "Christian Kurnub (Mampsis?)," *CNI* 17:4, 1966, pp. 17–23, fig., pls. 1–4; *id.*, "Mampsis in the Negev," *Ariel* 15, 1966, pp. 79–86; A. Biran, "Kurnub," *CNI* 18:1–2, 1967, p. 32; A. Negev, "Oboda, Mampsis and Provincia Arabia," *IEJ* 17, 1967, pp. 46–55, pls. 7–11; *id.*, "Kurnub," *IEJ* 17, 1967, pp. 121–123; *id.*, "A City of the Negev," *ILN*, September 14, 1968, pp. 32–33, figs. 1–8; *id.*, "A City of the Negev," *ILN*, September 21, 1968, pp. 25–27, figs. 1–10; *id.*, "Kurnub," *RB* 75, 1968, pp. 407–413, pls. 45–48; N. Glueck, *Rivers in the Desert*, 1968, pp. 207–210, fig. 14; J. C. Mann, "A Note on an Inscription from Kurnub," *IEJ* 19, 1969, pp. 211–214; A. Negev, "Seal-Impressions from Tomb 107 at Kurnub," *EI* 9, 1969, pp. 109–118, pls. 32–34a (Hebrew); *id.*, "Seal-Impressions from Tomb 107 at Kurnub (Mampsis)," *IEJ* 19, 1969, pp. 89–106, pls. 9–10; *id.*, "The Chronology of the Middle Nabataean Period," *PEQ* 1969, pp. 5–14; *id.*, "The Excavations at Kurnub," *Qadmoniot* 2, 1969, pp. 17–22, figs. (Hebrew); *id.*, "Kurnub," *BTS* 90, 1970, pp. 6–17, figs.; *id.*, "Kurnub," *EAEHL*, 1970, pp. 280–289, figs. (Hebrew); *id.*, "Mampsis: A Report on Excavations of a Nabataeo-Roman Town," *Archaeology* 24, 1971, pp. 166–171, figs.

Lachish, Tell ed-Duweir

Excavated by J. L. Starkey for the Wellcome-Colt Expedition, 1932, for the Wellcome-Marston Archaeological Expedition, 1933–1938, by C. H. Inge, 1938, and G. L. Harding, 1938–1940.

See *PEF* Index, 1911–1963; J. L. Starkey, "The Lachish Letters," *ILN*, August 10, 1935, pp. 240–242, figs. 1–14; *id.*, "Finds from Biblical Lachish," *ILN*, July 6, 1935, pp. 19–21, figs. 1–15; H. Torzcyner, *et al.*, *Lachish I: The Lachish Letters*, 1938; O. Tufnell, C. H. Inge, G. L. Harding, *Lachish II: The Fosse Temple*, 1940; O. Tufnell, *Lachish III: The Iron Age*, 2 vols., Text, Plates, 1953; O. Tufnell, *et al.*, *Lachish IV: The Bronze Age*, 2 vols., Text, Plates, 1958.

Temple excavated by Y. Aharoni and B. Boyd for the Hebrew University and the University of North Carolina, 1966.

A. Brunot, "Lakish," *BTS* 82, 1966, pp. 8–15, figs.; O. Tufnell, "Lachish," *AOTS*, 1967, pp. 296–308, pl. 13; Y. Aharoni, "Trial Excavation in the 'Solar Shrine' at Lachish," *IEJ* 18, 1968, pp. 157–169, figs. 1–3, pls. 9–12; P. R. S. Moorey, "Two Middle Bronze Age Brooches from Tell ed-Duweir," *Levant* 1, 1969, pp. 97–99, figs. 1–2; Y. Aharoni, "Excavations in the 'Solar Temple' at Lachish," *Qadmoniot* 2, 1969, pp. 131–134, figs. (Hebrew); *id.*, "Lakish," *RB* 76, 1969, pp. 576–578, pls. 31a, 32a; J. B. Pritchard, ed., *ANEP*, 1969, nos. 69, 150, 175, 271, 273, 279, 728, 731; O. Tufnell, "Lakish," *EAEHL*, 1970, pp. 290–298, figs. (Hebrew).

Laish, see Dan

Lod, Lydda, Georgiopolis

J. W. Crowfoot, *Early Churches in Palestine*, 1941, pp. 110, 116, 145.

Excavated by J. Kaplan for the Department of Antiquities, Israel, 1952.

M. Avi-Yonah, *The Madaba Mosaic Map*, 1954, pp. 61–62, pl. 7; J. Kaplan, "Lod," *EAEHL*, 1970, p. 289 (Hebrew).

Ma'abarot

Tombs excavated by R. Gophna for the Department of Antiquities, Israel, 1966–1968.

A. Biran, "Kibbutz Maᶜabarot," *CNI* 18:1–2, 1967, pp. 39–40; R. Gophna, "Maᶜabarot," *IEJ* 17, 1967, p. 119; *id.*, "Maᶜabarot," *RB* 75, 1968, pp. 268–269, pl. 34a; *id.*, "A Middle Bronze Age I Cemetery at Maᶜabarot," *Qadmoniot* 2, 1969, pp. 50–51, figs. (Hebrew); *id.*, "A Middle Bronze Age I Tomb with Fenestrated Axe at Maᶜabarot," *IEJ* 19, 1969, pp. 174–177, figs. 1–3, pl. 14b.

Madeba

C. Clermont-Ganneau, "The Mâdeba Mosaic," *PEFQS* 1897, pp. 213–225; J. W. Crowfoot, *Early Churches in Palestine*, 1941, pp. 101, 140; G. L. Harding, "Recent Discoveries in Trans-Jordan," *PEQ* 1948, pp. 118–120; S. Saller, B. Bagatti, *The Town of Nebo (Khirbet el-Mekhayyat)*, 1949, pp. 236–244, pls. 28, 38, 39, 40.

Tomb excavated by G. L. Harding for the Department of Antiquities, Jordan, 1950.

G. L. Harding, "An Early Iron Age Tomb at Madeba," *PEFA* 6, 1953, pp. 27–33, figs. 12–17, pls. 3–5; B. S. J. Isserlin, "Notes and Comparisons," *PEFA* 6, 1953, pp. 34–41; M. Avi-Yonah, *The Madaba Mosaic Map*, 1954; R. T. O'Callaghan, "Madaba (Carte de)," *Supplement au Dictionnaire de la Bible*, 1957, cols. 627–704, figs.; V. R. Gold, "The Mosaic Map of Madeba," *BA* 21, 1958, pp. 50–71, figs. 1–9; G. L. Harding, *The Antiquities of Jordan*, 1967, pp. 33, 38, 73–75, pls. 4a, 8a; H. Cüppers, H. Donner, "Die Restauration und Konservierung der Mosaikkarte von Madeba," *ZDPV* 83, 1967, pp. 1–33, pls. 1–12; U. Lux, "Eine altchristliche Kirche in Mādeba," *ZDPV* 83, 1967, pp. 165–182, pls. 26–40; *id.*, "Die Apostel-Kirche in Mādeba'," *ZDPV* 84, 1968, pp. 106–129, pls. 14–35, 1 plan; M. Noth, "Die Mosaikinschriften der Apostel-Kirche in Mādeba," *ZDPV* 84, 1968, pp. 130–142, figs. 1–4; *id.*, "Prosopographie die Bistums Medaba in spätbyzantinischer Zeit," *ZDPV* 84, 1968, pp. 143–158; J. Finegan, *The Archeology of the New Testament*, 1969, pp. xvii, 10, 11, 12, 24, 36, 169; S. Saller, "The Works of Bishop John of Madaba in the Light of Recent Discoveries," *LA* 19, 1969, pp. 145–167, figs. 1–15; U. Lux, "Madeba," *RB* 76, 1969, pp. 398–402, pls. 11b, 12a, 13a; V. R. Gold, "The Mosaic Map of Madeba," in E. F. Campbell, D. N. Freedman, eds., *The Biblical Archaeologist Reader*, 3, 1970, pp. 366–389, pl. 8b; M. Avi-Yonah, "Medva," *EAEHL*, 1970, pp. 321–323, figs. (Hebrew).

Ma'in

Excavated by R. de Vaux for the École Biblique et Archéologique Française, 1938.

R. deVaux, "Maᶜin," *QDAP* 8, 1939, pp. 161–162; *id.*, "Une Mosaique Byzantine a Maᶜin, Transjordanie," *RB* 47, 1938, pp. 227–258, figs. 1–4, pls. 10–16; J. W. Crowfoot, *Early Churches in Palestine*, 1941, pp. 141–146, pls. 25–26.

Makmish

Excavated by N. Avigad for Museum Haaretz and the Hebrew University, 1958–1960.

N. Avigad, "Makmish," *IEJ* 8, 1958, p. 276; *id.*, "A Phoenician Sanctuary in the Plain of Sharon," *ILN*, May 16, 1959, pp. 836–837, figs. 1–17; *id.*, "Excavations at Makmish, 1958," *IEJ* 10, 1960, pp. 90–96, pls. 9–12; *id.*, "Makmish," *RB* 67, 1960, pp. 381–382, pl. 25:2; *id.*, "Excavations at Makmish, 1960, Preliminary Report," *IEJ* 11, 1961, pp. 97–100, fig. 1, pl. 25; W. F. Albright, *Yahweh and the Gods of Canaan*, 1968, pp. 246–247; N. Avigad, "Makmish," *EAEHL*, 1970, pp. 325–326, figs. (Hebrew).

Mallaḥa, see ʻEinan

Mambre, see Ramat el-Khalil

Mampsis, see Kurnub

Maʻon, Nirim

Nirim synagogue excavated by S. Levy for the Department of Antiquities, Israel, 1957–1958.

S. Levy, "Nirim," *IEJ* 7, 1957, p. 265; J. Leibowitz, "Nirim," *CNI* 9:1–2, 1958, p. 29, pl. 4; S. Levy *et al.*, "The Ancient Synagogue of Maᶜon (Nirim)," *Bulletin Rabinowitz* 3, 1960, pp. 6–40, figs. 1–14, pls. 1–8; S. Levy, "The Ancient Synagogue at Maᶜon (Nirim)," *EI* 6, 1960, pp. 77–82, pl. 15 (Hebrew); L. Y. Rahmani, "The Maon Synagogue (the small finds and coins)," *EI* 6, 1960, pp. 82–85, pl. 16 (Hebrew); M. Avi-Yonah, "The Mosaic Pavement of the Maᶜon (Nirim) Synagogue," *EI* 6, 1960, pp. 86–93, pls. 17–22 (Hebrew); E. Kitzinger, *Israeli Mosaics of the Byzantine Period*, 1965, pp. 7, 17, pls. 22–24; D. Barag, "Maᶜon," *EAEHL*, 1970, pp. 333–334, figs. (Hebrew); *BTS* 130, 1971, fig. on p. 18.

Marissa, see Tell Sandahannah

Marwa

Tomb excavated by C. C. McCown for the American Schools of Oriental Research and the Trans-Jordan Department of Antiquities, 1935.

C. C. McCown, "A Painted Tomb at Marwa," *QDAP* 9, 1942, pp. 1–30, pls. 1–5; S. Applebaum, "Marwa," *EAEHL*, 1970, p. 397, fig. (Hebrew).

Masada

M. Avi-Yonah, "The Dead Sea Fortress Rock of Masada," *ILN*, November 5, 1955, pp. 784–787, figs. 1–12; *id.*, "Herod's Fortress-Palace of Masada," *ILN*, November 12, 1955, pp. 836–839, figs. 1–10; M. Avi-Yonah, N. Avigad, Y. Aharoni, I. Dunayevsky, S. Gutman, "The Archaeological Survey of Masada, 1955–56," *IEJ* 7, 1957, pp. 1–60, figs. 1–22, pls. 1–16; L. Kadman, "A Coin Find at Masada," *IEJ* 7, 1957, pp. 61–65, pl. 16e, f; A. Biran, "Bar Kochba Period," *CNI* 11:2, 1960, p. 16, pl. 1; Y. Yadin, "Masada: Herod's Fortress-Palace and the Zealots' Last Stand," *ILN*, October 31, 1964, pp. 693–697, figs. 1–19; A. Biran, "Masada," *CNI* 15:2–3, 1964, pp. 19–20.

Excavated by Y. Yadin for the Hebrew University, Israel Exploration Society, Department of Antiquities, Israel, 1963–1964.

Y. Yadin, "The Excavation of Masada, 1963–64," *IEJ* 15, 1965, pp. 1–120, pls. 1–24; *id.*, "Masada," *CNI* 16:1–2, 1965, pp. 23–30, pls. 1–8; *id.*, *The Ben Sira Scroll from Masada*, 1965; A. Biran, "Masada," *CNI* 17:1, 1966, p. 18; Y. Yadin, *Horizon* 8, 1966, pp. 2, 18–31, pls.; *id.*, Masada: *Herod's Fortress and the Zealots' Last Stand*, 1966; *id.*, "Masada: A Zealot Fortress," *Archaeological Discoveries in the Holy Land*, 1967, pp. 168–174, figs.; *id.*, "The Ben Sira Scroll from Masada," *EI* 8, 1967, pp. 1–45, pls. 1–9 (Hebrew); P. W. Lapp, *Biblical Archaeology and History*, 1969, pp. 77, 118, pls. 21–22; J. Strugnell, "Notes and Queries on 'The Ben Sira Scroll from Masada'," *EI* 9, 1969, pp. 109–119; Y. Yadin, "Mtsada," *EAEHL*, 1970, pp. 374–390, figs. (Hebrew).

Megiddo, Tell el-Mutesellim

Excavated by G. Schumacher, C. Steuernagel and C. Watzinger for the Deutscher Palästina-Verein and the Deutsche Orient-Gesellschaft, 1903–1905.

G. Schumacher, *Tell el-Mutesellim*, I, 2 vols., Text, Plates, 1908.

Excavated by G. A. Reisner, for Harvard University, 1908–1910.

Excavated for the Oriental Institute, University of Chicago, by J. H. Breasted, 1925, C. S. Fisher, 1925–1927, P. L. O. Guy, 1927–1935, G. Loud, 1935–1939.

C. S. Fisher, *The Excavation of Armageddon*, 1929; C. Watzinger, *Tell el-Mutesellim*, II, 1929; P. L. O. Guy, *New Light from Armageddon*, 1931; Bibliography, *QDAP* 1, 1932, pp. 140–141; R. M. Engberg, G. M. Shipton, "Another Sumerian Seal Impression from Megiddo," *PEFQS* 1934, pp. 90–93, pl. 6; *id.*, *Notes on the Chalcolithic and Early Bronze Pottery of Megiddo*, 1934; R. S. Lamon, *The Megiddo Water System*, 1935; H. G. May, *Material Remains of the Megiddo Cult*, 1935; P. L. O. Guy, *Megiddo Tombs*, 1938; G. Loud, *The Megiddo Ivories*, 1939; R. S. Lamon, G. M. Shipton, *Megiddo I*, 1939; G. Shipton, *Notes on the Megiddo Pottery of Strata VI-XX*, 1939; J. W. Crowfoot, "Megiddo — A Review," *PEQ* 1940, pp. 132–147; R. M. Engberg, "Megiddo — Guardian of the Carmel Pass," *BA* 3, 1940, pp. 41–51, figs. 1–5; *id.*, "Megiddo — Guardian of the Carmel Pass II," *BA* 4, 1941, pp. 11–16, figs. 13–16; G. Loud *et al.*, *Megiddo II*, 2 vols., *Text*, *Plates*, 1948; G. E. Wright, "The Problem of the Transition between the Chalcolithic and Bronze Ages," *EI* 5, 1958, pp. 37–45; M. Dothan, "Some Problems of the Stratigraphy in Megiddo XX," *EI* 5, 1958, pp. 38–40 (Hebrew); K. M. Kenyon, "Some Notes on the Early and Middle Bronze Age Strata of Megiddo," *EI* 5, 1958, pp. 51–60; S. Yeivin, "The Date of the Seal Belonging to Shemaᶜ (the) Servant (of) Jeroboam," *JNES* 19, 1960, pp. 205–212, figs. 1–3; R. Amiran, "The Pottery of the Middle Bronze Age I in Palestine," *IEJ* 10, 1960, pp. 204–225, figs. 1–10.

Excavated by Y. Yadin for the Hebrew University, 1960, 1965–1967.

Y. Yadin, "New Light on Solomon's Megiddo," *The Biblical Archaeologist Reader*, 2, 1964, pp. 240–247, pls. 19–20; G. E. Wright, "The Discoveries at Megiddo, 1935–39," in D. N. Freedman, E. F. Campbell, Jr., eds., *The Biblical Archaeologist Reader*, 2, 1964, pp. 225–240; C. Epstein, "An Interpretation of the Megiddo Sacred Area During Middle Bronze II," *IEJ* 15, 1965, pp. 204–221, fig. 1, pls. 39b, 40a; I. Dunayevsky, A. Kempinski, "Megiddo," *IEJ* 16, 1966, p. 142; Y. Yadin, "Megiddo," *IEJ* 16, 1966, pp. 278–280, D. Ussishkin, "King Solomon's Palace and Building 1723 in Megiddo," *IEJ* 16, 1966, pp. 174–186, figs. 1–5; Y. Yadin, "Megiddo," *IEJ* 17, 1967, pp. 119–121; J. N. Schofield, "Megiddo," *AOTS*, 1967, pp. 309–328; A. Biran,

"Megiddo," *CNI* 18:1–2, 1967, pp. 26–27; Y. Yadin, "Megiddo," *RB* 75, 1968, pp. 396–401, pl. 43; A. Biran, "Megiddo," *CNI* 19:3–4, 1968, pp. 39–40; H. O. Thompson, "Apsidal Construction in the Ancient Near East," *PEQ* 1969, pp. 69–86, figs. 1–11; K. M. Kenyon, "The Middle and Late Bronze Age Strata at Megiddo," *Levant* 1, 1969, pp. 25–60, figs. 1–29; J. B. Pritchard, ed., *ANEP*, 1969, nos. 60, 67, 68, 70, 125, 126, 128, 215, 276, 332, 467, 469, 494–497, 575, 582, 583, 586, 587, 589, 595, 663, 708, 711, 712, 721, 726, 729, 734, 735, 741–742, 743; D. Ussishkin, "On the Original Position of Two Proto-Ionic Capitals at Megiddo," *IEJ* 20, 1970, pp. 213–215, fig. 1, pl. 48a; T. L. Thompson, "The Dating of the Megiddo Temples in Strata XV-XIV," *ZDPV* 86, 1970, pp. 38–49; U. Müller, "Kritische Bemerkungen zu den straten XIII bis IX in Megiddo," *ZDPV* 86, 1970, pp. 50–86, figs. 1–3; Y. Yadin, "Megiddo of the Kings of Israel," *BA* 33, 1970, pp. 66–96, figs. 1–18; J. B. Pritchard, "The Megiddo Stables: A Reassessment," *NEATC*, 1970, pp. 269–276; Y. Yadin, "The Megiddo of the Kings of Israel," *Qadmoniot* 3, 1970, pp. 38–56, figs. (Hebrew); K. M. Kenyon, *Archaeology in the Holy Land*, 1970, pp. 341–342, 345–348; Y. Aharoni, "Mgiddo," *EAEHL*, 1970, pp. 299–307, figs. (Hebrew); Y. Yadin, "Mgiddo (Iron Age)," *EAEHL*, 1970, pp. 308–316, figs. (Hebrew).

Mene'iyeh, see Timna'

Meqabelein, see Amman

Meron

Excavated by C. W. Wilson for the Palestine Exploration Fund, 1866.

C. W. Wilson, "Notes on Jewish Synagogues in Palestine," *PEFQS* 1869, pp. 37–42; E. Atkinson, "Notes on the Ancient Synagogue at Meiron," *PEFQS* 1878, pp. 24–27, figs. 1–2; H. Kohl, C. Watzinger, *Antike Synagogen in Galilaea*, 1916, pp. 80–88, figs. 160–173, pls. 10–11; J. Garstang, *Joshua-Judges*, 1931, pp. 101–102, 191–195, fig. 3, map 14; E. R. Goodenough, *Symbols* 1, 1953, pp. 200–201; S. J. Saller, *A Revised Catalogue of the Ancient Synagogues of the Holy Land*, 1969, p. 77; D. Barag, "Meron," *EAEHL*, 1970, pp. 323–324, figs. (Hebrew); G. Foerster, "Les Synagogue de Galilée," *BTS* 130, 1971, fig. 4 on p. 9.

Meṣad Ḥashavyahu, see Yavneh-Yam

Meṣer

Excavated by M. Dothan for the Department of Antiquities, Israel, 1956, 1957.

M. Dothan, "Meṣer," *IEJ* 7, 1957, pp. 127–128; *id.*, "Excavations at Meṣer 1956, Preliminary Report on the First Season," *IEJ* 7, 1957, pp. 217–228, figs. 1–4, pls. 37–40; M. Avi-Yonah, "Meṣer," *CNI* 8:1–2, 1957, p. 25, pl. 2:1, 2; J. Leibovitz, "Meṣer," *CNI* 9:1–2, 1958, p. 25, pl. 3:2; M. Dothan, "Excavations at Meṣer, 1957, Preliminary Report on the Second Season," *IEJ* 9, 1959, pp. 13–29, figs. 1–9, pls. 1–3; H. O. Thompson, "Apsidal Construction in the Ancient Near East," *PEQ* 1969, pp. 69–86, figs. 1–11; P. W. Lapp, "Palestine in the Early Bronze Age," *NEATC*, 1970, pp. 101–131, esp. 106, 109, 126–127; M. Dothan, "Metser," *EAEHL*, 1970, pp. 395–396, figs. (Hebrew).

Montfort Castle, Qal'at el-Qurain

Excavated by B. Dean for the Metropolitan Museum of Art, 1926.

B. Dean, "A Crusaders' Fortress in Palestine, A Report of Explorations Made by the Museum, 1926," *Bulletin of the Metropolitan Museum of Art*, 1927, pp. 1–46, figs. 1–59; E. W. G. Masterman, "A Crusaders' Fortress in Palestine," *PEFQS* 1928, pp. 91–97, fig. 1; M. Benvenisti, *The Crusaders in the Holy Land*, 1970, pp. 331–337, figs.; *id.*, "Monfor," *EAEHL*, 1970, pp. 319–320, figs. (Hebrew).

Mount Carmel Caves

Excavated by P. L. O. Guy for the Department of Antiquities, Palestine, 1922.

P. L. O. Guy, "Mt. Carmel, an Early Iron-Age Cemetery near Haifa," *Palestine Museum Bulletin*, 1, 1924, pp. 47–53, pls. 1–3.

Excavated by F. Turville-Petre for the British School of Archaeology in Jerusalem, 1925–1926.

F. Turville-Petre *et al.*, *Researches in Prehistoric Galilee 1925–26*, 1927; D. A. E. Garrod, "Excavation of a Palaeolithic Cave in Western Judaea," *PEFQS* 1928, pp. 182–185; *id.*, "Excavations in the Mughâret el-Wad, near Athlit, April–June, 1929," *PEFQS* 1929, pp. 220–222.

Excavated by D. A. E. Garrod and T. D. McCown for the British School of Archaeology in Jerusalem and the American School of Prehistoric Research, 1929–1934.

G. M. FitzGerald, "Some Stone Age Sites Recently Investigated," *PEFQS* 1930, pp. 85–90; D. A. E. Garrod, "Excavations at the Mughâret el-Wad, 1930," *PEFQS* 1931, pp. 99–103, pls. 1–3; *id.*, "Excavations in the Wady el-Mughara, 1931," *PEFQS* 1932, pp. 46–51, pls. 1–3; *id.*, "Excavations at the Wady al-Mughara, 1932–3," *PEFQS* 1934, pp. 85–89, pls. 4–5; J. H. Iliffe, "A Nude Terra-cotta Statuette of Aphrodite," *QDAP* 3, 1934, pp. 106–111; D. A. E. Garrod, "Wādi Maghāra," *QDAP* 4, 1935, pp. 209–210; D. A. E. Garrod, D. M. A. Bate, *The Stone Age of Mount Carmel*, I, 1937; T. D. McCown, A. Keith, *The Stone Age of Mount Carmel*, II, 1939.

Excavated by M. Stekelis for the American Schools of Oriental Research, 1941.

M. Stekelis, "Preliminary Report on Soundings, Prehistoric Caves in Palestine," *BASOR* 86, 1942, pp. 2–10, figs. 1–7; W. F. Albright, "Observations on the Date of the Pottery-bearing Stratum of Mughâret Abu Uṣbaᶜ," *BASOR* 86, 1942, pp. 10–14, figs. 5–6; M. Stekelis, "Further Observations on the Chronology of Mughâret Abū Uṣbaᶜ," *BASOR* 89, 1943, pp. 22–24; *id.*, "Prehistoric Caves," *QDAP* 11, 1945, pp. 115–118.

Excavated by M. Stekelis for the Hebrew University and the Department of Antiquities, Israel, 1952, 1953.

M. Stekelis, G. Haas, "The Abu Usba Cave (Mount Carmel)," *IEJ* 2, 1952, pp. 15–47, figs. 1–17, pls. 1–4; M. Avi-Yonah, "Mount Carmel and the God of Baalbek," *IEJ* 2, 1952, pp. 118–124, pl. 8; M. Stekelis, "Kabbara," *IEJ* 2, 1952, pp. 141–142; *id.*, "Kabbara," *IEJ* 3, 1953, p. 262; D. A. E. Garrod, *The Natufian Culture: The Life and Economy of a Mesolithic People in the Near East*, 1957; F. C. Howell, "Upper Pleistocene Stratigraphy and Early Man in the Levant," *Proceedings of the American Philosophical Society* 103, 1959, pp. 1–65, figs. 1–34; B. Bagatti, "Mont Carmel," *RB* 67, 1960, pp. 388–389; E. Wreschner, M. Avnimelech, S. Angress, "The Geulah Caves, Haifa, Preliminary Report," *IEJ* 10, 1960, pp. 78–89, pls. 7–8, figs. 1–4; B. Bagatti, "The Monastery of St. Brocardus (Mount Carmel," *IEJ* 11, 1961, pp. 197–198; G. W. Van Beek, "Wadi el-Mugharah," *IDB*, 1962, pp. 455–456, figs. 73–76.

Mughâret esh-Shubabiq excavated by S. R. Binford for the National Science Foundation, 1962.

Geulah Cave excavated by E. Wreschner for the Department of Antiquities, Israel, 1962, 1964.

E. Wreschner, "Geulah Cave, Haifa," *IEJ* 13, 1963, p. 138; E. Anati, *Palestine Before the Hebrews*, 1963, pp. 44, 71–75, 97, 101–106, 119, 123–125, 148–149, 151–158, 163–167, 171–172, 230–231, figs., pls.; E. Wreschner, "Geulah Cave, Haifa," *IEJ* 14, 1964, pp. 277–278.

Excavated by M. Stekelis for the Hebrew University and the Department of Antiquities, Israel, 1964.

M. Stekelis, "Kabara Cave," *IEJ* 14, 1964, p. 277; A. Biran, "Kabara Cave," *CNI* 16:3, 1965, pp. 13–14; S. R. Binford, "Meᶜarat Shovakh (Mughâret esh-Shubbabiq)," *IEJ* 16, 1966, pp. 18–32, figs. 1–9; pp. 96–103; A. Ovadiah, "Elijah's Cave, Mount Carmel," *IEJ* 16, 1966, pp. 284–285; A. Biran, "Mount Carmel Caves," *CNI* 18:1–2, 1967, pp. 38–39, pl. 6:2; M. A. Ronen, "Sefounim (Iraq el-Barud)," *RB* 75, 1968, pp. 261–262; A. Ovadiah, "Mont Carmel, Grotte d'Élie," *RB* 75, 1968, pp. 417–418.

Cave of et-Tabun excavated by A. J. Jellinek for the Universities of Arizona and Michigan, 1969.

A. J. Jellinek, "et-Tabun," *IEJ* 19, 1969, pp. 114–115; K. M. Kenyon, *Archaeology in the Holy Land*, 1970, pp. 36–38, 41–42, pls. 1–3; T. Israeli, "Carmel Caves," *EAEHL*, 1970, pp. 335–339, figs. (Hebrew); A. Bar-Yosef, "Carmel Caves," *EAEHL*, 1970, pp. 366, 369, 372 (Hebrew); M. Stekelis, "Carmel Caves," *EAEHL*, 1970, pp. 367–369, figs. (Hebrew).

Mount Ebal, see Mount Gerizim

Mount Gerizim, Jebel et-Tur, Tananir, Tell er-Râs

Excavations conducted by C. W. Wilson for the Palestine Exploration Society, 1866.

C. W. Wilson, "Ebal and Gerizim, 1866," *PEFQS* 1873, pp. 66–71, pl. 1; C. K. Spyridonidis, "The Church over Jacob's Well," *PEFQS* 1908, pp. 248–253, figs. 1–3.

Excavated by A. M. Schneider for the Notgemeinschaft der Deutschen Wissenschaft, 1927–1928.

Bibliography, "Mount Gerizim," *QDAP* 1, 1932, p. 141; F. M. Abel, "Garizim et Ébal," *Géographie de la Palestine*, I, 1933, pp. 360–370, pl. 2:1; J. W. Crowfoot, *Early Churches in Palestine*, 1941, fig. 6 on p. 37, pp. 92–94, pls. 8b, 27a–b, 30d; A. M. Schneider, "Römische und Byzantinische Bauten auf dem Garizim," *ZDPV* 68, 1951, pp. 211–234, figs. 1–12, pls. 1–3; A. Reifenberg, "Mount Gerizim," *EI* 1, 1951, pp. 74–76 (Hebrew); V. R. Gold, "The Mosaic Map of Madeba," *BA* 21, 1958, pp. 50–71, figs. 1–6, esp. 63–64.

Tell er-Râs excavated by R. J. Bull for the American Schools of Oriental Research, Drew University, and the Department of Antiquities, Jordan, 1966, 1968.

R. J. Bull, "A Preliminary Excavation of an Hadrianic Temple at Tell er-Râs on Mount Gerizim," *AJA* 71, 1967, pp. 387–393, figs. 1–2, pls. 109–110; *id* ., "The Sixth Campaign at Balâtah (Shechem)," *BASOR* 190, 1968, pp. 1–41, figs. 1–17 (Tell er-Râs *passim*); *id.*, "Tell er-Râs (Garizim), *RB* 75, 1968, pp. 238–243, fig. 2, pls. 21–24; *id.*, "The Excavation of Tell er-Râs on Mt. Gerizim," *BA* 31, 1968, pp.

58–72, figs. 11–18; E. F. Campbell, Jr., "Tell er-Râs," *IEJ* 18, 1968, pp. 192–193.

Tananir excavated by R. G. Boling for the American Schools for Oriental Research, 1968.

R. G. Boling, "Tananir," *RB* 76, 1969, pp. 419–421, pls. 20–21; *id.*, "Bronze Age Buildings at the Shechem High Place: ASOR Excavations at Tananir," *BA* 32, 1969, pp. 81–103, figs. 1–16; A. Biran, "Mount Gerizim," *CNI* 20:3–4, 1969, pp. 44–45; J. Finegan, *The Archeology of the New Testament*, 1969, pp. 34–42, figs. 41–50; R. J. Bull, "Towards a Corpus Inscriptionum Latinarum Britannicarum in Palestina," *PEQ* 1970, pp. 108–110, pl. 16.

Mount Nebo

F. M. Abel, *Géographie de la Palestine*, I, 1933, pp. 379–384, fig.

Râs Siyâgha excavated by S. J. Saller and B. Bagatti for the Franciscan Custody of the Holy Land and the Department of Antiquities, Jordan, 1933, 1935, 1937.

S. J. Salier, "Râs Siyagha," *QDAP* 6, 1937, pp. 220–221, 229; J. W. Crowfoot, *Early Churches in Paestine*, 1941, pp. 55–56, fig. 11, pp. 72, 141–145, pls. 23–24; S. J. Saller, *The Memorial of Moses on Mount Nebo* (*Râs Siyâgha*), I, Text, 1941, II, Plates, 1941, III, Pottery, H. Schneider, 1950.

Khirbet el-Mekhayyet excavated by S. J. Saller and B. Bagatti for the Franciscan Custody of the Holy Land and the Department of Antiquities, Jordan, 1933, 1935, 1937, 1939, 1948.

S. J. Saller, B. Bagatti, *The Town of Nebo* (*Khirbet el-Mekhayyat*), *with a brief Survey of Other Ancient Monuments in Transjordan*, 1949; I. Lissner, "The Tomb of Moses is Still Undiscovered," *BA* 26:3, 1963, pp. 106–108; S. J. Saller, "Iron Age Tombs at Nebo, Jordan," *LA* 16, 1966, pp. 165–298, figs. 1–37; *id.*, "Hellenistic to Arabic Remains at Nebo," *LA* 17, 1967, pp. 5–64, figs. 1–4; E. Stockton, "Stone Age Culture in the Nebo Region, Jordan," *LA* 17, 1967, pp. 122–128, figs. 1–5; St. Yonick, "The Samaritan Inscription from Siyagha," *LA* 17, 1967, pp. 162–221, figs. 1–17; V. Corbo, "Nuovi Scavi Archeologici nella del Battistero della Basilica del Nebo (Siyagha)," *LA* 17, 1967, pp. 241–258, figs. 1–7; N. Glueck, *The Other Side of the Jordan*, 1970, pp. 141, 178, 179, 186, 188; B. Bagatti, "Har Nvo," *EAEHL*, 1970, pp. 138–140, figs. (Hebrew).

Mughâra, Wadi el-, see Mount Carmel Caves

Mughâret Abū Šinjeh, see Wâdī Dâliyeh

Mughâret Abu Uṣba', see Mount Carmel Caves

Mughâret el-Emireh, see Mount Carmel Caves

Mughâret el-Kebara, see Mount Carmel Caves

Mughâret el-Wad, see Mount Carmel Caves

Mughâret esh-Shubbabiq, see Mount Carmel Caves

Mughâret ez-Zuttiyeh, see Mount Carmel Caves

Munḥata, Ḥorvat Minḥa

Excavated by J. Perrot and N. Zori for the Mission Archéologique Française and the Department of Antiquities, Israel, 1962–1967.

N. Zori, "Neolithic and Chalcolithic Sites in the Valley of Beth-shan," *PEQ* 1958, pp. 44–51, figs. 1–3, pls. 2, 3a, 5c, esp. pp. 44–45; A. Biran, "Ha-Minha (Munḥata)," *CNI* 14:1, 1963, pp. 17–18, pl. 1:1; J. Perrot, "Ḥorvat Minḥah (Munḥata)," *IEJ* 13, 1963, pp. 138–140; *id.*, "Munhata," *RB* 70, 1963, pp. 560–563; J. Perrot, N. Zori, "Munḥata," *RB* 71, 1964, pp. 391–393, fig. 1, pl. 18a; A. Biran, "Tel Minha (Munḥata)," *CNI* 15:2–3, 1964, p. 32, pl. 5:3; J. Perrot, "Les Deux Premières Campagnes de Fouilles à Munḥatta (1962–1963)," *Syria* 41, 1964, pp. 323–345, figs. 1–6, pls. 21–24; A. Biran, "Horvat Minha," *CNI* 16:3, 1965, p. 14, pl. 1; J. Perrot, "Munhata," *IEJ* 15, 1965, pp. 248–249; *id.*, "La troisième Campagne de Fouilles à Munḥata (1964)," *Syria* 43, 1966, pp. 49–63, figs. 1–7, pls. 5–6; A. Biran, "Horvat Minha (Munhata)." *CNI* 17:2–3, 1966, p. 24; J. Perrot, "Munḥata (Kh. Minḥa)," *IEJ* 16, 1966, pp. 269–271; *id.*, "Munḥata," *RB* 74, 1967, pp. 63–67, pls. 5–6; *id.*, "Munhata," *BTS* 93, 1967, pp. 4–16, figs.; A. Biran, "Horvat Minha," *CNI* 18:1–2, 1967, p. 26; J. Perrot, "Munḥata," *RB* 75, 1968, pp. 263–264, pls. 31–32; A. Biran, "Horvat Minha (Munhata)," *CNI* 19:3–4, 1968, p. 38; G. A. Wright, A. A. Gordus, "Source Areas for Obsidian Recovered at Munḥata, Beisamoun, Hazorea and el-Khiam," *IEJ* 19, 1969, pp. 79–89, figs. 1–3; J. Perrot, "Ḥorvat Minḥa, A Prehistoric Village in the Middle Jordan Valley," *Qadmoniot* 2, 1969, pp. 52–56, figs. (Hebrew); J. Perrot, N. Zori, "Khirbet Minḥa," *EAEHL*, 1970, pp. 172–174, figs. (Hebrew).

Murabba'ât

Wâdī el-Murabbaᶜât excavated by R. de Vaux for the Palestine Archaeological Museum, American Schools of Oriental Research, École Biblique et Archéologique Française, Department of Antiquities, Jordan, 1952.

G. L. Harding, "Khirbet Qumran and Wady Murabaat," *PEQ* 1952, pp. 104–109, pls. 28–32; R. deVaux, "Wady el Marabaat," *ADAJ* 2, 1953, p. 85, pl. 13a; *id.*, "Les Grottes de Murabbaᶜat et leur documents," *RB* 60, 1953, pp. 245–267, figs. 1–4, pls. 8–11; *id.*, "Quelques Textes Hébreux de Murabaaᶜat," *RB* 60, 1953, pp. 268–275, pls. 12–13; P. Benoit, J. T. Milik, R. deVaux, *Discoveries in the Judaean Desert*, II, *Les Grottes de Murabbaᶜat*, 1961; F. M. Cross, Jr., *The Ancient Library of Qumran and Modern Biblical Studies*, 1961, pp. 17–19; *id.*, "Epigraphic Notes on Hebrew Documents of the Eighth–Sixth Centuries B.C. II. The Murabbaᶜât Papyrus and the Letter Found near Yabneh-yam," *BASOR* 165, 1962, pp. 34–46, fig. 1; E. Stern, "Wadi Murabbaᶜat," *EAEHL*, 1970, pp. 147–149, fig. (Hebrew).

Na'aran, see 'Ain Duq

Nablus, see Mount Gerizim, Samaria

T. Drake, "Mr. Tyrwhitt Drake's Reports," *PEFQS* 1872, pp. 190–193; L. Oliphant, "Notes on a Tomb Opened at Jebata, and on Monuments found at Nablous," *PEFQS* 1885, pp. 94–97, figs.

Excavated by F. M. Abel and L. H. Vincent for the Department of Antiquities, Palestine and the École Biblique et Archéologique Française, 1920–1921.

L. H. Vincent, "Un Hypogée antique à Naplouse. Nouvelles Diverses," *RB* 29, 1920, pp. 126–135, figs. 1–6; F. M. Abel, "Notre Exploration à Naplouse," *RB* 31, 1922, pp. 89–99, figs. 1–3, pls. 3–5.

Excavation carried out by G. M. FitzGerald for the British School of Archaeology in Jerusalem and the Department of Antiquities, Palestine, 1927.

G. M. FitzGerald, "A Find of Stone Seats at Nablus," *PEFQS* 1929, pp. 104–110, pl. 17; Bibliography, "Nablus," *QDAP* 1, 1932; 7, 1938, p. 57.

R. Dajani excavated tombs at Khirbet Blibus for the Department of Antiquities, Jordan, 1966.

R. Dajani, "Khirbet Blibus," *ADAJ* 11, 1966, p. 103.

Nabratein, Kfar Niburaya

C. W. Wilson, "Notes on Jewish Synagogues in Palestine," *PEFQS* 1869, pp. 37–42, plan.

Excavations conducted by H. Kohl and C. Watzinger for the Deutsche Orient-Gesellschaft, 1905.

H. Kohl, C. Watzinger, *Antike Synagogen in Galilaea*, 1916, pp. 101–106, figs. 192–203, pl. 14; E. R. Goodenough, *Symbols* 1, 1953, pp. 203–204; N. Avigad ,"A Dated Lintel-Inscription from the Ancient Synagogue of Nabratein," *Bulletin Rabinowitz* 3, 1960, pp. 49–56, figs. 1–3, pl. 13; *id.*, "Kfar Nvuriya," *EAEHL*, 1970, p. 276, figs. (Hebrew).

Naḥal Amud, see Wadi el-Amud

Naḥal ha-Besor, see Wadi Ghazzeh

Naḥal Ḥever, Wadi Habra

Y. Aharoni, "Ḥever Valley (Wadi Ḥabra)," *IEJ* 4, 1954, pp. 126–127; *id.*, "Ḥever Valley," *IEJ* 5, 1955, pp. 272–273.

The expedition to the Judaean Desert was undertaken by the Israel Exploration Society, Hebrew University and Department of Antiquities, Israel, 1960–1961.

Y. Yadin, "The Newly-Found Bar Kochba Letters," *CNI* 11:3, 1960, pp. 12–16, pls. 1–4; *id.*, "New Discoveries in the Judean Desert," *BA* 24, 1961, pp. 34–50, figs. 1–7; *id.*, "The Caves of Naḥal Ḥever," *ʿAtiqot* 3, 1961, pp. 148–162, figs. 1–10, pls. 20–23; M. Levin, S. Horowitz, "Textile Remains from the Caves of Naḥal Ḥever," *ʿAtiqot* 3, 1961, pp. 163–164, pl. 24; H. Nathan, "The Skeletal Material from Naḥal Ḥever," *ʿAtiqot* 3, 1961, pp. 165–175, pls. 25–27; Y. Yadin, "More on the Letters of Bar Kochba," *BA* 24, 1961, pp. 86–95, figs. 11–13; *id.*, "Finding Bar Kochba's Despatches," *ILN*, November 4, 1961, pp. 772–775, figs. 1–20; *id.*, "New Archives of the Revolt of Bar Kochba," *ILN*, November 11, 1961, pp. 820–822, figs. 1–14; Y. Aharoni, "Expedition B," *IEJ* 11, 1961, pp. 11–24, figs. 1–5, pls. 4–10; *id.*, "Expedition B — The Cave of Horror," *IEJ* 12, 1962, pp. 186–199, figs. 1–4, pls. 23–33; L. Y. Rahmani, "The Coins from the Cave of Horror," *IEJ* 12, 1962, p. 200; B. Lifshitz, "The Greek Documents from the Cave of Horror," *IEJ* 12, 1962, pp. 201–207; Y. Yadin, "The Nabataean Kingdom, Provincia Arabia, Petra and En-Geddi in the Documents from Naḥal Ḥever," *Jaarbericht Ex Oriente Lux* 17, 1964, pp. 227–241, pls. 5–6; H. J. Polotsky, "Three Greek Documents from the Family Archive of Babatha," *EI* 8, 1967, pp. 46–51, pls. 10–11; Y. Yadin, "New Discoveries in the Judean Desert," in E. F. Campbell, Jr., D. N. Freedman, *The Biblical Archaeologist Reader*, 3, 1970, pp. 254–278, fig. 4; Y. Aharoni, "Naḥal Ḥever," *EAEHL*, 1970, pp. 343–347, figs. (Hebrew).

Naḥal Mishmar, Wadi Mahras

The expedition to the Judaean Desert was undertaken by the Israel Exploration Society, Hebrew University and Department of Antiquities, Israel, 1960–1961.

P. Bar-Adon, "Expedition C," *IEJ* 11, 1961, pp. 25–35, figs. 1–4, pls. 11–17a; *id.*, "The Treasure Cave of Naḥal Mishmar," *ILN*, December 2, 1961, pp. 972–974, figs. 1–18; *id.*, "Expedition C — The Cave of the Treasure," *IEJ* 12, 1962, pp. 215–226, fig. 1, pls. 35–42; *id.*, "The Cave of the Treasure," *Archaeology* 16, 1963, pp. 251–259, figs.; Y. Yadin, *The Art of Warfare in Biblical Lands*, 1963, p. 126, fig.; P. Bar-Adon, "Caves of Naḥal Mishmar," *EAEHL*, 1970, pp. 354–359, figs. (Hebrew); D. Ussishkin, "The 'Ghassulian' Temple in Ein Gedi and the Origin of the Hoard from Naḥal Mishmar," *BA* 34, 1971, pp. 23–39, figs. 10–23.

Naḥal Oren, Mughâret Wadi Fallâh, Mount Carmel

Caves of Mount Carmel excavated by M. Stekelis for the American Schools of Oriental Research, and British School of Archaeology in Jerusalem, 1940–1941.

M. Stekelis, "Preliminary Report on Soundings in Prehistoric Caves in Palestine," *BASOR* 86, 1942, pp. 2–10, figs. 1–7; *id.*, "Prehistoric Caves (Mount Carmel)," *QDAP* 11, 1945, pp. 115–118; *id.*, "Oren Valley (Wadi Fallah)," *IEJ* 7, 1957, p. 125; *id.*, "Oren Valley (Wadi Fallah)," *IEJ* 8, 1958, p. 131; *id.*, "Oren Valley (Wadi Fallah)," *IEJ* 10, 1960, pp. 118–119, 258–259; A. Biran, "Earliest Remains (Mount Carmel)," *CNI* 12:1, 1961, p. 18, pl. 4:2, 3.

Excavated by M. Stekelis, T. Israeli for the Hebrew University and the Department of Antiquities, Israel and the Municipality of Haifa, 1951–1960.

M. Stekelis, T. Israeli, "Excavations at Naḥal Oren, Preliminary Report," *IEJ* 13, 1963, pp. 1–12, figs. 1–6, pls. 1–4; T. Israeli, "Naḥal Oren," *EAEHL*, 1970, pp. 406–410, figs. (Hebrew).

Naḥal Šoreq, see Apheq

Nahariyah

Excavated by I. Ben-Dor for the Department of Antiquities, Palestine, 1947.

I. Ben-Dor, "A Bronze-Age Temple at Nahariyah," *QDAP* 14, 1950, pp. 1–41, figs. 1–48, pls. 1–12; J. Waechter, "Note on the Flints from Nahariyah," *QDAP* 14, 1950, pp. 42–43, fig. 1; I. Ben-Dor, "A Canaanite Temple at Nahariya," *EI* 1, 1951, pp. 17–28, figs. 1–15, pls. 1–6 (Hebrew); M. Dothan, "Nahariyah," *IEJ* 4, 1954, pp. 301–302.

Excavated by M. Dothan for the Department of Antiquities, Israel, 1954–1955.

M. Dothan, "Nahariyah," *IEJ* 5, 1955, pp. 126–127; J. Leibovitch, "Nahariyah," *CNI* 6:3–4, 1955, pp. 32–33, pls. 1:2, 2; M. Dothan, "Nahariyah," *IEJ* 5, 1955, p. 272; *id.*, "The Excavations at Nahariyah, Preliminary Report (Seasons 1954/55)," *IEJ* 6, 1956, pp. 14–25, figs. 1–8, pls. 1–6; *id.*, "The Sacrificial Mound at Nahariya," *EI* 4, 1956, pp. 41–46, figs. 1–5, pls. 1–4; *id.*, "Some Aspects of Religious Life in Palestine During the Hyksos Rule," *A and S* 2, 1957, pp. 121–130, figs. 1–23; A. Biran, "Nahariya," *CNI* 16:4, 1965, p. 19; O. Negbi, "Dating Some Groups of Canaanite Bronze Figurines," *PEQ* 1968, pp. 45–55, figs. 1–3, pl. 19.

Caves excavated by D. Barag for the Department of Antiquities, Israel, 1968.

A. Biran, "Nahariya," *CNI* 20:3–4, 1969, p. 40, pl. 5:1; O. Negbi, "Metal Figurines in Israel and Neighboring Lands," *Qadmoniot* 3, 1970, pp. 78–87, figs., pls.

(Hebrew); D. Barag, "Tomb Caves at Khirbet ᶜEitayim (Nahariya)," *BMH* 12, 1970, pp. 124–126; M. Dothan, "Nahariya," *EAEHL*, 1970, pp. 404–406, figs. (Hebrew).

Naveh-Yam

Excavated by E. Wreschner and M. W. Prausnitz for the Department of Antiquities, Israel, 1968.

E. Wreschner, M. W. Prausnitz, "Naveh-Yam," *IEJ* 18, 1968, p. 192; *id.*, "Naveh Yam," *RB* 76, 1969, pp. 415–416.

Nazareth

G. Schumacher, "Recent Discoveries in Galilee. Nazareth. Discovery of Large Cave," *PEFQS* 1889, pp. 68–74, figs. 1–8, pl., plan.

Excavations conducted by the Franciscan Custody of the Holy Land, 1890–1909.

P. M. Viaud, *Nazareth et ses deux églises de l'Annonciation et de Saint-Joseph d'après les fouilles récentes*, 1910; A. Mansur, "An Interesting Discovery in Nazareth," *PEFQS* 1923, pp. 89–91, 1 fig.; E. T. Richmond, "A Rock-cut Tomb at Nazareth," *QDAP* 1, 1932, pp. 53–54, pls. 33–34, plan; C. Kopp, "Beiträge zur Geschichte Nazareths," *JPOS* 18, 1938, pp. 187–228, figs. pl. 44.

Excavated by B. Bagatti for the Franciscan Custody of the Holy Land, 1954.

B. Bagatti, "Ritrovamenti nella Nazaret evangelica," *LA* 5, 1955, pp. 5–44, figs. 1–23, 2 plans; *id.*, "Results of the Excavations at the Sanctuary of the Annunciation in Nazareth," *CNI* 6:3–4, 1955, pp. 28–31; T. F. Meysels, "Recent Archaeological Discoveries at Nazareth," *ILN*, December 22, 1956, pp. 1074–1075, figs. 1–11; M. Barash, "The Nazareth Capitals," *EI* 7, 1964, pp. 125–134, figs. 1–2, pls. 27–29 (Hebrew); E. Testa, "Le grotte mistiche dei Nazareni e i loro riti battesimali," *LA* 12, 1962, pp. 5–45, figs. 1–7; B. Bagatti, "Nazareth," *RB* 69, 1962, pp. 418–420, pl. 48b; *id.*, *Gli scavi di Nazaret*, I, *Dalle origini al sec. 12*, 1967; *id.*, "I Vetri del Museo Francescano di Nazaret," *LA* 17, 1967, pp. 222–240, figs. 1–7; A. C. Carola, "Esami di frammenti di Intonaci provenienti dalla grotta della Annunciazione di Nazareth," *LA* 19, 1969, pp. 168–193, pls. 1–25; J. Finegan, *The Archeology of the New Testament*, 1969, pp. 27–33, figs.; B. Bagatti, "Notsrat," *EAEHL*, 1970, pp. 420–421, figs. (Hebrew).

Nebi Rubin, see Yavneh-Yam

Nebo, see Mount Nebo

Nicopolis, see ʻEmmaus

Nirim, see Maʻon

Nitsanah, see ʻAuja el-Ḥafir

Palmaḥim, see Yavneh-Yam

Pella, Tabaqat Faḥil, Piḥil

W. F. Albright, "Peḥel-Faḥil," *AASOR* 6, 1926, pp. 39–42; F. M. Abel, *Géographie de la Palestine*, 2, 1938, pp. 405–406; J. Richmond, "Khirbet Faḥil," *PEFQS*

1934, pp. 18–31, figs. 1–3, pls. 1–5; N. Glueck, *AASOR* 25–28, 1951, pp. 254–257, fig. 85; H. N. Richardson, "Khirbet Faḥil (Pella)," *RB* 67, 1960, pp. 242–243.

Excavated by R. H. Smith for Wooster College, American Schools of Oriental Research, Department of Antiquities, Jordan, 1967.

R. J. Bull, "A Refuge for Christians," *ILN*, March 16, 1968, pp. 26–27, figs. 1–7; R. H. Smith, "Pella," *RB* 75, 1968, pp. 105–112, pls. 12–14; *id.*, "Pella of the Decapolis, 1967," *Archaeology* 21, 1968, pp. 134–137, figs.; *id.*, "Pella," *Wooster Alumni Magazine* 82, 1968, pp. 4–13, figs.; *id.*, "Pella," *PEQ* 1969, pp. 2–3; *id.*, "Pella," *PEQ* 1969, p. 55; *id.*, "The 1967 Excavations at Pella of the Decapolis," *ADAJ* 14, 1969, pp. 5–10, pls. 1–10; J. B. Pritchard, ed., *ANET*, 1969, nos. 243, 253, 329, 486; R. W. Funk, "Faḥil," *EAEHL*, 1970, pp. 484–485, figs. (Hebrew).

Petra

J. L. Burckhardt, *Travels in the Holy Land*, 1822, pp. 420–436, figs., map; C. L. Irby, J. Mangles, *Travels in Egypt and Nubia, Syria and Asia Minor*, 1823, pp. 403–441, figs., map; L. deLaborde et Linant, *Voyage de l'Arabie Petrée*, 1830; S. I. Curtiss, "High Place and Altar at Petra," *PEFQS* 1900, pp. 350–355, 2 pls., plan; R. E. Brünnow, A. von Domaszewski, *Die Provincia Arabia* 1, 1904; A. Musil, *Arabia Petraea*, 2, *Edom*, 1907, pp. 41–150; G. Dalman, *Petra und seine Felsheiligtümer*, 1908; H. Kohl, *Kasr Firaun*, 1910; G. Dalman, "The Khazneh at Petra," *PEFA* 1, 1911, pp. 95–107, fig. 1, pls. 15–17; W. H. Schoff, transl., *The Periplus of the Erythraean Sea*, 1912, pp. 29, 101–102; G. Dalman, *Neue Petra Forschungen und der heilige Felsen von Jerusalem*, 1912; T. Wiegand *et al.*, *Petra*, 1921; A. B. W. Kennedy, *Petra: Its History and Monuments*, 1925; A. Musil, *The Northern Ḥeǧâz*, 1926, pp. 262–266, 270–272; H. J. Orr-Ewing, "The Lion and the Cavern of Bones at Petra," *PEFQS* 1927, pp. 155–157, 1 pl.

Excavated by G. Horsfield, A. Conway and W. F. Albright for the Department of Antiquities, Transjordan, 1929–1936.

A. Kammerer, *Petra et la Nabatène*, 1929; T. Canaan, "Studies in the Topography and Folklore of Petra," *JPOS* 9, 1929, pp. 136–142, pls. 1–2; *id.*, "Additions to 'Studies in the Topography and Folklore of Petra'," *JPOS* 10, 1930, pp. 178–180; G. L. Robinson, *The Sarcophagus of an Ancient Civilization*, 1930; G. Horsfield, A. Conway, "Historical and Topographical Notes on Edom, with an Account of the First Excavation at Petra," *The Geographical Journal* 76, 1930, pp. 369–388, figs. 1–2, pls. 1–24, map; J. Cantineau, *Le Nabatéen*, I, 1930, II, 1932; D. Nielsen, "The Mountain Sanctuaries in Petra and its Environs," *JPOS* 11, 1931, pp. 222–240, figs. 1–5; *id.*, "The Mountain Sanctuaries in Petra and its Environs," *JPOS* 13, 1933, pp. 185–208, pls. 9–14; W. F. Albright, "The Excavation of the Conway High Place at Petra," *BASOR* 57, 1935, pp. 18–26, figs. 1–5.

Excavations by M. A. Murray for the British School of Archaeology in Egypt, 1937.

A. S. Kirkbride, "Note on New Type of AE Coin from Petra," *PEQ* 1937, pp. 256–257, pl. 11; G. Horsfield, A. Horsfield, "Sela-Petra, the Rock, of Edom and Nabatene," *QDAP* 7, 1938, pp. 1–42, pls. 1–74, figs. 1–10; M. A. Murray, "Petra," *QDAP* 7, 1938, pp. 46–47; G. Horsfield, A. Horsfield, "Sela, the Rock, of Edom and Nabatene," *QDAP* 8, 1939, pp. 87–115, figs. 1–18, pls. 43–56; M. A. Murray, *Petra, the Rock City of Edom*, 1939; M. Murray, J. C. Ellis, *A Street in Petra*, 1940; G. Horsfield, A. Horsfield, "Sela-Petra, the Rock, of Edom and Nabatene," *QDAP* 9, 1942, pp. 105–204, figs. 1–55, pls. 6–49B.

Excavated by D. Kirkbride, P. J. Parr and G. L. Harding for the Department of Antiquities, Jordan, 1955–1957.

R. Dussaud, *La pénétration des arabes en Syrie avant l'Islam*, 1955; J. Starcky, "The Nabataeans: A Historical Sketch," *BA* 28, 1955, pp. 84–106, figs. 1–8; W. H. Morton, "Umm el-Biyara," *BA* 19, 1956, pp. 26–36, figs. 1–6; P. J. Parr, "Recent Discoveries at Petra," *PEQ* 1957, pp. 5–16, pls. 1–15.

Excavated by P. J. Parr, D. Kirkbride, G. R. H. Wright and C. M. Bennett for the Department of Antiquities, Jordan and the British School of Archaeology in Jerusalem, 1958–1968.

P. C. Hammond, "Petra," *PEQ* 1958, pp. 12–15; *id.*, "The Nabataean Bitumen Industry at the Dead Sea," *BA* 22, 1959, pp. 40–48; P. J. Parr, "Rock Engravings at Petra," *PEQ* 1959, pp. 106–108, pls. 4–5; R. L. Cleveland, "The Conway High Place, Petra," *AASOR* 34–35, 1960, pp. 57–78, figs. 1–7, pls. 1–18; P. C. Hammond, "Petra," *BA* 23, 1960, pp. 29–32; D. Kirkbride, "Seyl Aqlat, Beida près de Pétra," *RB* 67, 1960, pp. 235–238, pl. 13; *id.*, "Wadi Musa et Wadi Madamagh," *RB* 67, 1960, p. 239; P. J. Parr, "Petra," *RB* 67, 1960, pp. 239–242, pl. 14; *id.*, "Excavations at Petra," *PEQ* 1960, pp. 124–135, fig. 1, pls. 16–24; D. Kirkbride, "The Excavation of a Neolithic Village at Seyl Aqlat, Beidha near Petra," *PEQ* 1960, pp. 136–145, figs. 1–2, pls. 25–30; *id.*, "A Short Account of the Excavations at Petra in 1955–56," *ADAJ* 4–5, 1960, pp. 117–122, pls. 7–9; P. J. Parr, "Nabataean Sculpture from Khirbet Brak," *ADAJ* 4–5, 1960, pp. 134–136, pls. 15–16.

Theater excavated by P. C. Hammond for the American Expedition, 1961–1962.

G. R. H. Wright, "Structure of the Qasr Bint Far'un, A Preliminary Review," *PEQ* 1961, pp. 8–37, figs. 1–11, pls. 1–2; A. Millard, "A Seal from Petra," *PEQ* 1961, p. 136, pl. 18b; G. R. H. Wright, "Petra — The Arched Gate," *PEQ* 1961, pp. 124–135, figs. 1–6, pls. 17–18a; D. Kirkbride, "Ten Thousand Years of Man's Activity Around Petra," *ILN*, September 16, 1961, pp. 448–451, figs. 1–21; *id.*, "Excavation of the Pre-pottery Neolithic Village at Seyl Aqlat, Beidha," *ADAJ* 6–7, 1962, pp. 7–12, figs. 1–7, pls. 1–4; P. J. Parr, J. Starcky, "Three Altars from Petra," *ADAJ* 6–7, 1962, pp. 13–20, pls. 5–7; P. J. Parr, "A Nabataean Sanctuary near Petra, A Preliminary Notice," *ADAJ* 6–7, 1962, pp. 21–23, pls. 8–11; G. R. H. Wright, "The Khazne at Petra: A Review," *ADAJ* 6–7, 1962, pp. 24–54, pls. 11–14; P. J. Parr, "Le 'Conway High Place' à Pétra," *RB* 69, 1962, pp. 64–79, pls. 2–6, plan; G. R. H. Wright, "Repair Work Among the Monuments of Petra, in Jordan," *ILN*, March 31, 1962, pp. 502–503, figs. 1–9; E. Probst, "Petra, die Felsenstadt der Nabatäer," *Atlantis* 8, 1962, pp. 453–461, figs., pls.; P. J. Parr, "Petra: The Discovery of the Earliest Buildings," *ILN*, November 10, 1962, pp. 746–749, figs. 1–16; *id.*, "Discoveries from the First Systematic Excavations at Petra," *ILN*, November 17, 1962, pp. 789–791, figs. 1–21; C. M. Bennett, "The Nabataeans in Petra," *Archaeology* 15, 1962, pp. 233–243, figs.; C. M. Bennett, P. J. Parr, "Soundings on Umm el-Biyara, Petra," *Archaeology* 15, 1962, pp. 277–279, figs.; P. C. Hammond, "Petra: The Excavation of the Main Theater," *The American Scholar*, Winter 1962–63, pp. 93–106; D. Kirkbride, "Seyl Aqlat, a Pre-pottery Neolithic Village near Petra," *ILN*, January 19, 1963, pp. 82–84, figs. 1–15; P. C. Hammond, "The Roman Theatre of Petra Excavated," *ILN*, May 25, 1963, pp. 804–805, figs. 1–7; P. J. Parr, "The Capital of the Nabataeans," *Scientific American* 209, 1963, pp. 94–102, figs.; J. M. C. Toynbee, "A Bronze Statue from Petra," *ADAJ* 8–9, 1964, pp. 75–76, pl. 3; P. C. Hammond, "The Rose-Red City of Petra," *Natural History* 73:2, 1964, pp. 14–24, pls.; *id.*, "The Excavation of the Main Theater at Petra," *BASOR* 174, 1964, pp. 59–66, fig. 1; J. Starcky, "Pétra et la Nabatène," *Supplement au Dictionnaire de la Bible*, fasc. 39,

1964, cols. 886–1017, figs. 691–705; *id.*, "Nouvelle Épitaphe Nabatéenne donnant le Nom Sémitique de Pétra," *RB* 72, 1965, pp. 95–97, pls. 5–6; C. M. Bennett, "Exploring Umm el-Biyara, the Edomite fortress-rock which dominates Petra," *ILN*, April 30, 1966, pp. 29–31, figs. 1–11; J. Starcky and J. Strugnell, "Deux nouvelles inscriptions Nabatéennes," *RB* 73, 1966, pp. 236–247, fig. 1, pls. 8–9; D. Kirkbride *et al.*, "Five Seasons at the Pre-Pottery Neolithic Village of Beidha in Jordan," *PEQ* 1966, pp. 8–72, figs. 1–22, pls. 1–22; C. M. Bennett, "Des Fouilles a Umm el-Biyarah: Les Édomites a Petra," *BTS* 84, 1966, pp. 1, 6–16, figs.; *id.*, "Fouilles d'Umm el-Biyara, Rapport preliminaire," *RB* 73, 1966, pp. 372–403, figs. 1–4, pls. 14–25; N. Glueck, *Deities and Dolphins*, 1965, *passim*; G. A. Larue, "Petra," in C. F. Pfeiffer, ed., *The Biblical World*, 1966, pp. 443–446, fig.; C. M. Bennett, "Umm el-Biyarah," *PEQ* 1966, pp. 123–126, pl. 30; G. R. H. Wright, "Structure et date de l'Arc monumental de Pétra," *RB* 73, 1966, pp. 404–419, pls. 26–28; D. Kirkbride, "Beidha," *Archaeology* 19, 1966, pp. 199–207, figs.; pp. 268–272, figs.; R. Stiehl, *Die Araber in der Alten Welt*, III, 1966; P. J. Parr, "La date du barrage du Sîq à Pétra," *RB* 74, 1967, pp. 45–49, fig. 1, pls. 1–3; D. Kirkbride, "Beidha 1965: An Interim Report," *PEQ* 1967, pp. 5–13, figs. 1–2, pls. 1–6; P. C. Hammond, "Desert Waterworks of the Ancient Nabataeans," *Natural History* 76:6, 1967, pp. 37–43, figs., pls.; D. Kirkbride, "Beidha: An Early Neolithic Village in Jordan," *ADHL*, 1967, pp. 9–18, figs.; C. M. Bennett, "The Nabataeans in Petra," *ADHL*, 1967, pp. 148–156, figs.; G. L. Harding, *The Antiquities of Jordan*, 1967, pp. 115, 137, pls. 14–17; P. J. Parr, "The Investigation of Some 'Inaccessible' Rock-cut Chambers at Petra," *PEQ* 1968, pp. 5–15, fig. 1, pls. 1–6; *id.*, "Découvertes Récentes au Sanctuaire du Qasr a Pétra, I. Compte Rendu des Dernières Fouilles," *Syria* 45, 1968, pp. 1–24, figs. 1–8, pls. 1–3; G. R. H. Wright, "Découvertes Récentes au Sanctuaire du Qasr a Pétra, II. Quelques Aspects de l'Architecture et de la Sculpture," *Syria* 45, 1968, pp. 25–40, figs. 1–3, pls. 4–7; J. Starcky, C. M. Bennett, "Découvertes Récentes au Sanctuaire du Qasr a Pétra, III. Les Inscriptions du Téménos," *Syria* 45, 1968, figs. 1–3, pls. 8–9; P. J. Parr, "Recent Discoveries in the Sanctuary of the Qasr Bint Far'un at Petra, 1. Account of the Recent Excavations," *ADAJ* 12–13, 1968, pp. 5–19, pls. 1–11; G. R. H. Wright, "Some Aspects Concerning the Architecture and Sculpture," *ADAJ* 12–13, 1968, pp. 20–29, pls. 12–20; J. Starcky, C. M. Bennett, "The Temenos Inscriptions," *ADAJ* 12–13, 1968, pp. 30–50, pls. 21–26; D. Kirkbride, "Beidha 1967: An Interim Report," *PEQ* 1968, pp. 90–96, figs. 1–2, pls. 23–28, plan; P. C. Hammond, "The Medallion and Block Relief at Petra," *BASOR* 192, 1968, pp. 16–21, figs. 1–2; P. J. Parr, "Petra, Jordanie," *RB* 76, 1969, pp. 393–394; G. R. H. Wright, "Strabo on Funerary Customs at Petra," *PEQ* 1969, pp. 113–116; P. W. Lapp, *Biblical Archaeology and History*, 1969, pp. 73, 116–117, pls. 7–11; H. J. Kellner, ed., *Die Nabatäer*, 1970, *passim*; W. Culican, "A Palette of Umm el-Biyara Type," *PEQ* 1970, pp. 65–67, pls. 13–14; G. R. H. Wright, "Petra — The Arched Gate, 1959–60: Some Additional Drawings," *PEQ* 1970, pp. 111–115, figs. 1–9, pl. 17; N. Glueck, *The Other Side of the Jordan*, 1970, pp. 29, 87–88, 196–204, 209–210, 213–214, 242–243, figs. 7, 38, 102–106, 117–118, 121, 144; P. J. Parr, "A Sequence of Pottery from Petra," *NEATC*, 1970, pp. 348–381, figs. 1–8, pls. 42–45; A. Negev, "Petra," *EAEHL*, 1970, pp. 486–495, figs. (Hebrew); F. Zayadine, "A New Commemorative Stele at Petra," *Perspective* 12:1–2, 1971, pp. 57–69, figs. 1–12.

Philadelphia, see 'Ammân

Philoteria, see Beth-Yeraḥ

Ptolemais-Akko, see Acre

Qalandia, see Kalandia

Qal'at el-Qurain, see Montfort Castle

Qaryet el'Enab, see Abu Ghosh

Qedumim, see Jebel Qafze

Qumran, see Khirbet Qumran

Qurnub, see Kurnub

Rabbath Ammon, see 'Ammân

Râmat el-Khalîl, Mambre

Excavated by E. Mader for the Görres-Gesellschaft, 1926–1928.

Bibliography, *QDAP* 1, 1932, pp. 142–143, 190; J. W. Crowfoot, *Early Churches in Palestine*, 1941, pp. 35–36; R. deVaux, "Mambre," *Supplement au Dictionnaire de la Bible*, 1957, cols. 753–758, figs. 542–543; E. Mader, *Mambre* (*Ḥaram Râmat el-Ḥalîl*, 1957; S. Applebaum, "Bet Ilanim," *EAEHL*, 1970, pp. 34–35, figs. (Hebrew).

Ramat Maṭred

Y. Aharoni, M. Evenari, L. Shanan, N. H. Tadmor, "An Israelite Agricultural Settlement at Ramat Maṭred," *IEJ* 10, 1960, pp. 23–36, figs. 1–10, pls. 3–6; pp. 97–111, figs. 11–17, pls. 13–16; T. Israeli, "Mesolithic Hunters' Industries at Ramat Matred (The Wilderness of Zin)," *PEQ* 1967, pp. 78–85, figs. 1–4; Y. Aharoni, "Ramat-Maṭred," *EAEHL*, 1970, p. 516, fig. (Hebrew).

Ramat Raḥel, Beth-haccherem

Excavated by Y. Aharoni for the Hebrew University, Israel Exploration Society, Department of Antiquities, Israel, and the University of Rome, 1954, 1959–1962.

Y. Aharoni, "Excavations at Ramat Raḥel, 1954, Preliminary Report," *IEJ* 6, 1956, pp. 102–111, figs. 1–6; pp. 137–155, figs. 7–18; L. Y. Rahmani, "Coins from Ramat Raḥel, I, Ptolemaic to Byzantine," *IEJ* 6, 1956, pp. 155–157; U. Ben-Horin, II, "Arab Coins," p. 157; Y. Aharoni, "Ramat Raḥel," *IEJ* 9, 1959, pp. 272–274; *id.*, "Excavations at Ramat Raḥel," *BIES* 24:2–3, 1960, pp. 1–47, figs. 1–24, pls. 1–8 (Hebrew); *id.*, "Ramat Raḥel," *IEJ* 10, 1960, pp. 261–262; *id.*, "Ramat Raḥel," *RB* 67, 1960, pp. 398–400, pl. 26; *id.*, "Hebrew Jar-Stamps from Ramat Raḥel," *EI* 6, 1960, pp. 56–60, 5 figs., pl. 7:3–6 (Hebrew); *id.*, "Ramat Raḥel," *ILN*, December 17, 1960, pp. 1096–1098, figs. 1–15; *id.*, "Excavations at Ramat Rahel," *ILN*, December 24, 1960, pp. 1140–1142, figs. 1–17; Y. Aharoni, "Ramat Raḥel," *BTS* 37, 1961, pp. 4–10, figs.; A. Biran, "Ramat Raḥel," *CNI* 12:2, 1961, pp. 13–14, pls. 1, 2:1; Y. Aharoni, "Ramat Raḥel," *IEJ* 11, 1961, pp. 193–195; *id.*, "Excavations at Ramat Raḥel," *BA* 24, 1961, pp. 98–118, figs. 1–15; Y. Aharoni *et al.*, *Excavations at Ramat Raḥel*, 1, *Seasons 1959–1960*, 1962; A. Biran, "Ramat Raḥel," *CNI* 13:2, 1962, pp. 15–17, pls. 1–2; Y. Aharoni, "Ramat Raḥel," *RB* 69, 1962, pp. 401–404, pl. 44a; A. Biran, "Ramat Raḥel," *CNI* 14:1, 1963, pp. 20–21, pls. 3:2, 4:1; Y. Aharoni, "Ramat Raḥel," *RB* 70, 1963, pp. 572–574, pls. 20b, 22a, b; Y. Aharoni *et al.*, *Excavations at Ramat Raḥel*, 2, *Seasons 1961–1962*, 1964; Y. Aharoni, "The Citadel of

Ramat Raḥel," *Archaeology* 18, 1965, pp. 15–25, figs.; A. F. Rainey, "Ramat Raḥel," in C. F. Pfeiffer, ed., *The Biblical World*, 1966, pp. 473–477, fig.; Y. Aharoni, "The Citadel of Ramat Raḥel," *ADHL*, 1967, pp. 77–88, figs.; *id.*, "Beth-haccherem," in D. W. Thomas, ed., *AOTS*, 1967, pp. 171–184, pl. 6; J. B. Pritchard, ed., *ANEP*, 1969, nos. 771, 799, 800; Y. Aharoni, "Ramat-Raḥel," *EAEHL*, 1970, pp. 517–522, figs. (Hebrew).

Ramle

Excavated by J. Kaplan, for the Department of Antiquities, Israel, 1949, 1956.

J. Kaplan, "Excavations at the White Mosque in Ramla," *ʿAtiqot* 2, 1959, pp. 106–115, figs. 1–4, pls. 15–16; L. A. Mayer, "Two Arabic Inscriptions from Ramla," *ʿAtiqot* 2, 1959, pp. 116–117, pl. 16:4.

Excavated by M. Rosen-Ayalon and A. Eitan for the Department of Antiquities and Museums, 1965.

A. Biran, "Ramle," *CNI* 17:2–3, 1966, p. 26, pl. 3; M. Rosen-Ayalon, A. Eitan, "Ramleh," *RB* 74, 1967, pp. 93–94, pl. 16b; *id.*, "Excavations at Ramle," *Qadmoniot* 1:4, 1968, pp. 138–140, figs. (Hebrew); J. Kaplan, "Ramle," *EAEHL*, 1970, pp. 514–516, figs. (Hebrew).

Ramm, Rumm, Iram

Excavations made in the Wadi Ramm by G. Horsfield, R. Savignac for the École Biblique et Archéologique Française and the Department of Antiquities, Transjordan, 1932–1933.

R. Savignac, "Le Sanctuaire d'Allat à Iram," *RB* 41, 1932, pp. 581–597, pls. 17–19; *id.*, "Le Sanctuaire d'Allat à Iram," *RB* 42, 1933, pp. 405–422, pl. 24; *id.*, "Le Sanctuaire d'Allat à Iram," *RB* 43, 1934, pp. 572–589; G. Ryckmans, inscriptions, pp. 590–591; R. Savignac, G. Horsfield, "Le Temple de Ramm," *RB* 44, 1935, pp. 245–278, pls. 7–13, plans; A. S. Kirkbride, G. L. Harding, "Hasma," *PEQ* 1947, pp. 7–26, figs. 1–3, plans 1–6.

Temple excavated by D. Kirkbride for the British School of Archaeology in Jerusalem and the Department of Antiquities, Jordan, 1959.

D. Kirkbride, "Le Temple Nabatéen de Ramm," *RB* 67, 1960, pp. 65–92, pls. 3–9, plan; pp. 230–231; *id.*, "A Stone Circle in the Deserts of Midian: Cryptic Carvings from the Wadi Rumm," *ILN*, August 13, 1960, pp. 262–263, figs. 1–10; N. Glueck, *Deities and Dolphins*, 1965, pp. 20, 114, 164, 243, 333–334, pls. 8b, 52; G. L. Harding, *The Antiquities of Jordan*, 1967, pp. 141, 144–147; A. Negev, "Eram," *EAEHL*, 1970, pp. 14–16, figs. (Hebrew).

Ramoth-Gilead, see Tell er-Rumeith

Râs el-ʿAin, see Apheq

Ras en-Naqura, see Rosh ha-Niqra

Râs Siagha, see Mount Nebo

Rekem, see Petra

Rephaim Baqa, see Jerusalem

Riḥâb

M. Avi-Yonah, "Greek Inscriptions from Riḥab," *QDAP* 13, 1948, pp. 68–72, pls. 27–28; U. Lux, "Der Mosaikfussboden der Menas-Kirche in Riḥâb," *ZDPV* 83, 1967, pp. 34–41, pls. 13–16, plans 1–2; S. Mittmann, "Die Mosaikinschrift der Menas-Kirche in Riḥâb," *ZDPV*, 83, 1967, pp. 42–45, pl. 17.

Risqeh

Excavated by D. Kirkbride for the British School of Archaeology in Jerusalem and the Department of Antiquities, Jordan, 1959.

D. Kirkbride, "Khirbet Rizqeh," *RB* 67, 1960, pp. 232–235, pl. 12; *id.*, "Ancient Arabian Ancestor Idols," *Archaeology* 22, 1969, pp. 116–121, figs.; pp. 188–195; T. H. Carter, "The Stone Spirits," *Expedition* 12:3, 1970, pp. 22–40, figs.

Rosh ha-'Ayin, see Apheq

Rosh ha-Niqra, Tell eṭ-Ṭaba'iq, Ras en-Naqura, Khirbet el-Musheyrife

Excavated by R. Amiran for the Department of Antiquities, Israel, 1951.

M. Prausnitz, "Rosh ha-Niqra," *IEJ* 2, 1952, p. 142; M. Tadmor, M. Prausnitz, "Excavations at Rosh Hanniqra," *ʿAtiqot* 2, 1959, pp. 72–88, figs. 1–7, pls. 10–11; M. Tadmor, "Tel-Rosh-Haniqra," *EAEHL*, 1970, p. 615, fig. (Hebrew).

Rumeileh, see Beth-shemesh

Safadi, see Bir es-Safadi

Sahab, see 'Ammân

Šalbit, Sha'albim

E. L. Sukenik, "The Samaritan Synagogue at Šalbit," *Bulletin Rabinowitz* 1, 1949, pp. 26–27, fig. 8, pls. 14–16; M. N. Todin, E. L. Sukenik, "On the Greek Inscription in the Samaritan Synagogue at Šalbit," *Bulletin Rabinowitz* 2, 1951, pp. 27–28, pl. 12; E. R. Goodenough, *Symbols* 1, 1953, pp. 262–263; M. Avi-Yonah, "Places of Worship in the Roman and Byzantine Periods," *A and S*, 2, 1957, pp. 262–272, figs. 1–14; D. Barag, "Shaʿalvim," *EAEHL*, 1970, pp. 548–549, figs. (Hebrew).

Samaria, Sebaste

Excavated by C. S. Fisher, D. G. Lyon, G. A. Reisner for Harvard University, 1908–1910.

G. A. Reisner, C. S. Fisher, D. G. Lyon, *Harvard Excavations at Samaria*, 2 vols., 1924; W. F. Albright, "The Administrative Divisions of Israel and Judah," *JPOS* 5, 1925, pp. 17–54, esp. 38–42; E. W. G. Masterman, "The Harvard Excavations at Samaria," *PEFQS* 1925, pp. 25–30; J. W. Jack, *Samaria in Ahab's Time: Harvard Excavations and their Results*, 1929.

Excavated by J. W. Crowfoot for the British School of Archaeology in Jerusalem, Harvard University, Palestine Exploration Fund, Hebrew University, 1930–1935.

J. W. Crowfoot, "Work of the Joint Expedition to Samaria-Sebustiya, April and May, 1931," *PEFQS* 1931, pp. 139–142, pls. 1–3; Bibliography, *QDAP* 1, 1932,

p. 143; J. W. Crowfoot, "Excavations at Samaria 1931," *PEFQS* 1932, pp. 8–34, pls. 1–7; pp. 63–70, pls. 1–6; *id.*, "Samaria," *PEFQS* 1932, pp. 132–133, pls. 1–4; pp. 134–137; M. Narkiss, "A Dioscuri Cult in Subustiya," pp. 210–212, fig. 1; J. W. Crowfoot, "Samaria Relics," *ILN*, January 21, 1933, pp. 84–85, figs. 1–10; J. W. and G. M. Crowfoot, "The Ivories from Samaria," *PEFQS* 1933, pp. 7–26, pls. 1–3; J. W. Crowfoot, "Samaria Excavations: The Stadium," *PEFQS* 1933, pp. 62–73, pls. 1–6; K. M. Kenyon, "Excavations at Samaria, The Forecourt of the Augusteum," *PEFQS* 1933, pp. 74–87, pls. 7–13; H. G. May, "A Supplementary Note on the Ivory Inlays from Samaria," *PEFQS* 1933, pp. 88–89; J. W. Crowfoot, "Samaria: Interim Report on the Work in 1933," *PEFQS* 1933, pp. 129–136; E. L. Sukenik, "Inscribed Hebrew and Aramaic Potsherds from Samaria," *PEFQS* 1933, pp. 152–156, pls. 1–4; *id.*, "Inscribed Potsherds with Biblical Names from Samaria," *PEFQS* 1933, pp. 200–204, fig. 5, pls. 9–10; J. W. Crowfoot, "Report of the 1935 Samaria Excavations," *PEFQS* 1935, pp. 182–194, pls. 7–10; E. L. Sukenik, "Potsherds from Samaria, Inscribed with the Divine Name," *PEFQS* 1936, pp. 34–37, pls. 1–2; *id.*, "Note on a Fragment of an Israelite Stele Found at Samaria," *PEFQS* 1936, p. 156, pl. 3; W. F, Albright, "Ostracon C1101 of Samaria," *PEFQS* 1936, pp. 211–215; J. W. Crowfoot, *Churches at Bosra and Samaria-Sebaste*, 1937; E. L. Sukenik, "A Further Note on an Inscribed Potsherd," *PEQ* 1937, pp. 140–141, 1 fig.; J. W. and G. M. Crowfoot, *Samaria-Sebaste, 2, Early Ivories from Samaria*, 1938; R. W. Hamilton, "The Domed Tomb at Sebasṭya," *QDAP* 8, 1939, pp. 64–71, figs. 1–3, pls. 38–40; J. W. Crowfoot, *Early Churches in Palestine*, 1941, pp. 67, 150, pl. 27c; J. W. Crowfoot, K. M. Kenyon, E. L. Sukenik, *Samaria-Sebaste, 1, The Buildings at Samaria*, 1942; B. Maisler, "The Historical Background of the Samaria Ostraca," *JPOS* 21, 1948, pp. 117–133, figs. 1–2; R. B. Y. Scott, "Another Griffin Seal from Samaria," *PEQ* 1954, pp. 87–90, fig. 6; J. W. and G. M. Crowfoot, K. M. Kenyon, *Samaria-Sebaste, 3, The Objects from Samaria*, 1957; A. Parrot, *Samaria the Capital of the Kingdom of Israel*, 1958; Y. Aharoni, R. Amiran, "A New Scheme for the Sub-Division of the Iron Age in Palestine," *IEJ* 8, 1958, pp. 171–184; W. F. Albright, "Recent Progress in Palestinian Archaeology: Samaria-Sebaste III and Hazor I," *BASOR* 150, 1958, pp. 21–25; G. E. Wright, "Israelite Samaria and Iron Age Chronology," *BASOR* 155, 1959, pp. 13–29; *id.*, "Samaria," *BA* 22, 1959, pp. 67–78, figs. 11–18; O. Tufnell, "Hazor, Samaria and Lachish, a Synthesis," *PEQ* 1959, pp. 90–105; W. F. Albright, *The Archaeology of Palestine*, 1960, pp. 128–129, 132, 135, 137–138, 150, 156–157, figs. 3, 40, 43, pl. 24; Y. Yadin, "Ancient Judaean Weights and the Date of the Samaria Ostraca," *Scripta Hierosolymitana* 8, 1961, pp. 9–25; F. M. Cross, Jr., "A New Reading of a Place Name in the Samaria Ostraca," *BASOR* 163, 1961, pp. 12–14, fig. 1; A. F. Rainey, "Administration in Ugarit and the Samaria Ostraca," *IEJ* 12, 1962, pp. 62–63; Y. Yadin, "A Further Note on the Samaria Ostraca," *IEJ* 12, 1962, pp. 64–66; Y. Aharoni, "The Samaria Ostraca — an Additional Note," *IEJ* 12, 1962, pp. 67–69; G. Van Beek, "Samaria," *IDB* 1962, pp. 182–188, figs. 8–18.

Excavated by F. Zayadine, P. W. Lapp for the Department of Antiquities, Jordan, 1965–1967.

F. Zayadine, "Early Hellenistic Pottery from the Theater Excavations at Samaria," *ADAJ* 11, 1966, pp. 53–64, fig. 1, pls. 27–31; Y. Aharoni, "The Use of Hieratic Numerals in Hebrew Ostraca and the Shekel Weights," *BASOR* 184, 1966, pp. 13–19, figs. 1–3; A. F. Rainey, "The Samaria Ostraca in the Light of Fresh Evidence," *PEQ* 1967, pp. 32–41; P. R. Ackroyd, "Samaria," in D. W. Thomas, ed., *AOTS*, 1967, pp. 343–354, pl. 14; F. Zayadine, "Une Tombe du Fer II à Samarie-Sébaste," *RB* 75, 1968, pp. 562–585, 1 fig., pls. 55–63; *id.*, "Samaria-Sebaste, Clearance and Excavations," *ADAJ* 12–13, 1968, pp. 77–80; "Iron-Age Tomb," p. 80, pls. 50–53.

Excavated by J. B. Hennessy for the British School of Archaeology in Jerusalem, 1968.

J. B. Hennessy, "Samaria-Sebaste," *RB* 76, 1969, pp. 417–419, pls. 18, 19; A. Biran, "Samaria," *CNI* 20:3–4, 1969, p. 43; J. Finegan, *The Archeology of the New Testament*, 1969, pp. 33–42, figs.; J. B. Pritchard, ed., *ANEP*, 1969, nos. 129, 130, 286, 566, 718, 720; *id.*, *ANET*, 1969, pp. 283–286, 292, 321, 492; G. E. Wright, *NEATC*, 1970, pp. 13–16; K. M. Kenyon, *Archaeology in the Holy Land*, 1970, pp. 262–269, 277–281, 318–319, figs. 61–64, pls. 51–53; A. F. Rainey, "Semantic Parallels to the Samaria Ostraca," *PEQ* 1970, pp. 45–51; Y. Aharoni, "Three Hebrew Ostraca from Arad," *BASOR* 197, 1970, pp. 16–42; J. B. Hennessy, "Excavations at Samaria-Sebaste, 1968," *Levant* 2, 1970, pp. iv–v, 1–21, figs. 1–15, pls. 1–12; J. B. Livio *et al.*, "Samarie," *BTS* 120, 1970, pp. 1–18, figs.; F. Zayadine, "Samarie," *BTS* 121, 1970, pp. 1–15, figs.; N. Avigad, "Shomron," *EAEHL*, 1970, pp. 527–538, figs. (Hebrew).

Samaria Papyri, see Wadi ed-Dâliyeh

Scythopolis, see Beth-shan

Sebaste, see Samaria

Sepphoris, Ṣippori, Saffûriyah, Diocaesarea

H. Kohl, C. Watzinger, *Antike Synagogen in Galilaea*, 1916, p. 146.

Excavated by L. Waterman and C. S. Fisher for the American Schools of Oriental Research and the University of Michigan, 1931.

M. Burrows, "Sepphoris," *BASOR* 45, 1932, pp. 21–22; Bibliography, *QDAP* 1, 1932, p. 143; M. Avi-Yonah, *QDAP* 3, 1934, pp. 39–40; L. Waterman, N. E. Manasseh, S. Yeivin, C. S. Bunnel, *Preliminary Report of the University of Michigan Excavations*, 1937; M. Avi-Yonah, "A Sixth Century Inscription from Sepphoris," *IEJ* 11, 1961, pp. 184–187, fig. 1, pl. 36d; S. Saller, *A Revised Catalogue of the Ancient Synagogues of the Holy Land*, 1969, pp. 57–58, fig. 20; M. Avi-Yonah, "Tsipori," *EAEHL*, 1970, pp. 496–498, figs. (Hebrew).

Sha'ar ha'aliya, see Shiqmona

Sha'ar ha-Golan

Excavation by M. Stekelis for the Israel Exploration Society, 1949–1953.

M. Stekelis, "The New Neolithic Industry: the Yarmukian of Palestine," *IEJ* 1, 1950, pp. 1–19, fig. 1, pls. 1–7, 17; p. 248; *id.*, "Two More Yarmukian Figurines," *IEJ* 2, 1952, pp. 216–217, pl. 16; pp. 252–253; *id.*, "Shaᶜar ha-Golan," *IEJ* 3, 1953, p. 132; *id.*, "On the Yarmukian Culture," *EI* 2, 1953, pp. 98–101, figs. 1–4, pls. 15–16 (Hebrew); E. Anati, *Palestine Before the Hebrews*, 1963, pp. 263–269, 276–277, figs.; M. Stekelis, *The Yarmukian Culture: Report on Excavations in a Neolithic Site near Kibbuz Shaᶜar ha-Golan, 1949–1952*, 1966 (Hebrew); *id.*, "Shaᶜar ha-Golan," *EAEHL*, 1970, pp. 549–551, figs. (Hebrew).

Sharuḥen, see Tell el-Far'ah (S)

Shavei Zion

Excavations conducted by M. W. Prausnitz for the Department of Antiquities and Museums, Israel, 1955, 1957, 1960, 1963.

M. W. Prausnitz, "Shavei Zion," *IEJ* 8, 1958, pp. 134–135; M. W. Prausnitz, M. Avi-Yonah, D. Barag, *Excavations at Shavei Zion: The Early Christian Church*, 1967; J. Leibovitch, "Shavei Zion," *CNI* 6:3–4, 1955, p. 35, pl. 4:1, 2; *id.*, "Shavei Zion," *CNI* 9:1–2, 1958, pp. 21–22, pl. 1; E. Kitzinger, *Israeli Mosaics of the Byzantine Period*, 1965, pls. 6, 7.

Shechem, Tell Balâṭah

Excavated by F. M. Th. Böhl, E. Sellin, H. H. Steckweh, G. Welter for the Vienna Academy of Science, Vorderasiatischägyptische Gesellschaft, German Archaeological Institute for the Notgemeinschaft der Deutschen Wissenschaft, Deutsche-Evangelischen Institut for Altertumswissenschaft des Heiliges Landes, 1913–1914, 1926–1927, 1928, 1931, 1934.

E. Sellin, "Die Ausgrabung von Sichem," *ZDPV* 49, 1926, pp. 229–236, pls. 29–31; *id.*, "Die Ausgrabung von Sichem," *ZDPV* 49, 1926, pp. 304–320, pls. 32–43; F. M. Th. Böhl, "Sichem Keilschrifttafeln," *ZDPV* 49, 1926, pp. 321–327, pls. 44–46, E. Sellin, "Die Ausgrabung von Sichem," *ZDPV* 50, 1927, pp. 205–211, pls. 11–21; *id.*, "Die Ausgrabung von Sichem," *ZDPV* 50, 1927, pp. 265–274, pls. 22–30; F. M. Th. Böhl, *De Opgraving von Sichem*, 1927; E. Sellin, "Die Masseben des el-Berit im Sichem," *ZDPV* 51, 1928, pp. 119–123, pls. 8–12; Bibliography, "Balata," *QDAP* 1, 1932, pp. 87, 189; E. Sellin, H. Steckweh, "Sichem," *ZDPV* 64, 1941, pp. 1–20, fig. 1, pls. 1–4; J. W. Crowfoot, *Early Churches in Palestine*, 1941, pp. 89–90; E. Nielsen, *Shechem, A Traditio-Historical Investigation*, 1955.

Excavated by G. E. Wright, E. F. Campbell, Jr. et al., *for the American Schools of Oriental Research, Austin, Drew, Garrett, McCormick Theological Seminaries, Department of Antiquities, Jordan, 1956, 1957, 1960, 1962, 1964, 1966.*

G. E. Wright, "The First Campaign at Tell Balâṭah (Shechem)," *BASOR* 144, 1956, pp. 9–20, figs. 1–6; G. E. Wright *et al.*, "Shechem," *BA* 20, 1957, pp. 2–32, figs. 1–10; H. C. Key, L. E. Toombs, "The Second Season of Excavation at Biblical Shechem," *BA* 20, 1957, pp. 82–105, figs. 1–13; G. E. Wright, "The Second Campaign at Tell Balâṭah (Shechem)," *BASOR* 148, 1957, pp. 11–28, figs. 1–5, plan; V. R. Gold, "The Mosaic Map of Madeba," *BA* 21, 1958, pp. 50–71, figs. 1–6; W. F. Albright, *The Archaeology of Palestine*, 1960, pp. 45–46, 88–90, 102, 104, 247; E. F. Campbell, Jr., "Excavations at Shechem," *BA* 23, 1960, pp. 101–110, figs. 1–4; R. J. Bull, "A Re-examination of the Shechem Temple," *BA* 23, 1960, pp. 110–119, figs. 5–7; G. R. H. Wright, "The Architectural Recording of the Shechem Excavation," *BA* 23, 1960, pp. 120–126, fig. 8; J. F. Ross, L. E. Toombs, "Three Campaigns at Biblical Shechem," *Archaeology* 14, 1961, pp. 171–179, figs.; L. E. Toombs, G. E. Wright, "The Third Campaign at Balâṭah (Shechem)," *BASOR* 161, 1961, pp. 11–54, figs. 1–20; S. H. Horn, "Scarabs from Shechem," *JNES* 21, 1962, pp. 1–14, fig. 1, pl. 1; G. E. Wright, "Archaeological Fills and Strata," *BA* 25, 1962, pp. 34–40; O. R. Sellers, "Coins of the 1960 Excavations at Shechem," *BA* 25, 1962, pp. 87–96, figs. 10–12; G. E. Wright, "Selected Seals from the Excavations at Balâṭah (Shechem)," *BASOR* 167, 1962, pp. 5–13, figs. 1–4; F. M. Gross, Jr., "An Inscribed Seal from Balâṭah (Shechem)," *BASOR* 167, 1962, pp. 14–15, 1 fig.; G. E. Wright, *Biblical Archaeology*, 1962, pp. 77–78; *id.*, "The Samaritans at Shechem," *The Harvard Theological Review* 55, 1962, pp. 357–366; E. F. Campbell, Jr., J. F. Ross, "The Excavation of Shechem and the Biblical Tradition," *BA* 26, 1963, pp. 1–27, figs.

1–10; L. E. Toombs, G. E. Wright, "The Fourth Campaign at Balâṭah (Shechem)," *BASOR* 169, 1963, pp. 1–60, figs. 1–26; G. E. Wright, "1600 Years of Shechem and its Pillars of the Covenant," *ILN*, August 10, 1963, pp. 204–208, figs. 1–27; N. Lapp, "Pottery from Some Hellenistic Loci at Balâṭah (Shechem)," *BASOR* 175, 1964, pp. 14–26, figs. 1–4, pls. 1–2; G. R. H. Wright, "Fluted Columns in the Bronze Age Temple of Baal-Berith at Shechem," *PEQ* 1965, pp. 66–84, fig. 1, pl. 20; *id.*, *Shechem: The Biography of a Biblical City*, 1965; R. J. Bull, J. A. Callaway, E. F. Campbell, Jr., J. F. Ross, G. E. Wright, "The Fifth Campaign at Balâṭah (Shechem)," *BASOR* 180, 1965, pp. 7–41, figs. 1–20; H Reviv, "The Government of Shechem in the el-Amarna Period and in the Days of Abimelech," *IEJ* 16, 1966, pp. 252–257; G. E. Wright, "Shechem (Tell Balata)," in C. F. Pfeiffer, ed., *The Biblical World*, 1966, pp. 518–522; V. I. Kerkhof, "An Inscribed Stone Weight from Shechem," *BASOR* 184, 1966, pp. 20–21, 1 fig.; G. E. Wright, "Shechem," in D. W. Thomas, ed., *AOTS*, 1967, pp. 353–370, pl. 15; G. R H. Wright, "The Place Name Balāṭah and the Excavations at Shechem," *ZDPV* 83, 1967, pp. 199–202; J. F. Ross, L. E. Toombs, "Six Campaigns at Biblical Shechem," *ADHL*, 1967, pp. 119–128, figs., plan; E. F. Campbell, Jr., "The Shechem Area Survey," *BASOR* 190, 1968, pp. 19–41, figs. 1–17; G. R. H. Wright, "Temples at Shechem," *ZAW* 80, 1968, pp. 1–35, figs. 1–4c; L. Wächter, "Salem bei Sichem," *ZDPV* 84, 1968, pp. 63–72, pls. 9–11, map on p. 68; E. F. Campbell, Jr., "Shechem," *IEJ* 18, 1968, pp. 192–193; G. R. H. Wright, "Another Fluted Column Fragment from Bronze Age Shechem," *PEQ* 1969, pp. 34–36, fig. 1, pl. 1; J. B. Pritchard, ed., *ANEP*, 1969, nos. 135, 713, 825, 866–868; K. M. Kenyon, *Archaeology in the Holy Land*, 1970, pp. 326–327; G. E. Wright, *NEATC*, 1970, p. 34; G. R. H. Wright, "The Mythology of Pre-Israelite Shechem," *VT* 20, 1970, pp. 75–82; *id.*, "The 'Granary' at Shechem and the Underlying Storage Pits," *ZAW* 82, 1970, pp. 275–278, figs. 1–2; G. E. Wright, "Shkhem," *EAEHL*, 1970, pp. 539–545, figs. (Hebrew).

Sheikh Abreiq, see Beth-She'arim

Shiloh, Seilûn

C. Clermont-Ganneau, *Archaeological Researches in Palestine* 2, 1896, pp. 299–301, figs.

Excavated by A. Schmidt for The National Museum of Denmark, Copenhagen, 1922.

W. F. Albright, "The Danish Excavations at Shiloh," *BASOR* 9, 1923, pp. 10–11; A. T. Richardson, "Notes and Queries," *PEFQS* 1925, pp. 162–163.

Excavated by H. Kjaer for The National Museum of Denmark, Copenhagen, 1926–1932.

A. T. Richardson, "The Site of Shiloh," *PEFQS* 1927, pp. 85–88; W. F. Albright, "The Danish Excavations at Seilun — a Correction," *PEFQS* 1927, pp. 157–158; H. Kjaer, "The Danish Excavation at Shiloh," *PEFQS* 1927, pp. 202–213, pls. 6–9; *id.*, "The Excavation of Shiloh 1929," *JPOS* 10, 1930, pp. 87–174, figs. 1–47, 3 plans; W. F. Albright, "Shiloh," *BASOR* 35, 1929, pp. 4–5; H. Kjaer, "Shiloh. A Summary Report of the Second Danish Expedition, 1929," *PEFQS* 1931, pp. 71–88, figs. 1–17, pls. 1–2; W. F. Albright, "Shiloh," *BASOR* 48, 1932, pp. 14–15; N. Glueck, "Shiloh," *AJA* 37, 1933, pp. 166–167; *id.*, "Shiloh," *BASOR* 52, 1933, pp. 30–31; *id.*, "Seilûn," *QDAP* 3, 1934, p. 180.

Excavated by S. Holm-Nielsen for The National Museum of Denmark, Copenhagen, 1969.

M. L. Buhl, S. Holm-Nielsen, *Shiloh*, 1969; A. Kampinski, "Shilo," *EAEHL*, 1970, pp. 546–548, figs. (Hebrew).

Shiqmona

Excavation of monastery by M. Dothan for the Department of Antiquities, Israel, 1951.

J. Leibovitch, "Shaʿar haʿAliya," *CNI* 4:2–3, 1953, p. 30, pl. 2:1, 2; M. Dothan, "Excavation of a Monastery near Shaʿar ha-ʿAliyah," *IEJ* 5, 1955, pp. 96–102, figs. 1–3, pls. 19–20.

Excavated by Y. Elgavish for the Haifa Municipal Museum of Ancient Art, 1962–1970.

A. Biran, "Shiqmona," *CNI* 15:2–3, 1964, p. 29, pls. 6:1, 7:1; Y. Elgavish, "Shiqmona," *CNI* 17:2–3, 1966, p. 24, pl. 1:2; A. Biran, "Shiqmona," *CNI* 18:1–2, 1969, pp. 28–29; Y. Elgavish, "Shiqmona," *RB* 75, 1968, pp. 416–417, pl. 50b; A. Biran, "Shiqmona," *CNI* 19:3–4, 1968, p. 41; Y. Elgavish, "Shiqmona," *RB* 76, 1969, pp. 412–413, pl. 15; A. Biran, "Shiqmona," *CNI* 20:3–4, 1969, p. 41; Y. Elgavish, "Shiqmona — a Biblical City," *Qadmoniot* 3, 1970, pp. 90–93, pls. (Hebrew); *id.*, "Shiqmona," *RB* 77, 1970, pp. 386–387, pl. 16; *id.*, "Shiqmona," *IEJ* 19, 1969, pp. 247–248; *id.*, "Shiqmona," *IEJ* 20, 1970, pp. 229–230.

Shivta, see Isbeita

Shukbah, see Mount Carmel Caves

Siloam, see Jerusalem

Ṣippori, see Sepphoris

Siyaghah, see Mount Nebo

St. Jean d'Acre, see Acre

Sûsîtâ, Hippos

Excavated by E. Anati, C. Epstein, for the Department of Antiquities, Israel, 1951–1952.

J. Leibovitch, "Sûsîtâ," *CNI* 4:2–3, 1953, p. 31, pl. 4:3; E. Anati, "Sûsîtâ-Hippos," *IEJ* 3, 1953, p. 133; M. Avi-Yonah, "Places of Worship in the Roman and Byzantine Periods," *A and S* 2, 1957, pp. 262–272, figs. 1–14; C. Epstein, "Susita," *EAEHL*, 1970, pp. 422–423, fig. (Hebrew).

Ta'anach

Excavated by E. Sellin for the Academy of Science, and Ministry of Education, Vienna, 1902–1904.

C. Wilson, "Austrian Excavations at Taanach," *PEFQS* 1904, pp. 388–391, pl. 1; W. F. Albright, "A Prince of Taanach in the Fifteenth Century B.C.," *BASOR* 94, 1944, pp. 12–27; Bibliography, "Tall Tiʿinnik," *QDAP* 1, 1932, pp. 147–148; W. F. Albright, *The Archaeology of Palestine*, 1960, pp. 32, 76, 102, 117; G. VanBeek, "Taanach," *IDB*, 1962, p. 497.

Excavated by P. W. Lapp for Concordia Theological Seminary and the American Schools of Oriental Research, 1963, 1968.

P. W. Lapp, "Palestine Known but Mostly Unknown," *BA* 26, 1963, pp. 121–134, figs. 6–10, esp. figs. 7, 9; *id.*, "The 1963 Excavation at Taʿannek," *BASOR* 173, 1964, pp. 4–44, figs. 1–24; D. R. Hillers, "An Alphabetic Cuneiform Tablet from

Taanach (TT433)," *BASOR* 173, 1964, pp. 45–50, figs. 1–3; C. Graesser, Jr., "Taanach," in C. F. Pfeiffer, *The Biblical World*, 1966, pp. 556–563, figs.; M. Weippert, "Zur Lesung der alphabetischen Keilschrifttafel vom Tell Taᶜannek," *ZDPV* 83, 1967, pp. 82–83; P. W. Lapp, "Taanach by the Waters of Megiddo," *BA* 30, 1967, pp. 1–27, figs. 1–14; *id.*, "The 1966 Excavations at Tell Taᶜannek," *BASOR* 185, 1967, pp. 2–39, figs. 1–26; F. M. Cross, Jr., "The Canaanite Cuneiform Tablet from Taᶜanach," *BASOR* 190, 1968, pp. 41–46, fig. 1; P. W. Lapp, "Tell Taᶜannak," *RB* 75, 1968, pp. 93–98, pls. 7–8; *id.*, "A Ritual Incense Stand at Taanak," *Qadmoniot* 2, 1969, pp. 16–17, figs. (Hebrew); *id.*, "The 1968 Excavations at Tell Taᶜannek," *BASOR* 195, 1969, pp. 2–49, figs. 1–32; A. F. Rainey, "A Clay Tablet from Taanach — A Ray of Light on Eretz-Israel on the Eve of Joshua's Conquest," *Qadmoniot* 2, 1969, pp. 89–90, figs. (Hebrew); A. Biran, "Tell Taᶜanach," *CNI* 20:3–4, 1969, pp. 41–43; P. W. Lapp, "Tell Taᶜannak," *RB* 76, 1969, pp. 580–586, pls. 33–38; *id.*, *Biblical Archaeology and History*, 1969, pp. 72, 79, 116, 119–120, pls. 4, 24, 29, 30; J. B. Pritchard, ed., *ANET*, 1969, pp. 235–236, 243, 488, 490; A. Kampinski, "Taᶜanakh," *EAEHL*, 1970, pp. 624–626, figs. (Hebrew); P. W. Lapp, "Taᶜanakh," *EAEHL*, 1970, pp. 626–628, figs. (Hebrew).

Tabaqat Faḥil, see Pella

Tabgha, see 'Ain eṭ-Ṭabgha

Tananir, see Mount Gerizim

Tanturah, see Dor

Tawilân

Excavated by C. M. Bennett for the British Academy, British School of Archaeology in Jerusalem, Department of Antiquities, Jordan, 1968–1970.

C. M. Bennett, "The Excavations at Tawilân, near Petra," *ADAJ* 12–13, 1968, pp. 53–55; *id.*, "Tawilân (Jordanie)," *RB* 76, 1969, pp. 386–390, pls. 6–7; *id.*, "Tawilan," *RB* 77, 1970, pp. 371–374, pl. 11; N. Glueck, *The Other Side of the Jordan*, 1970, pp. 29–32, figs. 8–9; C. M. Bennett, "An Archaeological Survey of Biblical Edom," *Perspective* 12:1–2, 1971, pp. 35–44, esp. 41–42; *id.*, "A Brief Note on Excavations at Tawilân, Jordan, 1968–70," *Levant* 3, 1971, pp. v–vii, pls. 1–2.

Tel Aviv

J. Kaplan, "Exploration archéologique de Tel Aviv-Jaffa," *RB* 62, 1955, pp. 92–99, 1 fig., pl. 1; *id.*, "A Cemetery of the Bronze Age Discovered near Tel Aviv Harbour," *ᶜAtiqot* 1, 1955, pp. 1–12, figs. 1–6, pl. 1; J. Leibovitch, "Description of the Scarabs Found in a Cemetery near Tel Aviv," *ᶜAtiqot* 1, 1955, pp. 13–18, fig. 6, pl. 2; J. Kaplan, *The Archaeology and History of Tel Aviv-Jaffa*, 1959.

Excavated by T. Israeli Noy for the Department of Antiquities, Israel, 1963–1964, 1970.

T. Israeli, "Ḥolon," *IEJ* 13, 1963, p. 137; J. Kaplan, "Tel-Aviv-Yafo," *IEJ* 16, 1966, pp. 282–283; T. Israeli, "A Lower Palaeolithic Site at Ḥolon, Preliminary Report," *IEJ* 17, 1967, pp. 144–152, figs. 1–3, pl. 35; J. Kaplan, "Two Samaritan Amulets," *IEJ* 17, 1967, pp. 158–162, figs. 1–2, pl. 36; T. Israeli-Noy, "The Prehistoric Site at Ḥolon," *Qadmoniot* 2, 1969, p. 14, fig. (Hebrew).

Excavated by J. Kaplan for the Museum of Antiquities and the Museum Haʿaretz, 1969–1970.

J. Kaplan, "The Excavations near Sdeh Dov, Tel Aviv," *BMH* 12, 1970, pp. 14–15, pl. 1b; T. Noy, A. Issar, "Ḥolon," *IEJ* 20, 1970, pp. 221–222. fig. 1; J. Kaplan, "Tel Aviv-Yafo," *IEJ* 20, 1970, pp. 225–226; *id.*, "Tel Aviv," *EAEHL*, 1970, pp. 563–565, figs. (Hebrew).

Teleilat el-Ghassul

Excavated by A. Mallon, R. Köppel for the Pontifical Biblical Institute, 1929–1938.

A. Mallon, "The Five Cities of the Plain, (Genesis XIV)," *PEFQS* 1932, pp. 52–56; J. G. Duncan, "Père Mallon's Excavation of Teleilat Ghassul," *PEFQS* 1932, pp. 71–77, pl. 1; A. Mallon, R. Köppel, R. Neuville *et al.*, *Teleilat Ghassul, compte rendu des fouilles de l'Institut Biblique Pontifical*, 1, 1934, 2, 1940.

Excavated by R. North for the Pontifical Biblical Institute, 1960.

R. North, "Teleilat Ghassul," *RB* 67, 1960, pp. 368–370; *id.*, "Ghassul 1960 Excavation Report," *Analecta Biblica* No. 14, 1961; E. Anati, *Palestine Before the Hebrews*, 1963, pp. 276–277, 306–314, 331, 333, figs., pls.; R. North, "Ghassul's New-Found Jar Incision," *ADAJ* 8–9, 1964, pp. 68–74, pls. 26–29.

Excavated by J. B. Hennessy for the British School of Archaeology in Jerusalem, 1967.

J. B. Hennessy, "Teleilat Ghassul," *RB* 75, 1968, pp. 247–250, fig. 5, pls. 26–27; *id.*, "Preliminary Report on a First Season of Excavations at Teleilat Ghassul," *Levant* 1, 1969, pp. vii–viii, 1–24, figs. 1–12, pls. 1–16; P. W. Lapp, *Biblical Archaeology and History*, 1969, pp. 73, 117, pl. 12; K. M. Kenyon, *Archaeology in the Holy Land*, 1970, pp. 70–76, 94, 97, 324, 333–334, figs. 6–9; R. North, D. Gilead, "Teleilat el-Ghasul," *EAEHL*, 1970, pp. 617–621, figs. (Hebrew); E. D. Stockton, "Non-Ghassulian Flint Elements at Teleilat Ghassul," *Levant* 3, 1971, pp. 80–81, figs. 1.

Tel Dan, see Dan

Tel Gat, see Tell esh-Sheikh Aḥmed el-ʿAreini

Tell Abu Ḥabil

N. Glueck, "Khirbet Abu Ḥabil," *AASOR* 25–28, 1951, Text, pp. 275–276, pls., pp. 432–435.

Excavated by H. deContenson for the Department of Antiquities, Jordan, 1953.

H. deContenson, "Three Soundings in the Jordan Valley," *ADAJ* 4–5, 1960, pp. 12–98, figs. 1–36; J. Mellaart, "Preliminary Report of the Archaeological Survey in the Yarmuk and Jordan Valley," *ADAJ* 6–7, 1962, pp. 126–158, pls. 24–31:15, 33, esp. 137–138; H. deContenson, "The Central Jordan Valley," *EAEHL*, 1970, pp. 460–461, 1 fig. (Hebrew).

Tell Abu Hawam, Salmonah

Excavated by R. Hamilton for the Department of Antiquities, Palestine, 1932–1933.

R. W. Hamilton, "Tall Abū Hawam," *QDAP* 3, 1934, pp. 74–80, pls. 19–23; *id.*, "Excavations at Tell Abû Hawâm," *QDAP* 4, 1935, pp. 1–69, figs. 1–416, pls. 1–39, plans; B. Maisler, "The Stratification of Tell Abû Hawâm on the Bay of Acre," *BASOR* 124, 1954, pp. 21–25.

Excavated by E. Anati for the Department of Antiquities, Israel, 1952, 1963.

E. Anati, "Excavations at the Cemetery of Tell Abu Hawam (1952)," *ᶜAtiqot* 2, 1959, pp. 89–102, figs. 1–9, pls. 12–14; M. Avnimelech, "Remarks on the Geological Features of the Surroundings of Tell Abu Hawam and the Cemetery in the Area of the Qishon Mouth," *ᶜAtiqot* 2, 1959, pp. 103–105, figs. 1–2; E. Anati, "Tell Abu Hawam," *IEJ* 13, 1963, pp. 142–143; *id.*, "Tell Abu Hawam, 1963," *Archaeology* 16, 1963, pp. 210–211; E. Stern, "The Dating of Stratum II of Tell Abu Hawam," *IEJ* 18, 1968, pp. 213–219, fig. 1.

Tell Abu Matar, see Beersheba

Tell ʻAbu Sultan, see Yavneh-Yam

Tell Abu Zureiq, see Hazorea'

Tell 'Aitun

Tombs excavated by V. Tsaferis, G. Edelstein, T. Dothan, D. Ussishkin for the Department of Antiquities, Israel, 1968.

T. Dothan, "Tell ᶜAitun," *IEJ* 18, 1968, pp. 194–195; G. Edelstein, "A Philistine Jug from Tell ᶜAitun," *Qadmoniot* 1, 1968, p. 100, fig. (Hebrew); V. Tsaferis, G. Edelstein, "Tel ᶜAitun," *RB* 76, 1969, pp. 578–579, pls. 31b, 32b; T. Dothan, "A Female Mourner Figurine from the Lachish Region," *EI* 9, 1969, pp. 42–46, figs., pl. 8 (Hebrew); A. Biran, "Tell ᶜAitun," *CNI* 20:3–4, 1969, p. 49, pl. 6a.

Tell Anafa

Excavated by S. S. Weinberg for the Museum of Art and Archaeology, University of Missouri-Columbia, 1968–1970.

S. S. Weinberg, "Tel Anafa," *IEJ* 18, 1968, pp. 195–196; *id.*, "Tel Anafa," *RB* 76, 1969, pp. 404–409, pl. 14; A. Biran, "Tell Anafa," *CNI* 20:3–4, 1969, p. 39; S. S. Weinberg, "Tell Anafa," *Muse* 3, 1969, pp. 16–23, figs.; *id.*, "Tell Anafa," *IEJ* 19, 1969, pp. 250–252; *id.*, "Tell Anafa," *RB* 77, 1970, pp. 381–383, pl. 13; *id.*, "Tel Anafa: The Second Season," *Muse* 4, 1970, pp. 15–24, figs. *id.*, "Tel Anafa: The Third Season of Excavations," *AJA* 75, 1971, pp. 216–217.

Tell Arad, see Arad

Tell Beit Mirsim, Debir, Kiriath-sepher

Excavated by W. F. Albright and M. G. Kyle for the American Schools of Oriental Research and Xenia Theological Seminary, 1926–1932.

W. F. Albright, "The Excavations at Tell Beit Mirsim," *BASOR* 23, 1926, pp. 2–14, figs. 1–19; *id.*, "The Second Campaign at Tell Beit Mirsim (Kiriath-sepher)," *BASOR* 31, 1928, pp. 1–11, 6 figs.; *id.*, "The American Excavations at Tell Beit Mirsim," *ZAW* 47, 1929, pp. 1–17; *id.*, "The Third Campaign at Tell Beit Mirsim," *BASOR* 39, 1930, pp. 1–10, 6 figs.; *id.*, "The Third Campaign at Tell Beit Mirsim and its Historical Results," *JPOS* 11, 1931, pp. 105–129; *id.*, "The Fourth Joint Campaign at Tell Beit Mirsim," *BASOR* 47, 1932, pp. 3–17, figs. 1–11; *id.*, *The Excavation of Tell Beit Mirsim in Palestine*, I, *The Pottery of the First Three Campaigns*, *AASOR* 12, 1932; *id.*, *The Excavation of Tell Beit Mirsim*, IA, *The Bronze Age Pottery of the Fourth Campaign*, *AASOR* 13, 1933, pp. 55–127; M. G. Kyle, *Excavating*

Kirjath-sepher's Ten Cities, 1934; W. F. Albright, *Archaeology of Palestine and The Bible*, 1932, pp. 63–126; *id.*, *The Excavation of Tell Beit Mirsim*, II, *The Bronze Age*, *AASOR* 17, 1938; *id.*, "Astarte Plaques and Figurines from Tell Beit Mirsim," *Mélanges syriens offerts à M. René Dussaud*, 1939, pp. 107–120; W. F. Albright, J. L. Kelso, *The Excavation of Tell Beit Mirsim*, 3, *The Iron Age*, *AASOR* 21–22, 1943; Y. Aharoni, "The Date of Casemate Walls in Judah and Israel and their Purpose," *BASOR* 154, 1959, pp. 35–39; R. Amiran, "The Pottery of the Middle Bronze Age I in Palestine," *IEJ* 10, 1960, pp. 204–225, figs. 1–10; W. F. Albright, *The Archaeology of Palestine*, 1960, pp. 81–84, 107–108, 118–119, 122, 129–133, 138–141; *id.*, "Debir," in D. W. Thomas, ed., *AOTS*, 1967, pp. 207–220; J. B. Pritchard, ed., *ANEP*, 1969, nos. 145, 214, 278, 469, 592, 596, 723, 724, 727; W. F. Albright, "Tel-Bet-Mirsim," *EAEHL*, 1970, pp. 567–572, figs. (Hebrew).

Tell Deir 'Alla

W. F. Albright, "Tell Deir ᶜAlla," *AASOR* 6, 1926, p. 46; *id.*, "Tell Deir ᶜAlla," *BASOR* 35, 1929, pp. 13–14; F. M. Abel, *Géographie de la Palestine* 2, 1938, p. 470.

Excavated by H. J. Franken for the Dutch Archaeological Expedition, 1960–1964.

H. J. Franken, "The Excavations at Deir ᶜAllā in Jordan," *VT* 10, 1960, pp 386–393, pls. 1–16; *id.*, "The Excavations at Deir ᶜAllā in Jordan," *VT* 11, 1961, pp. 361–372; *id.*, "The Excavations at Deir ᶜAllā in Jordan," *VT* 12, 1962, pp. 378–382; *id.*, "Clay Tablets from Deir ᶜAlla, Jordan," *VT* 14, 1964, pp. 377–379, p. 1; *id.*, "The Stratigraphic Context of the Clay Tablets Found at Deir ᶜAlla," *PEQ* 1964, pp. 73–78, figs. 1–3, pls. 14–15; *id.*, "A Bronze Age Shrine and Unknown Script," *ILN*, April 17, 1965, pp. 34–35, figs. 1–6; A. Vanden Branden, "Essai de déchiffrement des Inscriptions de Deir ᶜAlla," *VT* 15, 1965, pp. 129–150; H. J. Franken, "A Note on How the Deir ᶜAlla Tablets were Written," *VT* 15, 1965, pp.1 50–152; A. Vanden Branden, "Comment lire les textes de Deir ᶜAlla," *VT* 15, 1965, pp. 532–535; H. J. Franken, "A Reply," *VT* 15, 1965, pp. 535–536; *id.*, "Iron Age Jordan Village," *ILN*, May 1, 1965, p. 27, figs. 1–4; J. Naveh, "The Date of the Deir ᶜAllā Inscription in Aramaic Script," *IEJ* 17, 1967, pp. 256–258, fig. 1; H. J. Franken, "Texts from the Persian Period from Tell Deir ᶜAllā," *VT* 17, 1967, pp. 480–481; *id.*, "For the Old Testament: New Clues?" *ILN*, July 20, 1968, pp. 30–31, figs. 1–5; M. Kochavi, "The Excavations at Tell Deir ᶜAlla," *Qadmoniot* 1, 1968, pp. 130–131, figs. (Hebrew); P. W. Lapp, *Biblical Archaeology and History*, 1969, pp. 73, 110, 117, 125, pls. 14–16; H. J. Franken, *Excavations at Tell Deir ᶜAllā*, with contribution by J. Kalsbeek, 1969; P. W. Lapp, Review of H. J. Franken, *Excavations at Tell Deir ᶜAlla* 1, 1969, in *VT* 20, 1970, pp. 243–256; N. Glueck, *The Other Side of the Jordan*, 1970, p. 142; H. J. Franken, "Tel-Der-ᶜAla," *EAEHL*, 1970, pp. 579–580, figs. (Hebrew).

Tell Dothan, see Dothan

Tell ed-Duweir, see Lachish

Tell ej-Judeideh

Excavated by F. J. Bliss, R. A. S. Macalister, for the Palestine Exploration Fund, 1899–1900.

F. J. Bliss, "First Report on the Excavations at Tell ej-Judeideh," *PEFQS* 1900, pp. 87–101, 3 figs., pls. 1–2; *id.*, "Second Report on the Excavations at Tell ej-Judeideh," *PEFQS* 1900, pp. 199–222, pls. 1–7; R. A. S. Macalister, "Cupmarks at Tell ej-Judeideh," *PEFQS* 1900, p. 249, 1 pl.; F. J. Bliss, R. A. S. Macalister, "The Excavations at Tell ej-Judeideh," *Excavations in Palestine 1898–1900*, 1902, pp. 7–8, 44–51, figs. 22–24, pp. 107, 195, 199, pls. 10–14, 89; C. Watzinger, *Denkmäler Palästinas*, 2, 1935, pp. 28–30; I. Ben-Dor, "Two Hebrew Seals," *QDAP* 13, 1948, pp. 64–67, fig. 1, pl. 27:2; M. Broshi, "Tel Judeide," *EAEHL*, 1970, pp. 572–573, figs. (Hebrew).

Tell el-ʿAjjul, Beth Eglayim

Excavated by W. M. F. Petrie (as Gaza) for the British School of Archaeology in Egypt, 1930–1934.

W. M. F. Petrie *et al.*, *Ancient Gaza* 1, 1931, 2, 1932, 3, 1933, 4, 1934, 5, 1952; W. A. Heurtley, "A Palestinian Vase-Painter of the Sixteenth Century B. C.," *QDAP* 8, 1939, pp. 21–37, pls. 8–24; K. M. Kenyon, "Tombs of the Intermediate Early Bronze-Middle Bronze Age at Tell Ajjul," *ADAJ* 3, 1956, pp. 41–55, figs. 7–10 G. E. Wright, "Philistine Coffins and Mercenaries," *BA* 22, 1959, pp. 54–66, figs. 1–10; C. Epstein, "Bichrome Wheel-made Tankards from Tell el ᶜAjjul," *PEQ* 1961, pp. 137–142, figs. 1–2, pls. 19–20; A. Dajani, "Some of the Industries of the Middle Bronze Period: Weapons," *ADAJ* 6–7, 1962, pp. 55–66, pl. 15; O. Tufnell, "The Courtyard Cemetery at Tell el-ᶜAjjul, Palestine," *Bulletin of the University of London Institute of Archaeology* 3, 1962, pp. 1–37; E. Anati, *Palestine Before the Hebrews*, 1963, pp. 394, 418–419, figs.; A. K. Dajani, "Transportation in Middle Bronze Periods," *ADAJ* 8–9, 1964, pp. 56–67, pls. 23–25; C. Epstein, "Bichrome Vessels in the Cross Line Style," *PEQ* 1965, pp. 42–53, figs. 1–2, pls. 13–15; *id.*, *Palestinian Bichrome Ware*, 1966; T. C. Mitchell, "Philistia," in D. W. Thomas, ed., *AOTS*, 1967, pp. 405–427, fig. 11, pl. 18; O. Tufnell, "The Pottery from Royal Tombs I–III at Byblos," *Berytus* 18, 1969, pp. 5–33, figs. 1–7; R. Amiran, *Ancient Pottery of the Holy Land*, 1970, pp. 98, 110, 119, 122, 152–190, figs., pls.; K. M. Kenyon, "Tell Ajjul," *Archaeology in the Holy Land*, 1970, pp. 305, 322; O. Tufnell, "Bet-ᶜEglayim," *EAEHL*, 1970, pp. 54–60, figs. (Hebrew); *id.*, Review of O. Negbi, *The Hoards of Goldwork from Tell el-ᶜAjjul*, 1970, in *PEQ* 1971, pp. 53–54.

Tell el-Asawir, ʿArruboth

Tomb cleared by M. Dothan for the Department of Antiquities, Israel, 1953.

M. Dothan, "Tell Asawir," *IEJ* 3, 1953, p. 263; J. Leibovitch, "Tell Asawir," *CNI* 5:1–2, 1954, p. 25, pl. 1; D. Ferembach, "Le Peuplement du Proche-Orient au Chalcolithique et au Bronze ancien," *IEJ* 9, 1959, pp. 221–228, fig. 1; R. Amiran, "Assawir," *NEATC*, 1970, pp. 89, 99, pl. 7; *id.*, *Ancient Pottery of the Holy Land*, 1970, pp. 44–47, pl. 9; M. Dothan, "Tel el-Asawir," *EAEHL*, 1970, pp. 566–567, figs. (Hebrew).

Tell el-Farʿah (N)

W. F. Albright, "The Site of Tirzah and the Topography of Western Manasseh," *JPOS* 11, 1931, pp. 241–251.

Excavated by R. de Vaux for the École Biblique et Archéologique Française, 1946–1960.

R. deVaux, A. M. Stève, "La première Campagne de Fouilles à Tell el-Fârᶜah, près Naplouse," *RB* 54, 1947, pp. 394–433, figs. 1–11, pls. 10–20; *id.*, "La première Campagne de Fouilles à Tell el-Fârᶜah, près Naplouse," *RB* 54, 1947, pp. 573–589, figs. 1–6, pls. 21–27; *id.*, "La seconde Campagne de Fouilles à Tell el-Fârᶜah, près

Naplouse," *RB* 55, 1948, pp. 544–580, figs. 1–17, pls. 9–24; *id.*, "La deuxième Campagne de Fouilles à Tell el-Fârᶜah, près Naplouse," *RB* 56, 1949, pp. 102–138, figs. 1–13, pls. 1–10; G. E. Wright, "The Excavation at Tell el-Farᶜah," *BA* 12, 1949, pp. 66–68; R. deVaux, "La troisième Campagne de Fouilles à Tell el-Fârᶜah, près Naplouse," *RB* 58, 1951, pp. 393–430, figs. 1–13, pls. 5–19; *id.*, "La troisième Campagne de Fouilles à Tell el-Farᶜah près Naplouse," *RB* 58, 1951, pp. 566–590, figs. 1–14, pls. 20–27; J. Gray, "Tell el-Farᶜa by Nablus: A 'Mother' in Ancient Israel," *PEQ* 1952, pp. 110–113; R. deVaux, "La quatrième Campagne de Fouilles à Tell el-Fârᶜah, près Naplouse," *RB* 59, 1952, pp. 551–583, figs. 1–12, pls. 10–20; *id.*, "Les Fouilles de Tell el-Fârᶜah, près Naplouse," *RB* 62, 1955, pp. 541–589, figs., pls. 6–18; *id.*, "The Excavations at Tell el-Fârᶜah and the Site of Ancient Tirzah," *PEQ* 1956, pp. 125–140, pls. 23–26; *id.*, "Les Fouilles de Tell el-Fârᶜah, près Naplouse," *RB* 64, 1957, pp. 552–580, figs., pls. 6–13; *id.*, "Tell el-Fârᶜah," *RB* 67, 1960, pp. 245–247, pl. 16; *id.*, "Les Fouilles de Tell el-Fârᶜah," *RB* 68, 1961, pp. 557–592, figs. 1–4, pls. 31–46; *id.*, "Les Fouilles de Tell el-Fârᶜah," *RB* 69, 1962, pp. 212–253, figs. 1–7, pls. 16–38; G. E. Wright, *Biblical Archaeology*, 1962, p. 152; R. deVaux, "Tirzah," in D. W. Thomas, ed., *AOTS*, 1967, pp. 371–383, figs. 8–9, pl. 16; J. L. Huot, "Typologie et Chronologie Relative de la Céramique du Bronze Ancien a Tell el-Fârᶜah," *RB* 74, 1967, pp. 517–554, figs. 1–9; J. B. Pritchard, ed., *ANEP*, 1969, nos. 786, 865; P. W. Lapp, *Biblical Archaeology and History*, 1969, pp. 74, 79, 117–118, pl. 17; *id.*, "Tell el-Farᶜah," *NEATC*, 1970, pp. 109–110, 111, 113, 127, 128; K. M. Kenyon, *Archaeology in the Holy Land*, 1970, pp. 310, 335–336, 338; R. deVaux, "Tel el-Farᶜa," *EAEHL*. 1970. pp. 602–607, figs. (Hebrew).

Tell el-Far'ah (S), Sharuḥen

Excavated by M. W. F. Petrie (as Beth-pelet) for the British School of Archaeology in Egypt, 1927–1929.

W. M. F. Petrie *et al.*, *Beth-Pelet* I, 1930, II, 1932; G. E. Wright, "Philistine Coffins and Mercenaries," *BA* 22, 1959, pp. 54–66, figs. 1–10; W. F. Albright, *The Archaeology of Palestine*, 1960, pp. 39, 87; R. Gofna, "Iron Age I Ḥaṣerim in Southern Philistia," *ᶜAtiqot* 3, 1966, pp. 44–51, figs. 1–4, pl. 11; J. Waldbaum, "Philistine Tombs at Tell Fara and their Aegean Prototypes," *AJA* 70, 1966, pp. 331–340, figs. 1–16; J. B. Pritchard, ed., *ANEP*, 1969, nos. 137, 140, 820; W. H. Stiebing, Jr., "Another Look at the Origins of the Philistine Tombs at Tell el-Farᶜah (S)," *AJA* 74, 1970, pp. 139–143, figs. 1–4; K. M. Kenyon, *Archaeology in the Holy Land*, 1970, pp. 180, 225, 301, 309–310; Y. Israeli, "Tel Sharuhen," *EAEHL*, 1970, pp. 551–556, figs. (Hebrew); R. Gofna, "Ḥaṣerim near Sharuḥen," *EAEHL*, 1970, p. 557, fig. (Hebrew).

Tell el-Fukhar, see Acre

Tell el-Fûl, see Gibeah

Tell el-Ḥammeh, see Ḥammat-Gader

Tell el-Ḥesi

Excavated by W. M. F. Petrie and F. J. Bliss (as Lachish) for the Palestine Exploration Fund, 1890–1893.

W. M. F. Petrie, *Tell el-Ḥesy* (Lachish), 1891; F. J. Bliss, "Report on the Excavations at Tell el-Ḥesy . . . 1891," *PEFQS* 1892, pp. 36–38, 1 fig.; pp. 95–113, 16 figs., pls. 3–4; pp. 192–196; W. M. F. Petrie, "Notes on the Results at Tell el-Ḥesy," *PEFQS* 1892, pp. 114–115; F. J. Bliss, *A Mound of many Cities, Tell el-Ḥesy Excavated*, 1894; J. H. Zink, "Tell el-Ḥesy," in C. F. Pfeiffer, *The Biblical World*, 1966, pp. 566–569; O. Tufnell, "The Pottery from the Royal Tombs I–III at Byblos," *Berytus* 18, 1969, pp. 5–33, figs. 1–7; R. Amiran, "Tel-Ḥesi," *EAEHL*, 1970, pp. 584–586, figs. (Hebrew).

Excavated by J. Worrell for Oberlin College, Hartford Seminary Foundation, Albright Institute of Archaeological Research, 1970–1971.

Tell ʿEli

Excavated by M. W. Prausnitz for the Department of Antiquities, Israel, 1955–1959.

M. W. Prausnitz, "Alumoth," *IEJ* 5, 1955, p. 271; *id.*, "Alumoth," *IEJ* 7, 1957, pp. 263–264; *id.*, "The First Agricultural Settlements in Galilee," *IEJ* 9, 1959, pp. 166–174, figs. 1–4; *id.*, "Tell ᶜEli," *RB* 67, 1960, pp. 389–390, pl. 23a; *id.*, "Tell ᶜEli (Khirbet esh-Sheikh ᶜAli)," *IEJ* 10, 1960, pp. 119–120; E. Anati, *Palestine Before the Hebrews*, 1963, pp. 270, 273; M. W. Prausnitz, "Tel-ᶜEli," *EAEHL*, 1970, p. 594 (Hebrew).

Tell el-Ḥusn, see Beth-shan

Tell el-Ḥusn, see Ḥusn-el

Tell el-Jerisheh

Excavated by J. Ory for the Department of Antiquities, Palestine, 1925.

S. Tolkowsky, "Canaanite Tombs near Jaffa," *JPOS* 6, 1926, pp. 70–74; J. Ory, "A Bronze-Age Necropolis at Ramath Gan, near Tell el-Jerisheh (Jaffa District)," *Palestine Museum Bulletin* 2, 1926, pp. 7–9, pls. 3b, 4; S. A. Cook, "Notes on Recent Excavations," *PEFQS* 1929, pp. 114–115.

Excavated by E. L. Sukenik, for the Hebrew University, 1927, 1934, 1936, 1940.

E. L. Sukenik, "Tell el-Jerishe," *QDAP* 4, 1935, pp. 208–209; *id.*, "Tell el-Jerishe," *QDAP* 6, 1937, p. 225; J. Ory, "A Late Bronze Age Tomb at Tell Jerishe," *QDAP* 10, 1944, pp. 55–57, pls. 12–13; E. L. Sukenik, "Tell Jerishe," *QDAP* 10, 1944, pp. 198–199; K. M. Kenyon, *Amorites and Canaanites*, 1966, p. 67; M. Pearlman, Y. Yannai, *Historical Sites in Israel*, 1969, pp. 145–146; N. Avigad, "Tel Grisa," *EAEHL*, 1970, pp. 576–578, figs. (Hebrew).

Tell el-Jurn, see ʿEn Gedi

Tell el-Kheleifeh

F. Frank, "Aus der ᶜArabah, I: Tell el-chlēfi," *ZDPV* 57, 1934, pp. 243–245, pls. 41–44; N. Glueck, *AASOR* 15, 1935, pp. 41, 45–48, 51; *id.*, "Ezion-geber," *BASOR* 65, 1937, pp. 12–14.

Excavated by N. Glueck (as Ezion-geber: Elath) for the American Schools of Oriental Research, American Philosophical Society, Smithsonian Institution and the Department of Antiquities, Transjordan, 1938–1940.

N. Glueck, "Ezion geber: Solomon's Naval Base on the Red Sea," *BA* 1, 1938, pp. 13–16, figs. 1–5; *id.*, "The First Campaign at Tell el-Kheleifeh," *BASOR* 71, 1938, pp. 3–17, figs. 1–7; *id.*, "The Topography and History of Ezion-geber and Elath," *BASOR* 72, 1938, pp. 2–13, figs. 1–3; *id.*, "The Second Campaign at Tell el-Kheleifeh

(Ezion-geber: Elath)," *BASOR* 75, 1939, pp. 8–22, figs. 1–5; *id.*, "Ezion-geber: Elath, the Gateway to Arabia," *BA* 2, 1939, pp. 37–41, figs. 1–4; *id.*, "Ezion-geber," *AASOR* 18–19, 1939, pp. 3–7; *id.*, "The Third Season at Tell el-Kheleifeh," *BASOR* 79, 1940, pp. 2–18, figs. 1–10; *id.*, "Ostraca from Elath," *BASOR* 80, 1940, pp. 3–10, figs. 1–5; *id.*, "Ostraca from Elath," *BASOR* 82, 1941, pp. 3–11, figs. 1–6; W. F. Albright, "Ostracon No. 6043 from Ezion-geber," *BASOR* 82, 1941, pp. 11–15; C. C. Torrey, "On the Ostraca from Elath (Bulletin No. 80)," *BASOR* 82, 1941, pp. 15–16; *id.*, "A Synagogue at Elath?" *BASOR* 84, 1941, pp. 4–5; F. Rosenthal, "The Script of Ostracon No. 6043 from Ezion-geber," *BASOR* 85, 1942, pp. 8–9, fig. 1; N. Glueck, "The Excavations of Solomon's Seaport: Ezion-geber," *Smithsonian Report for 1941*, 1942, pp. 453–478, pls. 1–14; N. Avigad, "The Jotham Seal from Elath," *BASOR* 163, 1961, pp. 18–22, figs. 1–5; B. Rothenberg, "Ancient Copper Industries in the Western Arabah," *PEQ* 1962, pp. 5–65, figs. 1–18, pls. 1–16; N. Glueck, "Ezion-geber," *BA* 28, 1965, pp. 70–87, figs. 1–11; *id.*, "Further Explorations in the Negev," *BASOR* 179, 1965, pp. 6–29, figs. 1–10, esp. pp. 17–18; V. R. Gold, "Ezion-geber," in C. F. Pfeiffer, ed., *The Biblical World*, 1966, pp. 233–237, fig.; N. Glueck, "Some Edomite Pottery from Tell el-Kheleifeh, Parts I, II," *BASOR* 188, 1967, pp. 8–38, 11 figs.; *id.*, "Transjordan," in D. W. Thomas, ed., *AOTS*, 1967, pp. 428–453, fig. 12, pl. 19; *id.*, "Tell el-Kheleifeh," *BTS* 102, 1968, pp. 1–2, 6–16, 21, figs.; *id.*, *Rivers in the Desert*, 1968, pp. 158–168, figs. 10, 22–23; *id.*, "Some Ezion-geber: Elath Iron II Pottery," *EI* 9, 1969, pp. 51–59, figs. 1–3, pls. 6–12; *id.*, *The Other Side of the Jordan*, 1970, pp. 106–137, figs. 10, 11, 47–70; G. E. Wright, *NEATC*, 1970, p. 31; J. B. Pritchard, *NEATC*, 1970, p. 275, n. 1; E. K. Vogel, "Bibliography of Nelson Glueck," *NEATC*, 1970, pp. 382–394; R. Amiran, *Ancient Pottery of the Holy Land*, 1970, pp. 300–301; N. Glueck, "Tel-el-Khleife," *EAEHL*, 1970, pp. 581–583, figs. (Hebrew); *id.*, "Iron II Kenite and Edomite Pottery," *Perspective* 12:1–2, 1971, pp. 45–56, figs. 1–7; *id.*, "Tell el-Kheleifeh Inscriptions," in H. Goedicke, ed., *Near Eastern Studies in Honor of William Foxwell Albright*, 1971, pp. 225–242, pls. 1–14.

Tell el-Kudadi, Tell esh-Shuni

Fortress cleared by P. L. O. Guy, excavated by E. L. Sukenik, for the Department of Antiquities, Palestine, and the Hebrew University, 1937–1938, 1944–1945.

E. L. Sukenik, "Tell esh-Shuni (Tell el-Kudadi)," *QDAP* 8, 1939, pp. 167–168; *id.*, "Tell esh-Shuni," *QDAP* 11, 1945, p. 118.

Excavated by J. Kaplan for the Department of Antiquities, Israel, 1969.

J. Kaplan, "Tell Kedadi (esh-Shuni), 1969," *BMH* 12, 1970, p. 12, pl. 1a; N. Avigad, "Tel Kudadi," *EAEHL*, 1970, p. 587, fig. (Hebrew).

Tell el-Mutesellim, see Megiddo

Tell el'Oreimeh, see Kinneret

Tell el-Qadi, see Dan

Tell el-Qasîle

Excavated by B. Maisler (Mazar) for the Hebrew University and the Israel Exploration Society, 1948–1950.

B. Maisler, "Excavations at Tell Qasîle," *Bulletin of the Jewish Palestine Exploration Society* 15, 1949, pp. 8–18, 1 fig., pls. 1–5 (Hebrew); *id.*, "The Excavations at

Tell Qasîle," *IEJ* 1, 1950–51, pp. 61–76, figs. 1–3, pls. 18–19; *id.*, "The Excavations at Tell Qasîle," *IEJ* 1, 1950–51, pp. 125–140, figs. 1–8, pls. 25–30; *id.*, "The Excavations at Tell Qasîle," *IEJ* 1, 1950–51, pp. 194–218, figs. 1–14, pls. 34–40; *id.*, "The Excavations at Tell Qasîle," *EI* 1, 1951, pp. 45–80 (Hebrew); *id.*, "The Excavations at Tell el-Qasîle," *BA* 14, 1951, pp. 43–49, figs. 7–10; *id.*, "Two Hebrew Ostraca from Tell Qasile," *JNES* 10, 1951, pp. 265–267, pls. 11–12; *id.*, "A Philistine Seal from Tell Qasîle," *Yediot* 31, 1967, pp. 64–67, 2 figs., pls. 4–5 (Hebrew); J. B. Pritchard, ed., *ANEP*, 1969, no. 134; T. Dothan, I. Dunayevsky, "Tel-el-Qasile," *EAEHL*, 1970, pp. 610–614, figs. (Hebrew).

Tell el-Qedah, see Hazor

Tell en-Naṣbeh

Excavated by W. F. Badè and J. C. Wampler for the Palestine Institute of the Pacific School of Religion and the American Schools of Oriental Research, 1926–1927, 1929, 1932, 1935.

W. F. Badè, "The Excavations at Tell en-Naṣbeh," *PEFQS* 1927, pp. 7–13, pls. 1–2; E. Grant, "Tell en-Naṣbeh Expedition of the Pacific School of Religion," *PEFQS* 1927, pp. 159–161; W. F. Badè, *Excavations at Tell en-Naṣbeh, 1926 and 1927, A Preliminary Report*, 1928; *id.*, "The Tell en-Naṣbeh Excavations of 1929, A Preliminary Report," *PEFQS* 1930, pp. 8–19, pls. 1–3; Bibliography, "Tall en Nasba," *QDAP* 1, 1932, pp. 147, 191; J. P. Naish, "Tell en-Naṣbeh," *PEFQS* 1932, pp. 204–209; W. F. Badè, *A Manual of Excavation in the Near East*, 1934; C. C. McCown, J. C. Wampler, *Tell en-Naṣbeh*, 2 vols., 1947; G. E. Wright, "Tell en-Naṣbeh," *BA* 10, 1947, pp. 69–77, figs. 1–4; *id.*, Review of C. C. McCown and J. C. Wampler, *Tell en-Naṣbeh*, 1947 in *AJA* 52, 1948, pp. 470–472; O. Tufnell, Review of C. C. McCown and J. C. Wampler, *Tell en-Naṣbeh*, 1947 in *PEFQS* 1948, pp. 145–150; N. Avigad, "New Light on the MṢH Seal Impressions," *IEJ* 8, 1958, pp. 113–119, fig. 1, pl. 24; K. Branigan, "The Four-Room Buildings of Tell en-Naṣbeh," *IEJ* 16, 1966, pp. 206–208; J. H. Zink, "Tell en-Naṣbeh," in C. F. Pfeiffer, ed., *The Biblical World*, 1966, pp. 569–571, fig.; D. Diringer, "Mizpah," in D. W. Thomas, ed., *AOTS*, 1967, pp. 329–342; J. B. Pritchard, ed., *ANEP*, 1969, nos. 277, 716–717, 725; N. Avigad, "A Group of Hebrew Seals," *EI* 9, 1969, pp. 1–9, pls. 1–2 (Hebrew); F. M. Cross, Jr., "Two Notes on Palestinian Inscriptions of the Persian Age," *BASOR* 193, 1969, pp. 19–24, figs. 1–2; M. Broshi, "Mitspa," *EAEHL*, 1970, p. 391–394, figs. (Hebrew).

Tell er-Râs, see Mount Gerizim

Tell er-Rumeith, Ramoth-gilead

P. W. Lapp, "Tell er-Rumeith," *RB* 70, 1963, pp. 406–411; *id.*, "Tell er-Rumeith," *BA* 26, 1963, p. 128, fig. 8, sounding.

Excavated by P. W. Lapp, H. M. Jamieson, Jr., for the Pittsburgh Theological Seminary, American Schools of Oriental Research, Department of Antiquities, Jordan, 1967.

P. W. Lapp, "Tell er-Rumeith," *RB* 75, 1968, pp. 98–105, pls. 9–11; M. Ottosson, *Gilead, Tradition and History*, 1969, pp. 22, 32, 34, 184, 217; P. W. Lapp, *Biblical Archaeology and History*, 1969, pp. 78, 118–119, 127, n. 32, pl. 23; B. Oded, "Observations on Methods of Assyrian Rule in Transjordania after the Palestinian Campaign of Tiglath-pileser III," *JNES* 29, 1970, pp. 177–186.

Tell esh-Sheikh Aḥmed el-'Areini

Excavated by S. Yeivin for the Department of Antiquities, Israel, 1956–1961.

S. Yeivin, "Gath," *RB* 67, 1960, pp. 391–394, pl. 24a; *id.*, "Early Contacts Between Canaan and Egypt," *IEJ* 10, 1960, pp. 193–203, figs. 1–4, pls. 23–24; *id.*, *First Preliminary Report on the Excavations at Tel Gat*, 1961; A. F. Rainey, "Gath of the Philistines," *CNI* 17:2–3, 1966, pp. 30–38, fig. 1, pl. 4:3; 17:4, 1966, pp. 23–34, fig. 1; *id.*, "Tell Sheikh el-Areini," in C. F. Pfeiffer, *The Biblical World*, 1966, pp. 573–574; P. W. Lapp, "Palestine in the Early Bronze Age," *NEATC*, 1970, pp. 101–131; S. Yeivin, "Tel-ᶜErani," *EAEHL*, 1970, pp. 595–600, figs. (Hebrew).

Tell esh-Shuneh

Excavated by H. deContenson for the Department of Antiquities, Jordan, 1953.

H. deContenson, "Three Soundings in the Jordan Valley," *ADAJ* 4–5, 1960, pp. 12–98, figs. 1–36; *id.*, "Remarques sur le chalcolithique recent de Tell esh-Shuna," *RB* 68, 1961, pp. 546–556, fig. 1, pl. 30; *id.*, "La chronologie relative du Niveau le plus Ancien de Tell esh-Shuna (Jordanie) d'après les Découvertes récentes," *Mélanges de l'Université Saint Joseph*, 37, 1961, pp. 57–77, fig.; J. Mellaart, "Preliminary Report of the Archaeological Survey in the Yarmouk and Jordan Valley," *ADAJ* 6–7, 1962, pp. 126–158, pls. 24–33, esp. pp. 129, 131–133; H. deContenson, "The Central Jordan Valley," *EAEHL*, 1970, pp. 460–461, 1 fig. (Hebrew).

Tell esh-Shuni, see Tell el-Kudadi

Tell eṣ-Ṣâfi

Excavated by F. J. Bliss and R. A. S. Macalister for the Palestine Exploration Fund, 1899.

F. J. Bliss, "First Report on the Excavations at Tell es-Sâfi," *PEFQS* 1899, pp. 183–199, 2 figs., 1 pl.; *id.*, "Second Report on the Excavations at Tell eṣ-Ṣâfi," *PEFQS* 1899, pp. 317–333, 8 figs., 11 pls.; *id.*, "Third Report on the Excavations at Tell eṣ-Ṣâfi," *PEFQS* 1900, pp. 16–29, figs. 1–7; R. A. S. Macalister, "The Rock-Cuttings of Tell eṣ-Ṣâfi," *PEFQS* 1900, pp. 29–39, figs. 1–11; F. J. Bliss, R. A. S. Macalister, *Excavations in Palestine During the Years 1898–1900*, 1902, pp. 1–43, figs. 8–21; W. F. Albright, *Archaeology and the Religion of Israel*, 1969, pp. 62–63, 190, n. 94; E. Stern, "Tel-Tsafit," *EAEHL*, 1970, pp. 608–610, figs. (Hebrew).

Tell es-Sa'idiyeh, Zarethan

Excavated by J. B. Pritchard for the University Museum of the University of Pennsylvania, Department of Antiquities, Jordan, 1964–1967.

N. Glueck, "Three Israelite Towns in the Jordan Valley: Zarethan, Succoth, Zaphon," *BASOR* 90, 1943, pp. 2–23; J. B. Pritchard, Excavating a Biblical Site in Jordan: Joshua's and Solomon's Zarethan Identified," *ILN*, March 28, 1964, pp. 487–490, figs. 1–15; *id.*, "Reconnaissance in Jordan," *Expedition* 6:2, 1964, pp. 3–9, figs.; *id.*, "Two Tombs and a Tunnel in the Jordan Valley: Discoveries at the Biblical Zarethan," *Expedition* 6:4, 1964, pp. 2–9, figs.; *id.*, "Excavations at Tell es-Saᶜidiyeh," *ADAJ* 8–9, 1964, pp. 95–98; *id.*, "Sarthan," *BTS* 75, 1965, pp. 6–15, figs.; *id.*, "Excavations at Tell es-Saᶜidiyeh," *Archaeology* 18, 1965, pp. 292–294, figs.; *id.*, "A Cosmopolitan Culture of the Late Bronze Age," *Expedition* 7:4, 1965, pp. 26–33, figs.; *id.*, "The Three Ages of Biblical Zarethan," *ILN*, July 2, 1966, pp. 25–27, figs. 1–11; *id.*, "Tell es-Saᶜidiyeh, Jordan," *Archaeology* 19, 1966, pp. 289–290, figs.; *id.*, "An Eighth Century Traveller," *Expedition* 10:2, 1968, pp. 26–29, figs.; *id.*, "The Palace at Tell es-Saᶜidiyeh," *Expedition* 11:1, 1968, pp. 20–22, figs.; J. E. Huesman, "Tell es-Saᶜidiyeh," *RB* 75, 1968, pp. 236–238; N. Glueck, *The River Jordan*, 1968, pp. 67, 162–163, figs.; J. B. Pritchard, ed., *ANEP*, 1969, nos. 774, 784, 785, 840, 859, 860, 877; R. Hestrin, "Excavations at Tell es-Saᶜidiye," *Qadmoniot* 2, 1969, pp. 92–95, figs. (Hebrew).

Tell es-Sa'idiyeh el-Tahta

N. Glueck, *AASOR* 25–28, 1951, pp. 275–276, 292–295, 432, 435.

Excavated by H. deContenson for the Department of Antiquities, Jordan, 1953.

H. deContenson, "Three Soundings in the Jordan Valley," *ADAJ* 4–5, 1960, pp. 12–98, figs. 1–36; *id.*, "Tell es-Saᶜidiyeh el-Tahta," *ADAJ* 8–9, 1964, p. 37; *id.*, "The Central Jordan Valley," *EAEHL*, 1970, pp. 460–461, 1 fig. (Hebrew).

Tell es-Sultan, see Jericho

Tell eṭ-Ṭaba'iq, see Rosh ha-Niqra

Tell ez-Zakariya, Azekah

Excavated by F. J. Bliss and R. A. S. Macalister for the Palestine Exploration Fund, 1898–1899.

F. J. Bliss, "First Report on the Excavations at Tell Zakariya," *PEFQS* 1899, pp. 10–25, figs. 1–3, pl. 1; R. A. S. Macalister, "The Rock-Cuttings of Tell Zakariya," *PEFQS* 1899, pp. 25–36; F. J. Bliss, "Second Report on the Excavations at Tell Zakariya," *PEFQS* 1899, pp. 89–111, figs. 1–2, pls. 1–9; *id.*, "Third Report on the Excavations at Tell Zakariya," *PEFQS* 1899, pp. 170–187, fig. 1, pls. 1–6; C. W. Wilson, "A Visit to Tell Zakariya," *PEFQS* 1899, pp. 334–338, pl. 1a; F. J. Bliss, "Fourth Report on the Excavations at Tell Zakariya," *PEFQS* 1900, pp. 7–16, fig. 1, pls. 1–4; R. A. S. Macalister, "Further Notes on the Rock-Cuttings of Tell Zakariya," *PEFQS* 1900, pp. 39–53, pls. 1–4; F. J. Bliss, R. A. S. Macalister, *Excavations in Palestine*, 1902, pp. 12–27, figs. 3–7, pls. 1–6; D. C. Baramki, "An Early Iron Age Tomb at eẓ-Ẓāhiriye," *QDAP* 4, 1934, pp. 109–110, fig. 1, pls. 61–64; E. Stern, "ᶜAzeqa," *EAEHL*, 1970, pp. 431–433, fig. (Hebrew).

Tell Gath, see Tell esh-Sheikh Aḥmed el-'Areini

Tell Ḥalif

Excavated by A. Biran and R. Gophna for the Department of Antiquities and Museums, Israel, 1965.

A. Biran and R. Gophna, "Tell Ḥalif," *IEJ* 15, 1965, p. 255; *id.*, "Tel Halif," *RB* 74, 1967, pp. 77–78, pl. 16a; *id.*, "An Iron Age Burial Cave at Tel Ḥalif," *EI* 9, 1969, pp. 29–39, pls. 4–6 (Hebrew); A. Biran, R. Giveon, R. Gophna, "An Iron Age Burial Cave at Tell Ḥalif," *IEJ* 20, 1970, pp. 151–169, figs. 1–13, pls. 36–38.

Tell Hum, see Capernaum

Tell Iktanu

N. Glueck, *AASOR* 25–28, 1951, pp. 394–398; H. deContenson, "The 1953 Survey in the Yarmuk and Jordan Valleys," *ADAJ* 8–9, 1964, pp. 30–46, pls. 7–20, esp. pp. 39–40 and pls. 10:9–12, 20:1.

Excavated by K. Wright for the British School of Archaeology in Jerusalem and the Department of Antiquities, Jordan, 1968.

P. W. Lapp, *Biblical Archaeology and History*, 1969, pp. 73, 117, pl. 13.

Tell Isdar

Excavated by M. Kochavi for the Department of Antiquities, Israel, 1963–1964.

M. Kochavi, "Tel Isdar," *IEJ* 14, 1964, pp. 111–112; A. Biran, "Tell Isdar," *CNI* 15:2–3, 1964, pp. 21–22, pl. 4:1; M. Kochavi, "Tel Isdar," *RB* 72, 1965, pp. 560–561, pl. 29b–c; *id.*, "Excavations at Tel Esdar," *ʿAtiqot* 5, 1969, pp. 14–48, figs. 1–20, pls. 4–9 (Hebrew).

Tell Jemmeh, Yurza

W. J. Phythian-Adams, "Report on Soundings at Tell Jemmeh," *PEFQS* 1923, pp. 140–146, figs. 1–2, pls. 1–4.

Excavated, as Gerar, by W. M. F. Petrie for the British School of Archaeology in Egypt, 1926–1927.

W. M. F. Petrie, "Gerar," *PEFQS* 1927, pp. 129–140; *id.*, *Gerar*, 1928; B. Maisler, "Yurza, the Identification of Tell Jemmeh," *PEQ* 1952, pp. 48–51; Y. Aharoni, "The Land of Gerar," *IEJ* 6, 1956, pp. 26–32, fig. 1; G. E. Wright, "Philistine Coffins and Mercenaries," *BA* 22, 1959, pp. 54–66, figs. 1–10.

Excavated by G. W. Van Beek for the Smithsonian Institution, 1970–1971.

G. W. Van Beek, "Tell Gamma," *IEJ* 20, 1970, p. 230; R. Amiran, "Tel Jemme," *EAEHL*, 1970, pp. 574–576, figs. (Hebrew).

Tell Makmish, see Makmish

Tell Malḥata

Excavated by M. Kochavi for the Department of Antiquities, Israel, 1968.

M. Kochavi, "Tel Malḥata," *CNI* 19:3–4, 1968, pp. 45–46; *id.*, "The First Season of Excavations at Tel Malḥata," *Qadmoniot* 3, 1970, pp. 22–24, figs. (Hebrew).

Tell Megadim

Excavated by M. Broshi for the Department of Antiquities, Israel, Israel Exploration Society and Boston College, 1967–1969.

M. Broshi, "Tel Megadim," *IEJ* 17, 1967, pp. 277–278; A. Biran, "Tel Megadim," *CNI* 19:3–4, 1968, pp. 41–42, pl. 5a; M. Broshi, "Tel Megadim," *RB* 76, 1969, pp. 413–414, pls. 16b, 17; *id.*, "Tel Megadim," *IEJ* 19, 1969, p. 248; A. Biran, "Tel Megadim," *CNI* 20:3–4, 1969, p. 43; M. Broshi, "A Phoenician City and Roman-Byzantine Road-Station," *Qadmoniot* 2, 1969, pp. 124–126, figs. (Hebrew); *id.*, "Tell Megadim," *RB* 77, 1970, pp. 387–388.

Tell Mor, see Ashdod

Tell Nagila, Tell en-Najila

S. Bülow, R. A. Mitchell, "An Iron Age II Fortress on Tel Nagila," *IEJ* 11, 1961, pp. 101–110, figs. 1–5, pls. 26–27.

Excavated by R. A. Mitchell, R. Amiran, A. Eitan, for the Institute for Mediterranean Studies, Israel Exploration Society, Department of Antiquities, Israel, 1962–1963.

R. Amiran, "A Preliminary Note on the First Season of Excavations at Tell Nagila, 1962," *CNI* 13:3–4, 1962, pp. 24–26, pls. 1–4; R. Amiran, A. Eitan, "Tel Nagila," *IEJ* 13, 1963, pp. 143–144; pp. 333–334; R. Amiran, "Tell Nagila," *RB* 70, 1963, pp. 568–569; A. Biran, "Tell Nagila," *CNI* 15:2–3, 1964, pp. 22–23; R. Amiran, "Tell Nagila," *RB* 71, 1964, pp. 396–399; R. Amiran, A. Eitan, "A Krater of Bichrome Ware from Tel Nagila," *IEJ* 14, 1964, pp. 219–231, figs. 1–9, pls. 45–46; *id.*, "Two Seasons of Excavations at Tel Nagila," *Yediot* 28, 1964, pp. 193–203, 3 figs., pls. 18–19 (Hebrew); *id.*, "A Canaanite-Hyksos City at Tell Nagila," *Archaeology* 18, 1965, pp. 113–123, 20 figs.; *id.*, "A Canaanite-Hyksos City at Tell Nagila," *ADHL*, 1967, pp. 41–48, figs.; *id.*, "Tel Nagila," *EAEHL*, 1970, pp. 589–592, figs. (Hebrew).

Tell Poleg

Excavated by R. Gophna for the Department of Antiquities, Israel, 1959, 1962.

R. Gophna, "Tel Poleg," *IEJ* 14, 1964, pp. 109–111; A. Biran, "Tel Poleg," *CNI* 16:4, 1965, pp. 15–16; R. Gophna, "Tell Poleg," *RB* 72, 1965, pp. 552–553; P. J. Parr, "Tell Poleg," *ZDPV* 84, 1968, p. 27; R. Gophna, "Ichthyomorphic Vessels from Tel Poleg," *BMH* 11, 1969, pp. 43–45, 1 fig., pl. 9; *id.*, "Tel Poleg," *EAEHL*, 1970, p. 601, fig. (Hebrew).

Tell Râs el-ʻAin, see Apheq

Tell Sandahannah, Marissa, Beit Jibrin, Eleutheropolis

C. Clermont-Ganneau, *Archaeological Researches in Palestine*, 2, 1896, pp. 440–451, figs.

Beit Jibrin excavated by R. A. S. Macalister and F. J. Bliss for the Palestine Exploration Fund, 1900.

F. J. Bliss, "Report on the Excavations at Tell Sandahannah," *PEFQS* 1900, pp. 319–338, figs., plan; R. A. S. Macalister, "Preliminary Observations on the Rock-Cuttings of Tell Sandahannah," *PEFQS* 1900, pp. 338–341, 2 pls.; *id.*, "'Es-Sûk,' Tell Sandahannah," *PEFQS* 1901, pp. 11–19, fig. 1, pls. 1–2; C. Clermont-Ganneau, "Royal Ptolemaic Greek Inscriptions and Magic Lead Figures from Tell Sandahannah," *PEFQS* 1901, pp. 54–58, 3 figs.; F. J. Bliss, "The Excavations at Tell Sandahannah," *Excavations in Palestine*, 1902, pp. 52–61, figs. 25–29, pls.; R. Wünch, "The Limestone Inscriptions of Tell Sandahannah," in F. J. Bliss, *Excavations in Palestine*, 1902, pp. 158–187, 41 figs., pls. 15–19; J. Peters, H. Thiersch, "The Necropolis of Mareshah," *PEFQS* 1902, pp. 393–397; *id.*, *Painted Tombs in the Necropolis of Marissa*, 1905; W. J. Moulton, "An Inscribed Tomb at Beit Jibrin," *AJA* 19, 1915, pp. 63–70, 3 figs., 5 pls.

Excavations conducted at Beit Jibrin by the École Biblique et Archéologique Française, 1921–1924.

W. J. Moulton, "A Painted Christian Tomb at Beit Jibrin," *AASOR* 2–3, 1923, pp. 95–102, figs. 1–6, front., pls. 1–6, front., pls. 1–4; E. W. G. Masterman, "Beit

Jibrin and Tell Sandahannah," *PEFQS* 1926, pp. 176–185; E. L. Sukenik, "A Synagogue Inscription from Beit Jibrin," *JPOS* 10, 1930, pp. 76–78, pl. 6; J. H. Iliffe, "Greek and Latin Inscriptions in the Museum," *QDAP* 2, 1933, pp. 121–122; E. L. Sukenik, "Beit Jibrin," *Ancient Synagogues in Palestine and Greece*, 1934, p. 72; C. Watzinger, *Denkmäler Palästinas*, 2, 1935, pp. 12, 17–20; *id.*, "Beit Jibrin," *The Ancient Synagogue of el-Hammeh*, 1935, pp. 42, 46, 61; W. F. Albright, "Two Cressets from Marissa and the Pillars of Jachin and Boaz," *BASOR* 85, 1942, pp. 18–27, figs. 1–10; E. R. Goodenough, "Marissa," *Symbols* 1, 1953, pp. 65–75, 80, 127, 142–144, 212; W. F. Albright, *The Archaeology of Palestine*, 1960, pp. 152–153, fig. 51.

An archaeological survey was conducted at Marissa by E. Oren for the Department of Antiquities, Israel, 1961–1963.

Y. Ben-Arieh, "Caves and Ruins in the Beth Govrin Area," *IEJ* 12, 1962, pp. 47–61, figs. 1–3, pls. 7–8; B. Couroyer, "Inscription Coufique de Beit Gibrin," *RB* 71, 1964, pp. 73–79, pl. 3; E. Oren, "The Caves of the Palestinian Shephelah," *Archaeology* 18, 1965, pp. 218–224, figs.; E. Kitzinger, *Israeli Mosaics of the Byzantine Period*, 1965, pp. 7, 8, 16, 19, 23, pls. 4, 5; M. Avi-Yonah, "A Reappraisal of the Tell Sandaḥannah Statuette," *PEQ* 1967, pp. 42–44, fig. 1, pl. 7; E. Oren, "The 'Herodian Doves' in the Light of Recent Archaeological Discoveries," *PEQ* 1968, pp. 56–61, figs. 1–5, pls. 20–21; W. F. Albright, *Archaeology and the Religion of Israel*, 1969, pp. 140–143; J. Finegan, *The Archeology of the New Testament*, 1969, pp. 188–191, figs. 213–217; S. J. Saller, *A Revised Catalogue of the Ancient Synagogues of the Holy Land*, 1969, p. 18; M. Avi-Yonah, "Bet-Guvrin," *EAEHL*, 1970, pp. 39–42, figs. (Hebrew); *id.*, "Maresha," *EAEHL*, 1970, pp. 398–403, figs. (Hebrew).

Tell Ṣippor, Tell eṭ-Ṭuyur

Excavated by A. Biran, O. Negbi for the Department of Antiquities, Israel, 1963–1965.

L. Y. Rahmani, "A Hoard of Alexander Coins," *EI* 7, 1964, pp. 33–38, 2 figs., pls. 6–8; A. Biran, O. Negbi, "Tell Ṣippor," *RB* 71, 1964, pp. 399–400, pl. 20a, b; O. Negbi, "A Contribution of Mineralogy and Palaeontology to an Archaeological Study of Terracottas," *IEJ* 14, 1964, pp. 187–189, pls. 42–43; A. Biran, O. Negbi, "Tel Ṣippor," *IEJ* 14, 1964, pp. 284–285; *id.*, "Tell Ṣippor," *IEJ* 15, 1965, pp. 255–256; *id.*, "Tell Ṣippor," *CNI* 15:2–3, 1964, pp. 23–24, pl. 5:1–2; *id.*, "Tel Sippor," *RB* 72, 1965, pp. 555–556, pl. 28d; *id.*, "Tell Ṣippor," *CNI* 16:4, 1965, pp. 16–17, pl. 2; *id.*, "The Stratigraphical Sequence of Tell Ṣippor," *IEJ* 16, 1966, pp. 160–173, figs. 1–7, pls. 17b–23; O. Negbi, "A Deposit of Terracottas and Statuettes from Tel Ṣippor," *ʿAtiqot* 6, 1966, pp. 1–27, pls. 1–16; A. Biran, O. Negbi, "Tel Ṣippor," *RB* 74, 1967, pp. 76–77.

Tell Ta'anach, see Ta'anach

Tell Zeror

Excavated by K. Ohata and M. Kochavi for The Society for Near Eastern Studies in Japan, 1964–1966.

K. Ohata, M. Kochavi, "Tel Zeror," *IEJ* 14, 1964, pp. 283–284; K. Ohata, ed., *Tel Zeror I: Preliminary Report, First Season 1964*, 1966; K. Ohata, M. Kochavi, "Tel Zeror," *CNI* 16:3, 1965, pp. 16–17, pl. 4; M. Kochavi, "Tel Zeror," *RB* 72, 1965, pp. 548–551; A. Biran, R. Gophna, "Tel Zeror," *IEJ* 15, 1965, pp. 253–255; K. Ohata, M. Kochavi, "Tel Zeror," *IEJ* 16, 1966, pp. 274–276; A. Biran, "Tel Zeror," *CNI* 17:2–3, 1966, p. 22; *id.*, "Tel Zeror," *CNI* 18:1–2, 1967, pp. 29–30, pl. 3:2; K. Ohata, M. Kochavi, "Tel Zeror," *RB* 74, 1967, pp. 73–76, pl. 11a; K.

Ohata, ed., *Tel Zeror II: Preliminary Report of the Excavation, Second Season 1965*, 1967; K. Ohata, M. Kochavi, "Tell Zeror," *RB* 75, 1968, pp. 269–272, pl. 34b; M. Kochavi, "The Excavations at Tell Zeror," *Qadmoniot* 1, 1968, pp. 128–130, figs. (Hebrew); K. Ohata, ed., *Tel Zeror III: Report of the Excavation Third Season 1966*, 1970.

Teluliot Batashi

J. Kaplan, "Tuleil Batashi in the Sorek Valley," *IEJ* 5, 1955, pp. 273–274; *id.*, "Excavations at Teluliot Batashi in the Vale of Sorek," *EI* 5, 1958, pp. 9–24, pl. 1; *id.*, "Tluliyot-Betesh," *EAEHL*, 1970, p. 616, fig. (Hebrew).

Tiberias, see also Ḥammath-Tiberias, Ḥammath-Gader

Tombs excavated by V. Tsaferis for the Department of Antiquities, Israel, 1965.

"Tiberiade," *BTS* 76, 1965, pp. 16, 79; A. Biran, "Tiberias," *CNI* 17:2–3, 1966, p. 25; V. Tsaferis, "A Middle Bronze Age I Cemetery in Tiberias," *IEJ* 18, 1968, pp. 15–19, figs. 3–5, pl. 1; D. Ussishkin, "A Chalcolithic Basalt Chalice from Tiberias," *IEJ* 18, 1968, pp. 45–46, pl. 3b; J. Finegan, *The Archeology of the New Testament*, 1969, pp. 44–45, fig.

Timnaʻ, Meneʻiyeh

B. Rothenberg, "Excavations in the Early Iron Age Copper Industry at Timna (Wadi Arabah, Israel) May 1964," *ZDPV* 82, 1966, pp. 124–135, pls. 11–12; *id.*, *BMH* 7, 1965, pp. 19–28, pls. 1–2; *id.*, "The Chalcolithic Copper Industry at Timna and the Beginning of Metallurgy," *BMH* 8, 1966, pp. 86–93, pl. 8; B. Rothenberg, A. Lupu, "Excavations at Timna," *BMH* 9, 1967, pp. 53–70, pls. 5–10; B. Rothenberg, "Timnaᶜ," *RB* 74, 1967, pp. 80–85, pl. 12; B. Rothenberg, E. Cohen, "An Archaeological Survey of the Eloth District and the Southernmost Negev," *BMH* 10, 1968, pp. 25–35, pls. 6, 6a.

Egyptian temple excavated by B. Rothenberg for the Archaeological Institute of Tel Aviv University and the Museum Haaretz, 1969.

B. Rothenberg, "King Solomon's Mines No More," *ILN*, November 15, 1969, pp. 32–33, figs. 1–8; *id.*, "The Egyptian Temple of Timna," *ILN*, November 29, 1969, pp. 28–29, figs. 1–9; *id.*, "Egyptian Temple," *PEQ* 1969, pp. 57–59; *id.*, "Un temple égyptien découvert dans le Arabah," *BTS* 123, 1970, pp. 6–14, figs.; *id.*, "An Egyptian Temple of Hathor Discovered in the Southern ᶜArabah (Israel)," *BMH* 12, 1970, pp. 28–35, pls. 2–7; *id.*, "Timnaᶜ," *EAEHL*, 1970, pp. 622–624, figs. (Hebrew); N. Glueck, *The Other Side of the Jordan*, 1970, pp. 59, 85, 86, 91–94, 104, 115, figs.

Tulūl Abū el-ʻAlâyiq, see Jericho

ʻUbeidiya

Excavated by M. Stekelis, L. Picard, G. Haas, for the Hebrew University, 1960–1963.

M. Stekelis, "ᶜUbeidiya," *IEJ* 10, 1960, p. 118.

Excavated by O. Bar-Yosef, E. Tchernov, for the Israel Academy of Sciences and Humanities, 1964–1966, 1969.

M. Stekelis, *Archaeological Excavations at ᶜUbeidiya, 1960–63*, 1966; O. Bar-Yosef, "The Excavations at Tell ᶜUbeidiya," *Qadmoniot* 1, 1968, pp. 95–98, figs.

(Hebrew); O. Bar-Yosef, E. Tchernov, "ᶜUbeidiya," *IEJ* 19, 1969, pp. 234–235; M. Stekelis, "Tell ᶜOvadya," *EAEHL*, 1970, pp. 592–593, figs. (Hebrew).

Umm el-Biyarah, see Petra

Umm el-Qanatir

L. Oliphant, "Explorations North-East of Lake Tiberias and in Jaulan," *PEFQS* 1885, pp. 82–93, figs., esp. pp. 89–92, figs. 1–4; H. Kohl, C. Watzinger, *Antike Synagogen in Galilaea*, 1916, pp. 125–134, figs. 252–272, pl. 17; E. L. Sukenik, *The Ancient Synagogue of El-Ḥammeh*, 1935, pp. 85–87, pl. 19; M. Avi-Yonah, "Qanatir," *QDAP* 10, 1944, p. 140; E. R. Goodenough, *Symbols* 1, 1953, pp. 206–207; A. Biran, "Umm el-Qanatir," *CNI* 19:3–4, 1968, pl. 7a; M. Avi-Yonah, "Synagogues," *EAEHL*, 1970, pp. 100–106, figs. (Hebrew).

Wadi Dhobai

J. d'A. Waechter, V. M. Seton-Williams, D. M. A. Bate, L. Picard, "The Excavations at Wadi Dhobai 1937–1938 and the Dhobaian Industry," *JPOS* 18, 1938, pp. 1–23, fig. 1, pls. 1–13, plans 1–3, map; J. d'A. Waechter, V. M. Seton-Williams, "The Excavations at Wadi Dhobai, 1937–1938," *JPOS* 18, 1938, pp. 172–185, pls. 26–43; D. M. A. Bate, "Vertebrate Remains from Wadi Dhobai, 1938," *JPOS* 18, 1938, pp. 292–298; J. Perrot, "The Excavations at Tell Abu Matar, near Beersheba," *IEJ* 5, 1955, pp. 167–189, figs. 17–22; N. Glueck, "Dam in Wâdī Dhôbai," *AASOR* 25–28, 1951, pp. 49–53, figs. 39–41; E. Yeivin, "Wadi Dhobai," *EAEHL*, 1970, pp. 146–147 (Hebrew).

Wadi ed-Dâliyeh

Excavated by P. W. Lapp for the American Schools of Oriental Research, 1963–1964.

P. W. Lapp, "The Samaria Papyrii," *Archaeology* 16, 1963, pp. 204–206, figs.; F. M. Cross, Jr., "The Discovery of the Samaria Papyri," *CNI* 14:3–4, 1963, pp. 24–35, figs.; *id.*, "The Discovery of the Samaria Papyri," *BA* 26, 1963, pp. 110–121, figs. 1–5; *id.*, "Papyri of the Fourth Century B.C. from Dâliyeh," *New Directions in Biblical Archaeology*, 1969, pp. 41–62, pls. 34–39; P. W. Lapp, *Biblical Archaeology and History*, 1969, pp. 98, 119, 128, pls. 25–26; F. M. Cross, Jr., "The Discovery of the Samaria Papyri," in E. F. Campbell, Jr., D. N. Freedman, eds., *Biblical Archaeologist Reader* 3, 1970, pp. 227–239, pl. 1a.

Wadi el-'Amud, Mount Carmel, Naḥal 'Amud

F. Turville-Petre, *Researches in Prehistoric Galilee*, 1927, *passim.*

Excavated by H. Suzuki, H. Watanabe for the Tokyo University Expedition to Western Asia, 1961, 1964.

H. Watanabe, "Naḥal ᶜAmud," *IEJ* 11, 1961, pp. 189–191; A. Biran, "Neanderthal Man," *CNI* 13:1, 1962, pp. 16–17; H. Watanabe *et al.*, "Amud Cave," *IEJ* 15, 1965, pp. 246–247; S. R. Binford, "Meᶜarat Shovakh (Mughâret esh-Shubbabiq)," *IEJ* 16, 1966, pp. 18–32, figs. 1–9; pp. 96–103; O. Bar-Yosef, "Naḥal Amud," *EAEHL*, 1970, pp. 410–411, figs. (Hebrew).

Wadi el-Mughârah, see Mount Carmel

Wadi Ghazzeh, Naḥal Besor

M. Dothan, "High Loop-handled Cups and the Early Relations between Mesopotamia, Palestine and Egypt," *PEQ* 1953, pp. 132–137, fig. 4, pl. 45.

Excavated by J. Perrot for the Mission Archéologique Française, 1961–1962.

A. Biran, "Nahal Ha-B'sor," *CNI* 13:1, 1962, p. 18, pl. 2:2; J. Perrot, "Naḥal Besor (Wadi Ghazzeh)," *RB* 69, 1962, pp. 388–391.

Wadi Murabba'ât, see Murabba'ât

Wadi Rabah

Excavated by J. Kaplan for the Israel Exploration Society and the Museum of Ancient History of Tel-Aviv-Jaffa, 1952.

J. Kaplan, "Excavations at Wadi Rabah," *IEJ* 8, 1958, pp. 149–160, figs. 1–6; *id.*, "The Relation of the Chalcolithic Pottery of Palestine to Halafian Ware," *BASOR* 159, 1960, pp. 32–36, figs. 1–2; *id.*, "Wadi Rabba," *EAEHL*, 1970, p. 149, fig. (Hebrew).

Wadi Rumm, see Ramm

Yavneh-Yam

Cave excavated by L. A. Mayer for the Department of Antiquities, Palestine, 1925.

L. A. Mayer, "A Bronze Age Deposit from a Cave near Neby Rubin (Jaffa District)," *Palestine Museum Bulletin* 2, 1926, pp. 2–7, pls. 1, 2, 3a.

Tell ʿAbu Sultan excavated by J. Ory for the Department of Antiquities, Palestine, 1940.

J. Ory, "A Middle Bronze Age Tomb at el-Jisr," *QDAP* 12, 1946, pp. 31–42, figs., pls. 12–14; N. Glueck, "A Seal Weight from Nebi Rubin," *BASOR* 153, 1959, pp. 35–38, figs. 1–3.

Excavated by J. Naveh for the Department of Antiquities and the Israel Exploration Society, Israel, 1960.

J. Naveh, "A Hebrew Letter from the Seventh Century B.C.," *IEJ* 10, 1960, pp. 129–139, figs. 1–3, pls. 17–18; *id.*, "More Hebrew Inscriptions from Meṣad Ḥashavyahu," *IEJ* 12, 1962, pp. 27–32, figs. 1–2, pls. 5–6; F. M. Cross, Jr., "Epigraphic Notes on Hebrew Documents of the Eighth-Sixth Centuries B.C. II. The Murabaʿât Papyrus and the Letter Found near Yabneh-Yam," *BASOR* 165, 1962, pp. 34–46, fig. 1, esp. pp. 42–46; J. Naveh, "A Hebrew Letter from the Time of Jeremiah," *Archaeology* 15, 1962, pp. 108–111, figs.; J. P. Amusin, M. L. Heltzer, "The Inscription from Meṣad-Ḥashavyahu," *IEJ* 14, 1964, pp. 148–157; J. Naveh, "Some Notes on the Reading of the Meṣad Ḥashavyahu Letter," *IEJ* 14, 1964, pp. 158–159.

Excavated by J. Kaplan for the Museum of Antiquities of Tel Aviv-Yafo, 1966–1969.

A. Biran, "Yavneh-Yam," *CNI* 18:1–2, 1967, p. 41, pl. 7:2; J. Kaplan, "Yavneh-Yam," *IEJ* 17, 1967, pp. 268–269; *id.*, "The Fortifications of Jaffa, Yavneh-Yam and Ashdod-Yam," *BMH* 10, 1968, pp. 4–5, pl. 1.

Tombs excavated by R. Gofna and S. Lifshitz for the Department of Antiquities, Israel, 1968.

R. Gofna, "Palmaḥim," *IEJ* 18, 1968, pp. 132–133; J. B. Pritchard, ed., *ANEP*, 1969, no. 808; J. Kaplan, "Yavneh-Yam," *IEJ* 19, 1969, pp. 120–121; *id.*, "Tel-

Aviv-Yafo Excavations 1968," *BMH* 11, 1969, pp. 10–11, pl. 1; A. Biran, "Yavneh-Yam," *CNI* 20:3–4, 1969, p. 50; J. Kaplan, "Yavneh-Yam," *RB* 76, 1969, pp. 567–568, pl. 28b; *id.*, "Yavneh-Yam," *RB* 77, 1970, pp. 388–389, pl. 17; *id.*, "The Middle Bronze II Enclosure at Yavneh-Yam," *BMH* 12, 1970, pp. 13–15; J. Naveh, "Mtsad-Ḥashavyahu," *EAEHL*, 1970, pp. 373–374, figs. (Hebrew).

Yeruḥam

Excavations were carried out by M. Kochavi, 1963, and R. Cohen, 1967, for the Department of Antiquities, Israel.

M. Kochavi, "Har Yeruḥam," *IEJ* 13, 1963, pp. 141–142; A. Biran, "Har Yeruḥam," *CNI* 15:2–3, 1964, p. 21, pl. 8; M. Kochavi, *The Settlement of the Negev in the Middle Bronze (Canaanite) I Age*, doctoral dissertation for the Hebrew University, 1967, *passim*; A. Biran, "Mezad Yeroḥam," *CNI* 18:1–2, 1967, p. 33, pl. 4:1–2; N. Glueck, *Rivers in the Desert*, 1968, *passim*; M. Kochavi, "The Middle Bronze Age I (The Intermediate Bronze Age) in Eretz-Israel," *Qadmoniot* 2, 1969, pp. 37–44 and cover, figs. (Hebrew); *id.*, "Har Yroḥam," *EAEHL*, 1970, pp. 136–137, figs. (Hebrew).

Yurza, see Tell Jemmeh

Zarethan, see Tell es-Sa'idiyeh